# THE ANTI-COMMUNIST MANIFESTO

# JESSE KELLY

## WITH NICK RIZZUTO

Threshold Editions

New York   London   Toronto   Sydney   New Delhi

Threshold Editions
An Imprint of Simon & Schuster, Inc.
1230 Avenue of the Americas
New York, NY 10020

First Threshold Editions trade paperback edition February 2025

THRESHOLD EDITIONS and colophon are trademarks
of Simon & Schuster, Inc.

For information about special discounts for bulk purchases,
please contact Simon & Schuster Special Sales at 1-866-506-1949
or business@simonandschuster.com.

The Simon & Schuster Speakers Bureau can bring authors to your
live event. For more information, or to book an event, contact the
Simon & Schuster Speakers Bureau at 1-866-248-3049 or visit our website
at www.simonspeakers.com.

Interior design by Davina Mock-Maniscalco

Manufactured in the United States of America

10  9  8  7  6  5  4  3  2  1

Library of Congress Cataloging-in-Publication Data is available.

ISBN 978-1-6680-1087-7
ISBN 978-1-6680-1088-4 (pbk)
ISBN 978-1-6680-1089-1 (ebook)

To me.

# CONTENTS

I'm always talking about how evil communism is. One day, someone said to me, "Hey, you should write a book about it." So, here it is.

—Jesse Kelly

# THE
# ANTI-COMMUNIST
# MANIFESTO

Communism is an evil, demonic religion, and it has infected America to its bones. It will tear this nation apart if it is not driven from our shores.

America is on the verge of defeat, brothers and sisters. As a nation, she is unrecognizable from what she was a century ago. What she was a decade ago. A year ago. Yesterday. The ideals, principles, and foundations that once made her the envy of the free world have been eroded to the point of nonexistence. All that remains is for a gentle push to send her over the edge. Picture in your mind a person who has damaging information against the Clintons and is teetering on the edge of a cliff with Hillary in a three-point stance behind them. That's America right now.

I wish I could tell you that our nation stands at a crossroad. That things could go either way and the future of the country is up in the air. But that's not the case. America chose a path long ago. Now we stand within sight of the journey's dark end.

You no doubt see it every day on your television screens. In the news you read. In the entertainment you consume. In the incessant jabbering of the wildebeests on *The View*. In the syllabus your son or daughter brings home from school. You can practically taste it in the air around you. A bitter cocktail of divisiveness, self-hatred, perpetual victimhood, and degeneracy.

All the while, there has been someone leading the way. For generations, he's been guiding us. Sometimes he operates in the shadows, while at others he works in the open.

He seduces us, gently taking our hands and whispering in our ears stories of a better tomorrow.

He threatens us, shouting about the end of the world and warning of impending doom if we stray from the path.

Worst of all, he deceives us, clouding our judgment with lies and making false promises he never intends to keep.

He is the communist.

"But Jesse," I already hear you asking, "are our political enemies really 'communists' or are you just being dramatic?" I assure you that I'm not being dramatic. The enemy we face are *really* communists and, as I will demonstrate, they are just as devoted to this dangerous religion as their forebears in the Soviet Union or their contemporaries in the People's Republic of China.

So, where is he leading us and how will America's journey finally end if we allow the communist to remain our guide? Well, let me answer that question with a few uncomfortable questions of my own. Would you line up your husband or wife against a wall and shoot them? Would you shove the bodies of your parents into an unmarked mass grave? Would you sit down with your family and decide which one of you must be killed and eaten so the rest may survive?

Probably not . . . I mean, I hope not. If you would, perhaps consider putting this book down and seeking some professional help. But if you're anything like me, the very thought of doing any of those things horrifies you. Maybe the suggestion has already caused you to chuck this book across the room.

But as unthinkable as that all might be, you'd better listen to my warning, because what I'm about to tell you is true: the communist would do all those things. Time and again he has done all those things and worse. Worse still, he has no misgivings about making *you* do them.

The communist is the height of evil. He is walking death. I know this because I understand history. I understand what he is capable of and, as we speak, he is all around us.

I'm hoping to pass on that understanding to you in the pages ahead. I want you to understand why the communist is evil, how history demonstrates his depravity beyond a shadow of a doubt, and how he is currently operating in our midst.

People ask me all the time if they should be afraid. The answer to that question is yes. You should be very afraid.

However, you should know that there is hope. We don't have to sit idly by and continue to act as spectators of America's destruction. The communist is not invincible.

In the pages that follow, I will outline not only the challenges we face, but specific steps you can take to defeat the communist.

But we must act, and we must act now.

*Let us begin.*

# CHAPTER ONE

# The Communist and Anti-Communist

Have you ever been to the mountains? You might have seen a curious sight: a boulder, somehow shattered into a million pieces. It's a fascinating occurrence. When you lay eyes on it, the first thing that might cross your mind is to wonder what force of nature could possibly have destroyed a boulder so old, large, and strong. The answer to that question is water. Boulders will develop cracks over time, and inevitably rainwater or runoff from melting snow will seep into those cracks. A freeze will come. The water will expand. Ultimately, the force of that frozen water destroys the boulder.

So, who is the communist? The communist is the water. Your society is the boulder. Societies, over time, will develop cracks, just like the boulder. Little weaknesses that don't appear important at first, but they are everything to the communist. He will find them, fill them, freeze them, and destroy your society unless he is stopped.

The communist is not "the worker." He is not the aggrieved peasant. He doesn't have a specific label. He is the bitter, envious malcontent in your society.

Communism is the religion of the malcontent.

The malcontent is drawn to this religion because it promises him power. Power to take what isn't his. Power to exact vengeance on the neighbor who has what he wants. Power to satisfy whatever sadistic desires he feels compelled to carry out.

The communist's power comes from his commitment. If you think of the communist as a political ideologue, you are grossly underestimating his devotion and you will never defeat him. He is a religious zealot. He is as deadly committed to his god as the suicide bomber.

So, where did this religion come from?

Like every religion, it has a prophet and scripture. Its founding scripture, *The Communist Manifesto*, was first presented to the masses in 1848 and was authored by Karl Marx and his accomplice Friedrich Engels—the Moses and Aaron of communism. Over the courses of their lifetimes, the pair wrote countless volumes outlining and justifying their faith. A person could spend an entire lifetime studying what they and their successors wrote, but let me summarize the key points for you:

Human history is a war between two classes: workers and capitalists.

The capitalist class are the oppressors, the working class are their victims.

The working class will rise up and destroy the capitalist class and the society they've built and it will be replaced by a worker's paradise.

The outcome is preordained; the worker's victory is inevitable, and it will unfold across every corner of the world.

Marx's prophecy speaks to the loser because it sets him above all other people and tells him that he will inherit the world. He describes the communist as "the most advanced and resolute section of the working class parties of every country." This description is ironic if you understand who Marx and Engels were: two men who never engaged in any work themselves.

Karl Marx was a fat and lazy man who spent his days living off the generosity of his parents and wealthy friends. This self-described "advanced" member of the working class never shed a drop of sweat in his life (unless he had to walk a flight of stairs), and the only jobs he every held were as a journalist and writer. Even his output as a writer reveals his laziness, as a single book, *Das Kapital*, took him thirty years to produce. He was also a noted liar, a slob, and a serial adulterer who refused to take responsibility for children he fathered out of wedlock.

Marx's life of leisure was bankrolled, most notably, by his collaborator and frequent coauthor, Friedrich Engels. Engels was not a member of the working class, either (although by all accounts his hygiene was better than Marx's). He was the son of a wealthy factory owner. A dandy who spent his evenings carousing, boozing, and slumming it with working-class dimes. In other words, he was the type of man Joseph Stalin would have introduced to the business end of a pistol without blinking an eye.

I could sit here and bore you with the ramblings of a nineteenth-century German philosopher. But who cares about theory anyway? To save some time, I'll just present you with the summary Marx himself provided in *The Communist Manifesto*:

> The theory of the Communists may be summed up in the single sentence: Abolition of private property.

Read that again. Tattoo it on your mind. Marvel at its simplicity. This is what motivates the communist. His core belief sits in direct opposition to the principles of liberty, central to which is the right to own property and keep the fruits of your labor. He wants to destroy everything you have.

The communist lives to destroy: destroy property, destroy his opposition, and destroy the very foundations of society.

It's important to understand that communism is not an ideology but rather, as I've already said, a religion. In many ways, it's the polar opposite of Christianity. It starts in Armageddon and promises to end in the Garden of Eden.

Marx and his comrades believed that the overthrow of capitalism was inevitable. They told the faithful that victory had been preordained not by God, as a Christian believes, but by the laws of science. "Just as Darwin discovered the law of development of organic nature," Engels said in 1883, "so Marx discovered the law of development of human history." The worker's paradise, they argued, was not a matter of *if*, but of *when*. This is the endtimes prophecy that the communist preaches with all the same fervor of a priest telling his congregation about the coming of the kingdom of heaven.

So, with Marx as his prophet, a deep sense of entitlement in his mind, and with total confidence in his cause, nothing would stand in the communist's way. He believed he was the bringer of utopia and felt absolutely justified using any means necessary. He went forth into history to wreak havoc on the Western world and beyond.

And wreak havoc he did.

He established secret police. Imprisoned dissidents in concentration camps. Seized property by force. Sent forth death squads. Induced mass starvation in noncompliant populations. Wherever his religion took root, death and suffering followed. Instead of the paradise promised, the communist brought hell to earth.

We'll examine more of this handiwork later in the book, but let's take a moment here at the top to look at a small sample of the evil the communist brought to his fellow man.

- Shortly after taking power in 1918, Vladimir Lenin established a system of concentration and labor camps that would become known as the gulag system. The camps would house not only criminals, but political dissidents and "class enemies," a term that would apply to anyone who fell out of favor with the Communist Party. The network of camps eventually became a system of slave labor. At its height, the gulag system consisted of as many as 30,000 individual camps. The system is estimated to have incarcerated around 18 million people throughout the Soviet Union over the course of several decades. An estimated 1.7 million perished.

- In 1932, Joseph Stalin targeted the Ukrainian people for their stubborn resistance to Soviet rule and agricultural collectivization. In order to break them, he set unrealistically high grain-procurement quotas. When farms inevitably came up short, Stalin issued a decree known as "The Law of Five Stalks of Grain." The rule condemned anyone who took even a handful of grain, which was considered property of the state, to ten years' imprisonment or to death. An army of Soviet apparatchiks and secret police descended upon Ukrainian towns and villages. House-to-house searches were conducted. Hidden grain stores were seized.

- The resulting famine came to be known as the Holodomor, which is Ukrainian for "death by hunger." Ukraine's borders were closed off, preventing food from being imported. The people became desperate, with some turning to cannibalism. At its height, as many as 28,000 Ukrainians per day were dying of starvation. Families ate each other. Or lay in their beds and watched each other starve to death. The United Nations estimates that deaths attributed to the Holodomor range from anywhere between 7 and 10 million.

- In 1958, communist dictator Mao Zedong instituted a campaign known as the Great Leap Forward, the Chinese Communist Party's second five-year plan to transform the nation into a worker's paradise. The party outlawed private farming and instituted a policy of mandatory agricultural collectivization. Rural farming communities were reorganized into "people's communes." The people were organized into "production brigades."

- It was a total failure. Grain output dropped dramatically throughout China. The resulting famine, widely regarded as the greatest man-made disaster in human history, led to the death of tens of millions of people, with some estimates as high as 45 million.

- In addition to those who died from starvation, between 2 and 3 million were tortured to death or summarily executed by leaders, often for minor infractions. In one case, when a boy stole a handful of grain in a Hunan village, the local Communist Party boss, Xiong Dechang, forced his father to bury his son alive. In another instance of brutality, a man named Wang Ziyou was reported to the central leadership: one of his ears was chopped off, his legs were tied with iron wire, a ten-kilogram stone was dropped on his back, and then he was branded with a sizzling tool. His crime? Digging up a potato. Still another man, Liu Desheng, was found guilty of poaching a sweet potato. He was covered in urine, then tongs were used to pry open his mouth and he was forced to swallow excrement.

- In April 1975, the army of the Khmer Rouge, a communist movement led by Pol Pot, rolled into the Cambodian capital of Phnom Penh. In its attempt to socially engineer a classless communist society, the regime unleashed four years of brutality commonly referred to as the Cambodian Genocide. The regime abolished civil liberties and political rights. They confiscated private property and banned the use of money. The government established a system of prisons where countless people were tortured and executed. In the most notorious of these prisons, known as S-21, those accused by communists of being traitors were cataloged, tortured until they confessed to nonexistent crimes, and murdered. At least 12,000 people met their fate at S-21 under the cruelest of conditions.

- Between 1975 and 1979, the Khmer Rouge's rule would lead to the death of as many as 2 million Cambodians, or close to 25 percent of the nation's entire population.

Have you heard enough yet? Too bad. I've saved the worst for last.

- Between 1949 and 1951, the Romanian Communist Party, in conjunction with the Soviets, carried out what came to be known as the Pitesti Experiment. In a penal facility located in the Romanian city of Pitesti, thousands of political prisoners, mostly members of the Orthodox clergy, were subjected to a gruesome reeducation program. Christians were made to denounce their faith and shout blasphemies. Their heads were submerged to the point of near drowning in buckets of urine and excrement in a cruel mockery of the rite of baptism. Other prisoners were made to torture one another, often to the point of insanity or death. The assortment of torments to which they were subjected is too vast and repulsive to catalog here.

- It was in Pitesti prison that the communist's lust for death and cruelty reached its insane but logical endpoint. Not content to kill their enemies, the communist attempted to destroy their souls. Famed Russian writer and Soviet political prisoner Aleksandr Solzhenitsyn called the Pitesti Experiment one of "the most terrible acts of barbarism in the modern world."

As I said, this is just a small sampling of the atrocities the communist has committed in countries where he took power. But even nations where his religion was ultimately rejected were not safe from his cruelty. For example, he murdered thousands of priests in Spain and kidnapped some 30,000 children in Greece and sent them off to foreign lands to be reeducated.

All told, Marx's disciples racked up an estimated body count approaching 100 million over of the twentieth century, according to *The Black Book of Communism: Crimes, Terror, Repression.* That number continues to climb to this very day.

## RED, White, and Blue

Thankfully, America was spared the horrors that many other nations experienced. Our unique history, one that valued individual liberty and the Christian faith, proved an effective fortification against communism's rapid advance. But don't let this fact lull you into a false sense of security. The American communist is not some different, more genteel breed. While the communist failed to bring about the drama he created throughout Europe and Asia, he was, nonetheless, hard at work in America subverting resistance to his religion.

Agents of communism infiltrated virtually every major American government agency of military or diplomatic importance. Working on behalf of the Soviet Union, the infiltrators stole details of the atomic bomb project, passed along military secrets, and advised Soviet officials on how to frustrate U.S. interests.

American communists were eventually met with resistance, in large part through the efforts of the House Un-American Activities Committee (HUAC) and the Senate Committee on Government Operations, under the leadership of Senator Joseph McCarthy. Over the course of two decades, anti-communists managed to score some victories in unmasking Soviet spy rings and agents.

Famously, the husband-and-wife team of Julius and Ethel Rosenberg, an engineer for the U.S. Army and a census worker, respectively, were convicted of spying on behalf of the Soviet Union in 1951. The pair were instrumental in Stalin's efforts to build the atomic bomb, leading a cabal of spies who divulged sensitive information to the Soviet Union. The two were executed in 1953.

The extent of communist penetration wasn't limited to low-level civil servants like the Rosenbergs. In fact, the infiltration went all the way up to the highest levels of power.

Arguably the most prominent government figure revealed to have been a communist agent was Alger Hiss. Hiss was a government attorney who held numerous posts in the administration of Franklin D. Roosevelt, at the Departments of Agriculture, Justice, and State. He stood side by side with FDR at the Yalta Conference and later served as temporary secretary-general of the United Nations. In 1948, Hiss was accused of serving in the communist underground, an accusation he vehemently denied before a congressional hearing. When the testimony of reformed communist Whittaker Chambers proved indisputable proof of Hiss's activities, he was given a five-year prison sentence for perjury, the statute of limitations having run out on espionage.

Like most communists, Hiss showed little remorse for his activities and maintained his innocence until the day he died. He also remains a popular figure among academics. Bard College, a liberal arts school in upstate New York, even maintains an Alger Hiss chair in social studies in the unrepentant communist's honor.

The pull of the communist religion is potent, and contrition is rare among the faithful. In his 1952 autobiography, *Witness*, Whittaker Chambers, the reformed communist whose testimony led to the downfall of Hiss, wrote, "It is worth noting that not one communist was moved to break with communism under the pressures of the Hiss case. Let those who wonder about communism and the power of its faith ponder that fact."

While many had been exposed, the communist didn't throw

his hands up in surrender. Much to America's disservice, the anti-communist zeal eventually subsided. Communists settled into the long game, which began with the rewriting of history. Academics, historians, and Hollywood returned to the work of casting communists in a sympathetic light.

For decades, the post–World War II efforts to root out communism from the U.S. government and other American institutions were cast as nothing more than witch hunts.

Movie studios, for example, produced documentaries like *Hollywood on Trial*, which helped to fix the communists-as-martyrs narrative in American minds. They framed the efforts of Senator McCarthy and HUAC as assaults on freedom of conscience rather than what they were: attempts to root out the Soviet fifth column. More recently, Americans were treated to *Trumbo*, a fawning biography of screenwriter Dalton Trumbo (Communist Party USA card number 47187) that conveniently glosses over the fact that he was a Stalinist stooge.

The whitewashing was, and remains, a pack of lies.

In the 1990s, much of the suspicion that drove the anti-communist efforts in previous decades was confirmed by the revelation of the Venona Project, a secret U.S. counterintelligence program that decrypted messages from Soviet intelligence agencies. The documents confirmed the guilt of the Rosenbergs and Hiss and identified hundreds of spies throughout the U.S. government and military.

Though the truth had been revealed, it ultimately made no difference. Despite their vindication, the brave individuals who spoke out against the communists in their midst and "named names" were vilified. Efforts to uncover communism in the

U.S. are now derided as having been driven by the "red scare," the fever dream of conspiracy-mongers.

In their 1999 book, *Venona: Decoding Soviet Espionage in America*, historians John Earl Haynes and Harvey Klehr described communists' successful efforts to clean up history:

> A number of liberals and radicals pointed to the excesses of McCarthy's charges as justification for rejecting the allegations altogether. Anticommunism further lost credibility in the late 1960s when critics of U.S. involvement in the Vietnam War blamed it for America's ill-fated participation. By the 1980s many commentators, and perhaps most academic historians, had concluded that Soviet espionage had been minor, that few American Communists had assisted the Soviets, and that no high officials had betrayed the United States. Many history texts depicted America in the late 1940s and 1950s as a "nightmare in red" during which Americans were "sweat-drenched in fear" of a figment of their own paranoid imaginations. As for American Communists, they were widely portrayed as having no connection with espionage. One influential book asserted emphatically, "There is no documentation in the public record of a direct connection between the American Communist Party and espionage during the entire postwar period."

It wasn't long before the anti-anti-communist narrative had become accepted as fact by the left and right. Senator Joe McCarthy became universally reviled. His

name became synonymous on both sides of the political aisle with excessive government investigation.

And just like that, the communist went from being a vilified
subversive to a victim. Americans were lulled back to sleep, while
the communist remained awake and active.

He abandoned any notion of a popular uprising that would
overthrow the United States government and focused instead on
creating a soft revolution that would come with the passage of
time. He hunkered down and dedicated himself to "the long
march through the institutions," a phrase based on the ideas of
Italian Marxist Antonio Gramsci. "Socialism is precisely the religion that must overwhelm Christianity," Gramsci wrote. "In the
new order, Socialism will triumph by first capturing the culture
via infiltration of schools, universities, churches, and the media
by transforming the consciousness of society."

He started with the universities, where Marxism continues to
thrive. He influenced generations of young minds and pumped
out an army of revolutionaries. In turn, those young revolutionaries entered society to become teachers, journalists, artists,
and corporate executives. They infected schools, newsrooms,
and boardrooms.

So, just who is today's communist?

In short, the communist is who he's always been: a subversive, chipping away at the pillars that hold up American society.

In the twenty-first century, the communist does not neces-
sarily adhere to a rigid set of principles and doctrines like those
who came before him. He'd be hard-pressed to recite Marx chapter and verse. He's also unlikely to voice his support for many

past communist regimes, like Stalin's Soviet Union or Pol Pot's Cambodia.

After all, that wasn't "real communism," he'll assure you.

When the majority of American communists tell you they're not communists, understand that in their mind they're telling the truth. The communist genuinely believes he's a liberal, or left-leaning, or a Democrat, or an environmentalist, or a civil rights advocate, or a feminist, or any of the other countless labels he applies to himself. He doesn't realize that he's a photocopy of a photocopy of a photocopy of a communist stretching all the way back to Marx. The image may have become warped and blurry as it was run through the machine time and again, but beneath it all you can still make out the outlines of the original.

Over time, he altered his language to better appeal to American sensibilities. Socialism became "social justice." The forced redistribution of wealth became "equity." The destruction of tradition became "inclusiveness." Comrades became "allies."

The notion of the workers' revolution has also gone through a remodel. Sure, the communist still pays lip service to the working class, a nod to his Marxist roots. But today's communist has nothing but contempt for the working class. They consider them ignorant and apathetic. The working class, the communist will argue, doesn't vote in his own interest and clings too tightly to his superstitious religions. He stubbornly refuses to hate himself as the communist demands.

The communist has antipathy for the working class because the communist is no longer a product of the working class. In truth, he never was. The communist leaders of the past—including Lenin, Mao, and Pol Pot—were spoiled rich kids. He can't be motivated by the dream of breaking off the shackles of factory work because he's unlikely to have ever seen the inside of a factory. He has nothing in common with the people of this nation who work with their hands, wear hard hats, or punch in and out five days a week.

Today, the working class are just another obstacle for the communist. They're a group destined to be arranged in any way he likes when victory is finally achieved. "He'll do as we tell him to do," the communist says, "and when his factory is closed, his livelihood is destroyed, and his family is left in ruin, he'll learn to code."

The communist has swapped the working class as his fetish of choice and replaced it with classes defined primarily by race and sexuality. These are the groups he looks to agitate by scratching at the scar tissue of old wounds and constantly manufacturing fresh ones. To the communist, America's history is not something to be learned from, but a collection of sins against aggrieved groups that he intends to set right through his own cleansing fire.

Nearly every social movement was co-opted or created to advance their goals: feminism, racial justice, gay and trans rights. At a surface level, each movement speaks to the American fixation on equality—a fixation so deeply ingrained in our national soul that nineteenth-century writer Alexis de Tocqueville observed that Americans are "far more ardently and tenaciously attached to equality than to freedom."

Feminism is just equality for women, right? Racial justice is just about giving a fair shake to minorities, right? The gay rights movement is just about giving homosexuals equal access to traditional institutions, right? The trans rights movement is just about acknowledging those who are different than us, right? After all, the only thing that makes a man a man is the ability to parallel park, right?

But beneath the seemingly innocuous façade, each of these movements is intertwined with the radical communist religion and class struggle. Feminism seeks to redefine women and pit them against men. The racial justice movement seeks to stoke anger, division, and antipathy for America so the communist can conquer it more easily. The gay movement seeks to destroy traditional institutions like marriage and family, which serve as foundations for strong nations. The trans insanity is nothing short of an assault on reason and truth itself.

Having integrated himself into society, the communist now has many faces. He may wear a sport coat and speak in passive tones to an auditorium full of students. He may sit in a board-room and quietly nod in approval as his subordinates explain mandatory equity and diversity training. He may wear a uniform bearing stars and ribbons and concern himself with the study of white privilege rather than the study of war. He may even don a black hoodie and mask and set fire to businesses.

Whatever his vision for the future, he believes America, as constituted by the founders, stands in the way. At the center of it all is an abiding hatred of his nation, her history, and the foundations upon which she is built. That hatred unifies the disparate groups that compose the modern communist movement.

What, then, does he seek? I assure you, it's not equity. It isn't a classless society. It's not even trans rights or any of the other nonsense to which he attaches himself. He hungers for something far simpler. To the communist everything is a means to achieve one thing: destruction. Destruction of your communities. Destruction of your children. Destruction of you. Destruction of everything.

This is the communist.

## The Anti-Communist

Who, then, is the anti-communist?

If you picked up this book, there's a good chance that you already dislike communism—at least, what you know about it. That's a good start, but simply not liking communism is not what makes someone an anti-communist. It takes no effort to believe communists sucks. There's more to it than that.

Being an anti-communist might have been straightforward in the early to mid-twentieth century, when communism was ascendant internationally and embodied by aggressive countries like the Soviet Union. For your average person who would wear the anti-communist label, the enemy was visible. You could point to him on a map. You could chart his advance like red tentacles expanding over a globe.

Back then, efforts by anti-communists to weed out the pinkos in our midst were viewed as part of a geopolitical struggle. It was Soviet agents who had infiltrated our institutions or the Communist Party USA, which was loyal to a foreign power. Once the evil empire was defeated, the agents of communism would shrink back into the holes from which they had come, never to return, right? Communism, it was believed, could never survive such a rebuke.

At least, that was the theory promoted by the smartest people in the room. Take, for example, Francis Fukuyama, a man

widely considered to be one of America's most brilliant political scientists. In his 1992 book, *The End of History and the Last
Man*, published less than a year after the fall of the Soviet Union,
Fukuyama declared final victory over communism. He claimed
that liberal democracy represented an "end point of mankind's
ideological evolution" and the "final form of human government,"
and as such constituted the "end of history."

What a complete load of nonsense.

Today's anti-communist knows that Fukuyama and the
rest of the people who spiked the ball were dead wrong. The
fall of the Soviet Union was not even a bump in the road for
the faithful. As a matter of fact, it worked to his benefit, as
the communist was freed from his association with a nation
whose human rights abuses and failures had become so obvious
to the world at large.

The beliefs of Fukuyama and his ilk notwithstanding, the
communist is as great a threat as ever. He is homegrown and
operating from within. Worst of all, he has a massive head start
on us. If he is not stopped and repelled, the communist will
tear down the foundations of our nation and foster a collapse
of American society as we know it.

The anti-communist must understand that the enemy we
face represents a greater existential threat to the American people
than the one faced by the founders of this nation. America would
have been better off losing the Revolutionary War and returning
to the fold of the British Empire than having these monsters
attain total power over you and your children.

With all of this in mind, the anti-communist knows his
opponent must be pulled out of the institutions root and branch.

Therefore, we can safely summarize the guiding principle of the anti-communist in a single sentence:

Defeating the communist is all that matters.

That's it. That's all you must understand as an anti-communist. No remorse. No misgivings. Just an unwavering commitment to this purpose.

It's not going to be easy.

We're not going to win by merely slowing the advance of communism. We're going to have to destroy it. Think of it like a feminist might think of an all-you-can-eat buffet. Every morsel on every steam tray must be devoured. Every spoon licked clean of gravy. All that will remain is a memory, residual heartburn, and the impotent protests of Golden Corral's evening shift manager.

That's what we must do to the communist. We're going to take from him everything he holds dear. All the gains he's made in this country must be ripped from his hands. Victory comes the day the communist can no longer openly practice his demonic religion.

Achieving victory will require us to use all the tools at our disposal. This is, after all, a war. You can't go to war and conduct yourself the way you would in peacetime. The struggle is not served by unread white papers from Washington, D.C., think tanks about the marginal tax rates. The nation will not be saved by editorials in the *Wall Street Journal*. To quote the most clear-sighted anti-communist in the history of cinema, Colonel Walter E. Kurtz from *Apocalypse Now*, "Horror has a face . . . and you must make a friend of horror."

Anti-communism is not passive. It is not just something

you are, it is something you *do*. It is exercising the power you have—in your places of business, in your school districts, in your houses of worship, and in your home—to help bring about the defeat of communists. Only when one adopts this active mindset can they truly count themselves among the ranks of the anti-communist. You cannot "live and let live" your way out of communism.

It doesn't matter where you fall on the political spectrum of the right—whether you call yourself a libertarian, nationalist, conservative, or neoconservative. Anti-communism comes first. It supersedes them all, and for one reason: the communist will destroy all of them together if he's not stopped. We can argue over the ultimate destination once we've removed the murderous horde blocking our path.

One more thing: whether you're nine or ninety, you're never going to see final victory. You're climbing Mount Everest but you, personally, will never make the summit. Learn to love the climb. It has taken the communist one hundred years to get us here and it will take us one hundred years to claw our way back.

The fight itself is what matters today. Embrace the struggle. Find joy in it. This is the time in history God has given us. You were uniquely made for it. Wade into it with the knowledge that we are the good guys.

# CHAPTER TWO

# The University System:
# America's Communist Factory

D id you know that American communists had a plan to slaughter tens of millions of Americans? Probably not. And if you did, you certainly didn't learn about it in school.

Let me explain why with a little anecdote.

In March 1970, Terry Robbins and Diana Oughton were hard at work in the furnace room of a town house in New York City's Greenwich Village. The location had become a makeshift bomb factory for America's premier communist terror organization, the Weather Underground. The pair were hastily assembling bombs made of water pipes, dynamite, and roofing nails in preparation for a bombing campaign whose targets included police stations, ROTC buildings, and a noncommissioned officers' dance at Fort Dix in New Jersey.

In the eyes of the group's founders, including a twenty-five-year-old radical named Bill Ayers, the bombings would just be the beginning, an opening salvo in a plan to overthrow the United States government and bring about a communist revolution. When all was said and done, the group estimated that 25 million Americans would need to be executed, an ocean of blood its members were more than willing to spill in pursuit of its twisted goals.

So, where are these dangerous, genocidal maniacs now? Surely they're all rotting in prison cells somewhere, right? Did they do the Epstein twitch at the end of rope while the guards "napped" and the surveillance cameras died? Nope. They're currently teaching your children at that university you're paying for.

---

Throughout his writings, Karl Marx describes a series of key events that would take place at the outset of the communist revolution. Arguably, the most important of these events would be the seizure by the working class of the means of production. This was the communist's first step in eliminating private property. Once this seizure was achieved, the factories and capital goods used to supply the masses would be centralized in the hands of the state, ushering in the so-called dictatorship of the proletariat.

During the Bolshevik Revolution in Russia, workers seized control of metalworks, textile factories, and oil fields. They kicked out overseers and foremen and established workers' committees to manage operations. Similar steps were taken during communist revolutions across the world.

But in the United States and other nations, the communist failed to hypnotize the working class. Communism couldn't achieve the industrial foothold needed to bring about its dictatorship. America's working class simply had it too good. It was impossible to convince enough American workers they were victims. The communist was forced to reevaluate. Why had so many workingmen of the world rejected him? Why hadn't they all rallied to the cause?

The problem, the communist concluded, was the working class itself. They were too old. Too set in their ways. Too drenched in a lifetime of capitalist propaganda. So, if they couldn't have the workers of the world, they'd take their children.

Education of the nation's youth is the lynchpin of the communist's efforts. The communist knew he had to adopt the mindset of Joe Biden looking for someone to sniff: get them young. If he could do so, he could infect impressionable minds and send them off into the system to do his bidding.

So, instead of taking over the steelworks and textile mills, the communist set his sights on a new factory: the university. The product that would roll off the assembly line was new communists.

It made perfect sense. The universities and colleges are the pipeline through which all other elite institutions are fed. The students of today will be the teachers, CEOs, industrialists, and politicians of tomorrow. Roughly 4 million people graduate from American universities every year. Don't think of those people as kids. Think of them as the communist does: reinforcements.

## The Long March Through the Universities

The name Bill Ayers will likely set off alarm bells for anyone who was around for the 2008 presidential election. Ayers resurfaced when his relationship with then–presidential candidate Barack Obama came under scrutiny. The Weather Underground founder had established himself as an esteemed figure in Chicago's educational community, where he crossed professional and political paths with Obama on numerous occasions. The fact that they were even breathing the same air should give you chills. How could the culture of American universities become so thoroughly radicalized that a known founder of a communist terror organization was able to rub elbows with the future president of the United States?

Well, the communist takeover of American universities didn't happen overnight. Efforts by radical socialists have been going on for well over a hundred years. Those efforts even predate the rise of communism as a political force in Europe.

There were various socialist clubs at the turn of the twentieth century, but the first major organization to arise was the Intercollegiate Socialist Society (ISS), which was established in 1905. The group was the brainchild of writer Upton Sinclair, the socialist muckraker whose novel *The Jungle* exposed unsanitary conditions in the meatpacking industry. According to Sinclair, the group was established "for the purpose of promoting an intelligent interest in Socialism among college men, graduate and undergraduate, through the formation of study clubs in the colleges and universities, and the encouraging of all legitimate endeavors to awaken an interest in Socialism among the educated men and women of the country." The group quickly attracted several high-profile socialist intellectuals, including novelist Jack London and lawyer Clarence Darrow. It became the de facto youth wing of the Socialist Party of America.

Although the organization faced initial resistance from some conservative college administrators, it quickly expanded. By 1913 the ISS had grown to seventy-six chapters around the country, with more than 1,700 members. The group became a powerful force for student activism. John Reed, a member of the Harvard chapter of the ISS, described the movement: "All over the place radicals sprang up . . . the more serious college papers took on a socialistic, or at least progressive tinge."

Despite its early success, the group would just as quickly lose momentum. The popularity of socialism in the U.S. took a nosedive in 1917 with the Bolshevik Revolution in Russia and America's entry into World War I. With membership dwindling and chapters shuttering across the country, the group eventually rebranded as the Student League for Industrial Democracy (SLID) to deemphasize its connection to socialism. According to the SLID, its purpose was to promote "a classless cooperative society in which men will have an equal opportunity to achieve the good things of life." While the language might have been slightly different, its goal was virtually indistinguishable from the central principle of communism. So similar were their goals, the SLID eventually merged with the expressly communist and pro-USSR National Student League.

The group would survive the anti-communist fervor of the 1940s and '50s, once again changing its name in 1960, to Students for a Democratic Society (SDS). The group swelled during the radical decade, eventually growing to over three hundred campus chapters and thirty thousand members by 1968.

It was with the rise of the SDS that the radical "New Left" began taking shape. They were the second generation of American communists, the children of the radicals of the 1930s. These were the so-called red-diaper babies. They rejected the kinder, gentler communism that their parents had espoused. Many openly embraced Marx, Lenin, and Mao.

In 1969, the SDS gave rise to a militant faction, the Marxist-Leninist Weather Underground. In the group manifesto, it

THE ANTI-COMMUNIST MANIFESTO    31

declared itself "a revolutionary communist party" ready to "seize power and build the new society." The organization's cofounder Bernardine Dohrn stated that the group's aim was "to lead white kids into armed revolution."

The Weather Underground embraced violence and declared war on the United States government. The group remained busy throughout the 1970s and into the early '80s, carrying out a campaign of terrorism in numerous cities.

On February 12, 1970, the group detonated two pipe bombs in a parking complex for the Berkeley, California, police department. The resulting explosions injured seven police officers. A Weather Underground member later recalled that they "were angry that a policeman didn't die."

On June 9 of that same year, the group bombed the New York City Police Department headquarters. The blast injured seven people.

On March 1, 1971, the group detonated a bomb in the U.S. Capitol Building in Washington, D.C., causing an estimated $300,000 in damage.

On May 19, 1972, the Weather Underground placed a bomb in the women's bathroom in the Air Force wing of the Pentagon. The date was chosen in honor of Vietnam's communist dictator Ho Chi Minh's birthday.

On January 29, 1975, the headquarters of the U.S. State Department in Washington, D.C., were bombed.

There were no casualties, but the bombing created extensive damage.

On October 20, 1981, several members of the Weather Underground murdered a Brinks security guard and stole more than a million dollars from an armored car in Nanuet, New York. Shortly after the robbery, the group was engaged by local police. Nyack, New York, police sergeant Edward O'Grady and Officer Waverly Brown were killed in the ensuing gun battle.

Over the course of a decade, the Weather Underground carried out at least twenty-five bombings. Among those killed by the group's activities were three of its own members. Terry Robbins and Diana Oughton were torn to shreds when a nail bomb they had built exploded in the group's Greenwich Village bomb factory. Another member of the group was killed when the building's façade came crashing down on his head. Now, I generally hate fireworks displays. But this was one that I can certainly get behind.

In subsequent years, the group's former leaders have attempted to rewrite history. Bill Ayers would claim that the group never intended to kill anybody. According to him, they were nothing more than wayward youths playing revolutionaries. But Ayers's account of the group's aims is contradicted by other members. In Bryan Burrough's 2015 book, *Days of Rage*, fellow Weather Underground member and alleged bomb maker Howard Machtinger put the lie to Ayers's whitewash. Machtinger said, "The myth, and this is always Bill Ayers's line, is that Weather never set out to kill people, and it's not true—we did."

Larry Grathwohl, an undercover FBI informant who in-filtrated the Weather Underground, said the group's aims and rhetoric went beyond sowing terror and killing a few cops. They were committed to genocide in the name of communist revo-lution. During an interview for the 1982 documentary *No Place to Hide*, Grathwohl recalled the answer he received when he asked Ayers what would happen after the group overthrew the U.S. government:

[They] believed that their immediate responsibility would be to protect against what they called the counter-revolution. They felt that this counter-revolution could best be guarded against by creating and establishing re-education centers in the southwest, where we would take all the people who needed to be re-educated into the new way of thinking and teach them how things were going to be. I asked, "well, what is going to happen to those people we can't re-educate that are die-hard capi-talists?" And the reply was that they'd have to be elimi-nated. And when I pursued this further, they estimated that they would have to eliminate 25 million people in these re-education centers. And when I say "eliminate," I mean kill.

Despite a mountain of damning evidence against the group, many of its leaders and some of its members managed to evade justice, eventually becoming celebrities in academic circles.

All charges were dropped against Ayers because of prosecu-torial misconduct, including improper FBI surveillance. Ayers became a professor of education at the University of Illinois at Chicago. The *Los Angeles Times* described Ayers as "very respected and prominent in Chicago [with] a national reputation as an educator."

In 1980, Ayers's wife, Bernardine Dohrn, was fined $1,500 for her activities and was placed on probation for three years. She became an associate clinical professor at Northwestern University School of Law, and for twenty-three years was the director of the school's Children and Family Justice Center.

In 2003, Kathy Boudin, one of the perpetrators of the 1981 Brinks robbery that led to the death of two police officers and a security guard, was paroled after serving twenty-two years for her part in the murders. In 2008 she was appointed as an adjunct professor at the Columbia University School of Social Work. It's also worth noting that Chesa Boudin, Kathy's son with fellow Brinks robbery alum David Gilbert, and who was the adopted son of Ayers and Dohrn, became the district attorney of San Francisco in 2020. Chesa was ultimately ousted from the position in 2022, but not before his policies helped turn San Francisco into more of a drug- and crime-infested city than it already was.

Alleged bomb maker Howard Machtinger became a professor at North Carolina Central University. Eleanor Raskin, who was indicted for bomb making (though the charges were eventually dropped), became an adjunct professor at Albany Law School. Susan Rosenberg, who was busted in New Jersey with 740 pounds of dynamite and weapons, had her sentence commuted by President Bill Clinton and went on to teach literature at John Jay College of Criminal Justice. Weather Underground leader Mark Rudd, who turned himself in to authorities in 1977 but was never convicted of the crimes of which he was accused, became a mathematics instructor at Central New Mexico Community College.

Just to recap: the two founders of a genocidal terrorist organization, an accessory to the murder of several police officers, and several bomb makers were returned to college campuses to teach your children. *And you're paying them to do it.*

By the late 1980s, the radical red-diaper babies of the 1960s and '70s had come of age, becoming professors, instructors, and administrators on campuses around the country. At about the time some Eastern Bloc nations were shooting their communist leaders in the face, Marxism had become entrenched in academia. "Marxism is dead everywhere except American universities" became a common joke following the fall of the Soviet Union.

In a *New York Times* article titled "The Mainstreaming of Marxism in U.S. Colleges," published in October 1989, Felicity Barringer wrote, "As Karl Marx's ideological heirs in Communist nations struggle to transform his political legacy, his intellectual heirs on American campuses have virtually completed their own transformation from brash, beleaguered outsiders to assimilated academic insiders."

The prevalence of communists on campus is only part of the problem. As communists' influence has increased in academia, all opposition has been pushed out. Professors who are inclined to teach theories that support the American system have been relegated to the dark corner of the universities. They are actively denied tenure and promotions because they are conservatives.

In 2007, associate professor of criminology Mike Adams sued officials at the University of North Carolina at Wilmington after he was denied full professorship. Adams claimed officials denied the promotion because he was outspoken about his conservative and Christian beliefs. After a seven-year legal battle, a jury in a federal court found in his favor. He was ultimately awarded full professorship and received seven years of back pay.

A quick look at the data shows that Adams's case is not unique. According to a study from the Center for the Study of Partisanship and Ideology, one in three conservative academics have been threatened with disciplinary action for expressing their beliefs. A further 70 percent of conservative academics reported that their department created a hostile environment for conservative ideas. More than half admit that they self-censor in their research and teaching. The universities you're sending your kids to aren't just adding communists, they're actively purging anyone who might teach them your values.

Not only does the widespread harassment and discrimination influence academics who are currently employed by universities, it prevents new conservative graduate students from pursuing careers in academia. This is, no doubt, the intended effect.

As a result of the persecution, conservative academics are a dying breed. A survey by *Econ Journal Watch* in September 2016 that investigated the voter registration of 7,243 professors at forty leading U.S. universities found that Democrats outnumber Republicans by an average of 11.5 to 1. The picture looks even more grim when broken down into fields of study. Republicans are most represented in the field of economics, where they're only outnumbered 4.5 to 1. In law, Democrats outnumber Republicans 8 to 1. In psychology, the ratio is 17.4 to 1. In journalism/communication, 20 to 1. In history, 33.5 to 1.

We are not merely surrounded, we are enveloped. We are the thong on Lizzo's body.

Many colleges have managed to eliminate conservatives altogether. The National Association of Scholars found in 2018 that among top-tier liberal arts colleges, 39 percent had no registered Republican professors in the entire school.

Think about what all of this means. If you're a Republican who is sending your kid to an elite university, there is a worse than 1-in-11 chance that your son or daughter is being instructed by someone who shares your values. This is nothing short of social suicide. Worse still, you are paying for it or saddling your children with hundreds of thousands of dollars in nondischargeable debt for the privilege.

Let's frame this another way. The body count of communism far exceeds what the evil Nazis were able to do. Mao alone is estimated to have killed around 65 million people. Yet if Nazi professors outnumbered conservatives in a particular university, would you send your son or daughter to attend that school? If Nazi professors outnumbered conservatives in a particular field of study, would you want your son or daughter to major in that field? Of course you wouldn't. But for some reason, we've accepted the idea that we're going to send our children off to be instructed by these ideological monsters. That's the extent to which communism has been normalized in American university life.

The bearded Marxists aren't the only problem. Those who promote communist ideas in their classrooms don't often apply the label to themselves. For every professor who declares his allegiance to Marx's twisted religion, there are still more whose beliefs incorporate aspects of Marxism. They call themselves Democratic socialists, progressives, or plain old Democrats.

"Some of my young colleagues call themselves neo-Marxists," Princeton historian Lawrence Stone told the *New York Times* in 1989. "I can't see much difference between their views and mine, and I call myself a liberal Democrat."

Whatever they call themselves, they are united in their hostility toward America and their hatred of you, your values, and everything you care about, make no mistake.

Which brings us to China. As if the homegrown communist threat wasn't enough, academia has welcomed the world's foremost communist nation onto American campuses with open arms. China's influence can be felt in many top-tier universities as they pump massive amounts of cash into these institutions.

According to a Bloomberg analysis of U.S. government data, about 115 colleges have received monetary gifts, contracts, or both from sources in mainland China since 2013. Harvard University alone has raked in $93 million, mostly in gifts, from China. And that's just the money we know about. Some universities have failed to disclose their foreign cash, as is required by law. In 2020, the U.S. Department of Education opened investigations into Yale and Harvard universities for failing to disclose hundreds of millions of dollars in gifts and contracts from foreign sources. The Department of Education alleged that Yale failed to disclose a total of $375 million in foreign money.

Since 2004, the Chinese government has funded the establishment of so-called Confucius Institutes in colleges and universities around the world, including twenty-seven that were still operational at the start of 2022. These institutes are supposedly centers for teaching American students Chinese language and courses on Chinese arts. In reality, they are designed to shape

American attitudes about Communist China. According to a report from the National Association of Scholars, the institutes "avoid Chinese political history and human rights abuses, present Taiwan and Tibet as undisputed territories of China, and develop a generation of American students with selective knowledge of a major country." The Chinese Communist Party (CCP) has called these institutes "an important part of China's overseas propaganda set-up."

What if the Soviet Union had acted so boldly? Could you imagine "Lenin Institutes" dotting U.S. campuses throughout the 1940s and '50s, offering courses in the Russian language and chugging crappy vodka while softening the image of communism? People would have never stood for it. Yet, here we are years later with the most powerful communist nation in the world operating in broad daylight in American schools.

In addition to being a threat to our students, the cozy relationship between academia and our sworn enemy has turned our colleges into soft targets for Chinese espionage. China is no different from the Soviet Union in that regard. The CCP is using universities to steal corporate and military secrets.

According to a 2018 report by the Australian Strategic Policy Institute, China's People's Liberation Army (PLA) routinely sends its soldiers to Western universities to collect military secrets. Students hide their affiliation with the PLA and collaborate on cutting-edge technologies like hypersonic missiles and advanced navigation techniques, a process the Chinese military refers to as "picking flowers in foreign lands to make honey in China." You think you're sending money to Harvard so little Aiden, Jaiden, and Alexis can get a good job one day.

But really, you're building the hypersonic missile that will potentially land in New York in the coming years.

## The Commie Curriculum

So, what exactly are they teaching on college and university campuses? Not surprisingly, the data suggest that communists are teaching . . . communism.

According to data from the Open Syllabus Project, which tracks books and other works assigned to students, Karl Marx is the single most assigned economist in U.S. college courses. The father of modern capitalism, Adam Smith, comes in at a distant second. Noted left-wing economist/doofus Paul Krugman comes in at third place. Marx has essentially become the baseline for students of economics. Just to be clear on this: American parents are sending their children to college, and those children are learning that the superior economic system is communism. *Communism*. The "land of the free" is teaching generation after generation about the greatness of communism.

There would be no problem in teaching Marx if the goal was to instruct students as to how destructive his theories were. It's useful to understand how a man could inspire the murder of almost 100 million people. But that's clearly not what's happening here. They're not learning *about Marxism*, they're learning *to be Marxists*.

This is demonstrated by the fact that Marx isn't taught in tandem with the great thinkers of the free West. For example, according to the Open Syllabus Project, *The Communist Manifesto* is the fourth most assigned book in U.S. colleges, outpaced only by a handful of writing manuals. Now, look at where the foundational works of freedom fall on that list. John Locke's *Second Treatise of Government*, the work that first declared that all men had a natural right to "life, liberty, and property," is the 32nd most assigned work on campuses. Adam Smith's *The Wealth of Nations*, which first described how the "invisible hand" of capitalism generated massive social benefits, is further down the list at 44. And the Declaration of Independence? Thomas Jefferson's masterpiece is buried at number 165. As a result, your son or daughter is as likely to be able to recognize the texts that were critical to America's founding as they are to recognize a WNBA player.

Now, I don't want to give the impression that communists in American universities focus exclusively on the works of Marx. Modern communism is not an orthodox religion rooted in fidelity to the German thinker. He's more like the soil from which the twisted tree of modern communist studies sprouted.

The most common form of Marxism being evangelized on campuses today is often referred to as "cultural Marxism." You see, the communist understood that all this "bourgeoisie" talk didn't work here. But he didn't change his religion. He changed his language. Cultural Marxism considers Western civilization to be a system of racism, white supremacy, and oppression. Cultural Marxism is thoroughly anticapitalist and replaces individual sovereignty with identity politics, victimology, and multiculturalism. This is the final form the Marxist ideology has taken after more than a century of evolution—the virulent strain of the communist disease that has come to infect all other institutions throughout the nation.

The origin of cultural Marxism can be traced back to a group of Marxist scholars in interwar Germany. Initially intending to call themselves the Institute for Marxism, the group ultimately became known as the Institute for Social Research in Frankfurt, or, as they're commonly called, the Frankfurt School. Although founded in Germany, the school was eventually moved to Columbia University in New York following the rise of the Nazi Party.

The school's most important contribution to the communist religion was called Critical Theory. I won't bore you, or myself, with the finer details of this philosophy, but the Heritage Foundation put together a handy list of the takeaways:

Marxist analysis of society made up of categories of oppressors and oppressed.

Language does not accord to an objective reality, but is an instrument of power dynamics.

The idea that the oppressed impede revolution when they adhere to the cultural beliefs of their oppressors— and must be put through re-education sessions.

Societal norms should be dismantled through relentless criticism.

The replacement of all systems of power and even the descriptions of those systems with a worldview that describes only oppressors and the oppressed.

These points are the keys to understanding communism in its current form. To take power, the communist believes the oppressed must be reeducated, communists must take control of the language, and they must bring an end to societal norms.

If you've ever questioned why communists seem hell-bent

on destroying everything, it's because that is exactly what they are doing. Get used to this because it will be a consistent theme: they are trying to burn it all down. Everything. The destruction is intentional. Critical Theory isn't just a challenge to the ideas that gave birth to the free world: it's the polar opposite. It reduces people to members of either an oppressor or oppressed group. This explains why the communist is so hostile to the idea of liberty. They no longer see value in individual rights because they no longer view people primarily as individuals. Instead, their group affiliation informs their identity.

The incorporation of Critical Theory also explains the communist's obsession with language. It's the reason we see a rise in speech codes on college campuses. It's why nearly everything that challenges the prevailing thought is considered "hate speech." It's given rise to concepts like "microaggressions," which encourages students to find offense in even the most innocent interactions.

In the communist's efforts to dismantle societal norms, traditional relationships are discouraged. Sexual deviance, for example, is seen as an alternative to traditional romantic arrangements. People are encouraged to have open or "poly-queer" relationships. Monogamous, heterosexual relationships are viewed as a tool of male power, otherwise known as "the patriarchy." This is why your daughter leaves for college as a normal teenager and returns as a pierced, pansexual, blue-haired land whale.

In short, Critical Theory is the dark heart of a modern university education. It is the source code for the new communist that rolls off the university assembly line.

Of course, not all classes involve hard-core indoctrination.

There's only so much a young mind can take, after all. The universities, therefore, also serve their students a ton of filler. If communism is the juicy burger, these classes are the useless lettuce and tomato that you would just as soon toss in the trash, where they belong. Let's take a gander at some of the lowlights:

- At Indiana University you can take a course on "Food, Sex, and Gender." According to the course description, the course "explores how food reflects and creates gender and promotes and expresses sexuality." I've been reliably informed that this class is not about Jell-O wrestling.

- At the University of Michigan, students can study "Eco/Queer/Feminist Art Practices." The class "investigates ecofeminist, queer ecological, and global feminist environmental justice art in visual art, sculptural practice, creative writing, performance, dance, somatic movement, and more." I have nightmares about what the "and more" may consist of.

- The University of Nebraska offers a course in "Saints, Witches, and Madwomen," which emphasizes how women "have been labelled in different periods as saintly, as witches, or as insane." The texts for the class are useless considering that the "witches" chapter makes no mention of Elizabeth Warren, and Maxine Waters fails to appear in the chapter about "madwomen." At least, I assume that's the case.

- At the University of Pennsylvania, vapid pop sing-
  ers take center stage in "Family Feuds: Beyoncé,
  Jay-Z and Solange and the Meaning of American
  Music." The course is a deep dive into Beyoncé's
  song "Lemonade," Solange's "A Seat at the Table,"
  and Jay-Z's "4:44." Perhaps students will finally
  learn the answer to Jay-Z's groundbreaking question, "What good is a ménage-à-trois when you
  have a soul mate?"

- Williams College offers "Buddhism, Sex, & Gender:
  #MeToo Then and Now." The course will help
  students answer the age-old riddle, "How did the
  Buddha's inner revolution produce a set of practices that both reject and reinforce existing bina-
  ries and social hierarchies of sex and gender?"

- And at Ohio State University, they're preparing
  students for World War Z with "Zombies: The
  Anthropology of the Undead."

These classes might appear innocuous at first, but I assure
you they're not. They're all part of the communist subversion
process.

In the 1980s, former KGB press and propaganda agent Yuri
Bezmenov gave a series of lectures in which he described
the process that the Soviet Union used to subvert or "demor-
alize" foreign nations. When it came to the education system,
he explained that the goal of the KGB was to promote useless
ideas in schools. "Distract them from learning something that

is constructive, pragmatic, efficient," Bezmenov said. "Instead of mathematics, physics, foreign languages, chemistry, teach them the history of urban warfare, natural food, home economy, and sexuality." With all due respect to Mr. Bezmenov, I fear a history of urban warfare will become increasingly relevant as the students of sexuality take the levers of power.

## The Communist Factories Bear Fruit

So, what has the steady diet of communist propaganda and useless crap in the universities produced? Exactly what was intended. Young people are increasingly viewing communism as an acceptable alternative to Western values.

According to a survey from YouGov conducted in 2020, 36 percent of millennials now say that they approve of communism. The report also showed that 22 percent of millennials believe "society would be better if all private property was abolished." Seventy percent of millennials say they are likely to vote for a socialist political candidate. Another poll carried out by Campus Reform found that 44 percent of millennials would rather live in a socialist country, while another 7 percent would prefer to live in a communist state.

This infatuation with communism is reflected in student activities on campus. Recent years have seen an acceleration in the growth of pro-communist student organizations. According to the Young Democratic Socialists of America, the youth and student wing of the Democratic Socialists of America, the organization expanded from 25 to 84 registered chapters between 2016 and 2019. As of January 2021, the group now claims 130 chapters on campuses around the country.

The shift toward radicalism has turned campuses into closed systems. Many now have the appearance of miniature communist states, directing hostility and violence toward anyone who challenges orthodoxy.

Since 2016, students have disinvited or attempted to disinvite 197 speakers from prominent colleges because of their political views, according to a database kept by the Foundation for Individual Rights and Expression. The vast majority of those disinvitations were against right-leaning speakers, at the bidding of the radical left.

When disinvitations don't occur, there have been numerous occasions where students responded with riots and violence.

In February 2017, a riot erupted on the University of California, Berkeley, campus over a planned speaking event featuring conservative commentator Milo Yiannopoulos. Rioters wearing masks threw commercial-grade fireworks and rocks at police. At least two College Republicans were physically assaulted while conducting an interview. UC Berkeley ultimately put a stop to the event, removing Yiannopoulos from the scene. According to administrators, the riot caused $100,000 worth of damage to the campus.

A similar scene played out at UC Berkeley two years later in November 2019, when half a dozen protesters were arrested while attempting to physically block people from entering a speech delivered by Ann Coulter. The mob reportedly chanted, "Go home, Nazis!" "Shame!" and "You're not getting in!"

The harassment is not limited to outside speakers. Students who don't toe the communist line are increasingly alienated and ostracized for their beliefs. A survey of one thousand Republican and Republican-leaning college students by College Pulse in

2019 found that nearly three-quarters of them have withheld their political views in class for fear that it would affect their grades. Some admitted to submitting essays that run counter to their beliefs to avoid scrutiny by professors. Others choose topics that they consider to be safe. One University of Louisville student admitted, "I would be crucified. I heard enough horror stories from friends and family to keep my mouth shut and avoid politics in class if at all possible."

## Shutting Down the Communist Factories

They have your children, America. For several generations now you've been sending your sons and daughters to colleges and universities in the hope that they were being prepared for a bright future. Instead, what emerged were vicious communists with more piercings than job skills. Now comes the difficult question: How do we begin to reverse the damage?

In a perfect world we would fire every university employee, seize their endowments, raze the old campuses, salt the earth, and replace them all with animatronic statues of Senator Joe McCarthy clapping his hands in approval. But I'm a practical man, and that all seems highly unlikely. For now, anyway.

When it comes to universities and colleges, the first step you must take as an anti-communist is to change your thinking about what these institutions are. That requires giving the devil his due. I'll be the first to admit it: the communist was right.

Are you surprised? Don't be. You're going to hear me say that a lot. The communist is right about a lot of things. Sure, his religion is pure evil, and he'd step over your corpse just as soon as he'd look at you, but it's important to admit when his methods have served him well. This is especially true when it comes to higher education.

Universities and colleges aren't just places where students go to learn. Nor are they four years of expensive day care for young adults who haven't yet decided what they want to do with their lives. They are workshops in which young minds are given shape. They are the most critical pipeline through which society is fed its future elites. No nation can survive with its universities and colleges teaching its students to hate it.

Too often, folks on the right are content with half measures but there can be no half measures when it comes to our universities. Eliminate any thoughts you may have about "real intellectual diversity" on campus. We don't need higher education to be fair and balanced. We need it to be dominated by people who value Western civilization and reject radical Marxist dogma. And just as the communist sought to use the universities to produce more communists, we must seek to have them produce a new generation of anti-communists.

Our first order of business is to stop the assembly line.

That process begins by keeping your own houses in order. Let me be perfectly clear: as an anti-communist, you need to stop sending your kids to these schools. Trust me, your life and the lives of your children will be much better for having done so.

Americans have been taught to believe that a degree from a college or university is the key to a prosperous future. You need to break this way of thinking both in yourself and your children. Would you take your child to the zoo and throw him into the gorilla enclosure? If the answer is no (and I really hope it is), then why would you send them to a university that hates you and hates them?

Every high school graduate should be encouraged to consider a skilled trade and attend vocational school or take on an apprenticeship. In doing so, they are guaranteed to begin developing an in-demand skill at a young age, which is more than can be said about many of their college-bound peers.

Furthermore, you'll be preventing your children from becoming saddled with massive amounts of student loan debt that will take them decades to pay off. This issue is only made worse by diminishing job prospects for young people who've chosen to pursue degrees with no practical use. According to *U.S. News & World Report*, the average student loan debt for recent college graduates in 2021 is nearly $30,000. If you are sending your kids to elite schools, that debt can be considerably higher. Servicing this much debt is crippling, especially if they end up majoring in art history with a minor in gender studies.

Now, while preventing your children from attending these institutions should be your first recourse, I understand that as a practical matter this isn't going to work for everyone. Many young people will choose to enter fields that require degrees. So, if you must send your son or daughter to one of these institutions, you have to be purposeful in inoculating them against the influence of Marxist professors.

Parents often forget how much influence they have over their own children or, even worse, they decide to relinquish that influence because of some ill-conceived notion of letting them develop a sense of personal independence. The truth is that if you don't use the influence you have over your own children, others will fill the void and do the job for you.

You need to leverage your parental influence to counter-balance the influence of Marxist professors and you need to start the process early. Don't wait until little Billy comes home with a tattoo of a hammer and sickle on his neck and a girlfriend with a penis before you start to act. It's already too late by then. The psychological damage will have already been done, and tattoo removal is painful and expensive.

You should begin introducing your children to the ideas of liberty when they're young. You'd be surprised at how much a basic understanding of individual rights and free market economics can go in preventing a kid from going down the communist path. Familiarize them with the Declaration of Independence. Assign your own reading based on their interests. If they have an interest in economics, pick up a copy of Milton Friedman's *Freedom to Choose* or Thomas Sowell's *Basic Economics*. Have them listen to the world-famous *Jesse Kelly Show*; after all, he is the greatest thinker of the modern era. In all cases, make sure they've read *The Anti-Communist Manifesto* by Jesse Kelly, which makes a great Christmas gift and will look very stylish on anyone's bookshelf or coffee table.

There's another important source of leverage that you have: your dollar. Your love for your children may be unconditional, but your financial support does not have to be. If you've promised to pay for your son's or daughter's education, that means you get a say in what they are learning. I know this may be difficult to hear, but if little Sally tells you she plans on majoring in women's literature or little Billy wants a degree in ethnic studies, you are perfectly within your rights to say no—and if you are a committed anti-communist, I would say that you have an obligation to say no.

The benefits of this approach will be twofold. First and foremost, you will be sparing your son or daughter from entering a field of study with no practical applications, only to emerge four years later with a degree that few employers are looking for. Second, you will be denying the communist more grist for the mill. By preventing young students from choosing academic tracks dominated by Marxist and neo-Marxist professors, we can help to dry up the demand for these fields.

Furthermore, all potential college students—even the gifted ones who are destined for elite universities—should be encouraged to consider two years of community college before they decide what path they want to take. There's no reason anyone should hand over thousands of dollars to a major university for a handful of undergraduate credits they can just as easily get for a fraction of the price at a community college. Ultimately, few future employers will care if an applicant received his associate's degree at a local college before transferring to a more prestigious school.

While preventing our sons and daughters from becoming communist foot soldiers is important, it's only part of this battle. We also must choke off the communist factory's money supply.

Again, this one starts at home. Stop sending money to your alma mater. Your alma matter probably sucks. The fond memories you have of getting high and playing Frisbee golf are hardly a valid excuse for you to fund your ideological enemy. If your alma mater is employing communists (which, let's face it, it is) and you're opening your wallet to them, then you are part of the problem. It would be preferable for you to toss your cash into a bonfire before funding a university that's churning out the next generation of communists.

I'm proud to have set an example in this regard. Despite being their most famous near graduate, I've never sent a dime to Pima County Community College. Of course, they've never asked me to, but that's because they've lost my address. Probably.

Government action will also be an important aspect of fighting back against the commie factories.

"But wait, Jesse," I already hear you saying. "Don't you believe in limited government?"

I want government small. You want government small. But government is not small. We must deal with life as it is, not as we want it to be. We can't allow our enemy to use our political principles to handcuff us, especially when he has no principles himself. As I've said, we need to use every weapon in our arsenal, and the government is nothing if not a powerful weapon.

State lawmakers should craft and pass legislation to limit the scope of funding to higher education with the goal of turning off the money valve to disciplines that produce communists. Remember when the government deemed certain jobs nonessential and prevented many people from going to work or opening their businesses during Covid-19 lockdowns? This is exactly the thinking we should be applying to state-run colleges and universities.

Fields of study that have little practical application should be deemed nonessential and excluded from all government funding. The government's focus should be on hard science, technology, engineering, and mathematics—the so-called STEM disciplines. Without state funding, many schools will be forced to shut down nonessential majors or find a source of funding elsewhere, helping to consign gender studies textbooks to the bargain shelf of Barnes & Noble with giant 80 percent off stickers on them.

State funded scholarships and student aid should come with similar conditions. Our tax dollars should not be going toward four years of indoctrination. It should be reserved for students who will emerge from college with useful skills that will be valuable to the economy.

In addition, we must shut down the university system's biggest source of easy money: student loans that are guaranteed by the federal government. For decades now, secured financing of student loans has allowed colleges and universities to consistently raise their prices, comfortable in the knowledge that the government will pick up the tab if the borrower is ultimately unable to pay. In turn, this has enabled schools to give lavish salaries to its professors, expand administrative bureaucracies, and offer more courses in pseudo-Bolshevism. If colleges and universities are going to sell useless diplomas to students, then *they* should cover the loss when their customers can't repay the loans—not the taxpayer.

Student loans have also had the effect of turning graduates into debt slaves. More than 40 million graduates together now owe more than $1.6 trillion as of the third quarter of 2021, according to the Federal Reserve Board. Many students are emerging from college with massive amounts of debt, with nothing more than a useless piece of paper to show for it. These graduates are likely to remain underwater for years, struggling to make ends meet while facing wage garnishment should they fall behind in their payments. This is sending them straight into the arms of socialist politicians who promise to alleviate their indentured servitude.

Not that our politicians would ever try something like that . . .

Also, stop taking out loans unless you have a rock-solid

plan to pay them back. Burying yourself in debt for a useless college degree from a communist university is no more responsible than an unemployed idiot taking at a loan to buy an eighty-five-inch television. In fact, it's even worse—at least the guy who bought the television can watch *I'm Right with Jesse Kelly* every weekday night at 9 p.m. Eastern/8 p.m. Central on The First TV.

But this doesn't go far enough. Colleges and universities must pay a steep price for churning out generations of communists and preying upon taxpayers and students.

I've seen many proposals to bring an end to higher education's predatory behavior, but anti-communists should rally behind the solution proposed by lawyer and conservative writer Will Chamberlain: seize the endowments. Many of these colleges and universities are swimming in money. Schools with the top ten endowments alone have close to $210 billion in assets to their name. A significant portion of this money is ill-gotten. Chamberlain writes:

> "Seize the Endowments" will help open the door for real policies to relieve the burden of student loans: we could make the debt dischargeable in bankruptcy, and write laws allowing the government to claw back assets to help compensate for the writedown. It also opens up the space for generally shutting off the river of government money to the universities, which seems moderate in comparison to simply seizing the endowment.

The best part of this proposal is that it isn't just practical, it's a punishment.

Finally, there's the issue of the cozy relationship between Communist China and American academia.

Colleges and universities should be forced to disclose any financial ties to China and any initiatives that are directly or indirectly funded by the CCP. They are already legally required to do so, but a report from the Senate's Permanent Subcommittee on Investigations found that nearly 70 percent of schools receiving more than $250,000 from organizations related to the Chinese government have failed to do so. Noncompliance should result in swift punishment.

All Confucius Institutes should be shuttered immediately. The world's foremost communist power can no longer be allowed to operate ideological beachheads on American soil.

These recommendations are far from a complete strategy to shut down America's communist factories. Think of them as our first strike, a good starting point in making sure that after eighteen years of loving our kids, we don't send them off to people who hate us. Remember, if you send your child to college, they're going to come out the other end with either your values or theirs. Make sure they're yours.

# ANTI-COMMUNIST ACTION ITEMS

- Introduce your children to the ideas of liberty when they're young.

- Stop sending your children to universities and colleges that hate you. Encourage your son or daughter to consider a skilled trade and attend vocational school or take on an apprenticeship.

- If you must send your children to a university or college, encourage them to spend two years in community college.

- Stop sending money to your alma mater.

- Cut off student loans for nonessential majors like gender and women's studies.

- Seize the endowments of universities and colleges.

- Punish universities and colleges that fail to disclose their financial ties to China and shutter all "Confucius Institutes."

# CHAPTER THREE

---

# Cultural Destruction

*Put destruction first, and in the process you have construction.*
—Mao Zedong

What if I showed up at your front door today, rang the doorbell, and asked you if I could burn your house to the ground? Would you let me?

Of course not. You'd probably call the cops and/or stick a gun in my face. You'd have good reason to do so. You love your home. Your home has value to you. You have memories in your home. There are pictures, plates, furniture, and decorations in there that are precious to you. Even that couch your wife has ruined by adding too many pillows and blankets has meaning to you. Your house is where you sleep at night. It's where you grew up. It's where you raised a family. It's where you celebrated birthdays and holidays. You won't let me burn down your home because you are *moored* to your home.

Your nation is also your home. Just like your house, its value comes from its familiarity, the protection it provides, the memories it invokes, and the pride it makes you feel. And that's precisely why the communist wants to burn it to the ground.

The communist is smart enough to know you're not just going to let him burn your house down. He knows he must first unmoor you from your home. If he can do that, if he can separate you from those memories and make your home nothing more than a building, he won't even have to burn down your home. You'll light the match yourself. So, he doesn't show up with a can of gasoline asking if he can torch the place. He shows up and asks if you'll let him in so he can improve the place.

You start by bringing him into your living room. Here you'll show him the photos on the wall of your family. Your parents, who raised you. Your grandparents, who told you stories about the old days. The black-and-white portraits of older generations whom you only know through family legend. The communist will look at the images and say, "Don't you remember that your father was a workaholic and your mother spanked you? Don't you realize your grandfather was an alcoholic and your grandmother was an enabler? And don't get me started on these awful racists who came before them."

Venturing farther into the home, you enter your kitchen. Here you'll tell the communist about the times you baked cookies with your children during the holidays and all the delicious meals you prepared for your family. The communist will tell you, "Don't you remember that time you burned your hand on the oven rack? Or the time you sliced your finger with the paring knife? What a dangerous place this kitchen is—filled with horror stories of scorched skin and bloody countertops."

Then you'll take him into the backyard. You'll share the memories of birthday celebrations and Independence Day cookouts. The communist will look around and reply, "Isn't that the tree your son was climbing when he fell and broke his arm? Isn't that the spot where your daughter burned her hand with a sparkler on the Fourth of July?"

Finally, you'll take the communist into your basement. Before you can even get a word out, he'll yell, "Termite damage!"

You might tell the communist how awful a guest he's been and kick him out of your house at that point. But another thought might creep into your mind: maybe he's right. Maybe you have been viewing your house through rose-colored glasses this whole time. This is exactly what the communist wants. The communist has alienated you from your house. He's convinced you to hate it so that the next time he shows up at your front door, you'll be begging him to set a match to the place.

This is what the communist is doing to your nation. Every time he tells you that the founders were white supremacists or that Christopher Columbus was a genocidal madman, he's undermining your love for your home. Every time he vandalizes a monument, pulls a statue down off its pedestal, or builds one for a drug dealer, he's unmooring the American people from the country's foundations. Rest assured, he is doing this on purpose and he's doing this so he can be permitted to destroy this country.

## Dominating the Past

The arrival of the communist is heralded by a simple word: destruction. Destroying monuments to the past and perverting history are his way of making sure you hate yourself and your country enough to let him destroy it. It's not just a tactic he uses in his quest for power, it's the base tenet of his sick religion. As you will hear me say repeatedly, the communist lives to destroy. He is devoted to it. That's why everything he touches turns to ash. You don't have to understand this way of thinking. But you most definitely *do* have to understand that's how he thinks.

To discover the truth, we must go back to the source. Marx declared in *The Communist Manifesto* that in a capitalist society, "the past dominates the present; in Communist society, the present dominates the past." Marx elaborated on this idea in 1852, writing, "The tradition of all dead generations weighs like a nightmare on the brains of the living." The communist views the past as an obstacle. Like all other obstacles in his path, it must be torn down. What came before him must be wiped clean before the new revolutionary order can be established. A people's connection to their history informs their present, so the communist seeks to break that connection to replace it with something different.

By destroying statues, monuments, and icons, the communist is attempting, in Marx's words, to dominate the past. He is eliminating the bedrocks that anchor people to their history. This is a process I call cultural destruction.

It's a bit of a cliché to quote George Orwell, but in his book *1984,* he absolutely nails it when he describes the ultimate goal of cultural destruction. Orwell's protagonist, Winston Smith, is employed at the Ministry of Truth, where his job is to rewrite history to reflect the current "truth" as dictated by the ruling party. Winston explains that "every picture has been repainted, every statue and street building has been renamed. . . . History has stopped. Nothing exists except an endless present in which the Party is always right." This is what the communist seeks to achieve. He wants a present that is free from the influence of the past, and an ignorant population that believes the communist's truth is the only one that exists. (In case you believe that's not happening here in the United States, just remember, the vaccine is totally effective at stopping the spread of coronavirus . . .)

The same story plays out in every nation where communism takes root: not long after the ruling party seizes power, they go to work eliminating everything that came before them. They attack political tradition by destroying reminders of the former political order. They attack martial tradition by toppling monuments of long-dead military leaders. They attack moral tradition by destroying religious icons, churches, and tributes to martyrs. Once gone, they are all replaced by statues of communist leaders, monuments to a new generation of martyrs, and icons of his own godless faith that the people will be forced to venerate. If you visit New York City today, you can no longer enjoy a statue of Teddy Roosevelt. He's been taken down. But you *can* take in a brand-new statue of their sainted George Floyd.

Whether it's a statue of Thomas Jefferson or Robert E. Lee, the rage you see directed at statues and monuments celebrating our past is part of the same story. And it's not a happy story. More of the kind of story where everyone you love dies in the end—and not even in a heroic way. But before we dive into statues being toppled in American parks, it'll be helpful to take a detour into history to watch the communist at work erasing the cultures that had once stood in his way.

## The Remaking of Russia

When looking at the destructive nature of communism, it's always best to start with the Russian Revolution, since the policies of the Bolsheviks in the early twentieth century would become the template for communist revolutions across the world.

For the newly installed Marxist-Leninist government, the influence of Russia's czars was the first thing that needed to be swept away. After Czar Nicholas II, his wife, and his children were yanked from their beds in the middle of the night, lined up against a basement wall, and shot by communists in 1918 by order of Vladimir Lenin, monuments to the czars were toppled across the nation.

- In 1918, a statue of Alexander III in front of Moscow's Cathedral of Christ the Savior was beheaded and dismantled. Several years later, the cathedral in front of which it stood would be reduced to rubble and turned into a swimming pool.

- In the city of Samara, a towering monument to Alexander II met a similar fate. Ironically, the statue was a tribute to the man who had emancipated Russia's serfs in 1861. It was replaced by a statue of Lenin.

- A statue of Czar Peter the Great in St. Petersburg— which depicted the Russian leader as a young carpenter in Holland—fell to the Bolsheviks less than a decade after it had been installed. The statue was melted down to provide munitions for the Red Army.

- In 1920, a monument to Alexander II in Kyiv was removed. The monument was ultimately replaced by an eight-meter figure of a Red Army soldier made of plywood.

This is just a small sampling of the czarist-era statues that were destroyed in the wake of the Bolshevik takeover. In their place, thousands of statues of Lenin, Marx, Stalin, and other communist heroes arose across the Soviet Union.

Statues weren't the only monuments to the czars that had to be eliminated. After taking power, the communists went on a city-renaming spree across Russia. Shortly after the death of Vladimir Lenin in 1924, the Bolsheviks rechristened the city of St. Petersburg, named in honor of Czar Peter the Great, Leningrad, as a tribute to their dearly departed leader. In 1925, Lenin's successor, Joseph Stalin, changed the name of the city of Tsaritsyn to Stalingrad. The city of Ekaterinburg, originally named for Czarina Catherine the Great, became "Sverdlovsk" after Bolshevik leader Yakov Sverdlov. In the end, the names of hundreds of cities and towns across Russia would be changed to suit the communists' needs.

Russian streets, infrastructure, and parks were given the same treatment. If you were visiting a Russian city during Soviet rule, it was likely that you would travel down Karl Marx Street, drive across Friedrich Engels Bridge, or spend the day in Lenin Park. There was also a good chance that you would be doing so in a car or bus that rolled off the assembly line of a factory named after Stalin. (Not that names would ever be changed in this country, right? By the way, if you're looking for directions to Occidental College, take a right when you get off President Barack H. Obama Highway.)

It's probably worth mentioning that in addition to all the damage the Bolsheviks did to Russia's cultural heritage, they also went ahead and killed millions of people—an estimated 20 million by one count.

While the Bolsheviks initially set the standard for cultural destruction, the Chinese Communist Party took it to a new level in 1966. That year, CCP chairman (and modern icon of the professor who's currently teaching your child in college) Mao Zedong ushered in the Cultural Revolution. While the party had already made efforts to stamp out pre-communist ideas in China, Mao believed those efforts had not gone far enough. "Chairman Mao often says that there is no construction without destruction," read a circular released by the CCP. "Put destruction first, and in the process you have construction."

At the heart of this new Cultural Revolution was what became known as the destruction of the "Four Olds": old customs, old cultures, old habits, and old ideas. Let's pause for a moment, because this is a helpful juncture if you want to understand the methods of the communist. What exactly do those four "olds" mean? They're pretty vague, right? Why wasn't Mao more specific about what he wanted destroyed? He didn't give specifics, for the same reason nobody can seem to define *equity* or how to achieve it today. They don't *want* specifics. Specifics put limits on them. Since their destruction is without end, you'll never get specifics.

The Four Olds movement was enthusiastically embraced by the militant Red Guard, young communists drawn largely from universities and high schools. Here's how the *Peking Review*, an official newspaper of the CCP, described the opening days of Mao's Cultural Revolution:

> Beating drums and singing revolutionary songs, detachments of Red Guards are out in the streets doing propaganda work, holding aloft big portraits of Chairman Mao, extracts from Chairman Mao's works, and great banners with the words: We are the critics of the old world; we are the builders of the new world. They have held street meetings, put up big-character posters, and distributed leaflets in their attack against all the old ideas and habits of the exploiting classes. As a result of the proposals of the Red Guards and with the support of the revolutionary masses, shop signs which spread odious feudal and bourgeois ideas have been removed, and the names of many streets, lanes, parks, buildings, and schools tainted with feudalism, capitalism, or revisionism or which had no revolutionary significance have been replaced by revolutionary names.

The first symbols of traditional China to go were the names of roads, parks, and places across the country. Traditional street names were replaced on the map with names like Great Leap Forward Road, Red Sun from the East Road, or Red Guard Road. Parks were given names like Worker-Peasant-Soldier Park or People's Park. Blue Sky clothing store became Defending Mao Zedong clothing store. Peking Union Medical College Hospital became Anti-Imperialist Hospital. The street in front of the embassy of the Soviet Union—whom the Chinese communists considered to be insufficiently revolutionary—was renamed Oppose Revisionism Street.

The statues were next to fall. Monuments to former emperors were vandalized, dismantled, and destroyed. In their place arose statues of Mao Zedong.

It's probably worth mentioning that in addition to all the damage the communists did to China's cultural heritage, they also went ahead and killed millions of people—an estimated 65 million by one account.

The only revolution to compare to Mao's Cultural Revolution in terms of pure savagery was that of the Khmer Rouge in Cambodia. Just as the Chinese Communist Party had come to believe that the Soviet Union had not gone far enough in implementing its vision for a classless utopia, the Cambodian communists believed the CCP had not been radical enough. (You see this concept all over America today. "We just haven't gone far enough." Mad about inflation and the national debt? We just have to spend even more. Transsexual children committing suicide at an alarming rate? That doesn't mean we should discourage such things. We just haven't encouraged it *enough*. That's how the communist thinks.)

Either way, immediately after the Khmer Rouge took control of the Cambodian capital of Phnom Penh, the group's leaders set about erasing history and hitting the reset button on Cambodian society, officially declaring that 1975 would be "year zero." The new Cambodia, Khmer Rouge leader Pol Pot declared, would start from scratch.

Not long after deposing Cambodia's previous government, the communists announced the nation would be renamed

Democratic Kampuchea. Major cities were systematically evacuated, with all citizens forced to relocate to agricultural labor camps in the countryside.

The concept of year zero became more than a declaration of war against the past: it was a governing philosophy of the Khmer Rouge. Monuments to the nation's deposed royal family were smashed. The regime abolished money, markets, and private property. As the group's chief ideologue, Khieu Samphân, explained, "Zero for him and zero for you—that is true equality."

All knowledge of the nation's history before year zero was to be eliminated. Libraries and books were burned. Cultural sites were looted and national treasures were vandalized or destroyed.

It's probably worth mentioning that in addition to all the damage the communists did to Cambodia's cultural heritage, they also went ahead and killed millions of people—an estimated 2 million by one account.

## The Red Religion vs. the Competition

While erasing the national heritage of a nation is a significant part of the communist's agenda, there's another pillar of culture he takes particular pleasure in destroying: the faith of the masses.

To Marx, religion was yet another means of control that the bourgeois used to keep the working class oppressed. "Religion is the sigh of the oppressed creature, the heart of a heartless world, just as it is the spirit of a spiritless situation," Marx declared. "It is the opium of the people. The abolition of religion as the illusory happiness of the people is required for their real happiness."

Marx's criticism of religion was enthusiastically embraced by Vladimir Lenin, who called it "the cornerstone of the entire ideology of Marxism." Lenin declared that all religions and churches were "the organs of bourgeois reaction, used for the protection of the exploitation and the stupefaction of the working class." It's no surprise, then, that the toppling of statues and renaming of streets appears quaint compared to Lenin's ruthless campaign against the Russian Orthodox Church.

Seeking to replace religion of the Russian people with "scientific atheism," Lenin officially dissolved the relationship between the church and the state shortly after taking power. According to the Russian Communist Party, their aim was "the complete destruction of links between the exploiting classes and . . . religious propaganda, while assisting the actual liberation of the working masses from religious prejudices and organizing the broadest possible education-enlightening and anti-religious propaganda."

Church property was nationalized and seized by communist soldiers. Church doors were shuttered or appropriated for use by the state. Seeking to eliminate any trace of what they considered to be superstition, the communist minions plundered holy relics from monasteries and attempted to prove they were frauds. When citizens and church leaders defended the holy sites, they were often arrested or mercilessly gunned down.

In China, the communists engaged in a similar campaign, targeting Buddhism, Taoism, and Confucianism. Statues of Buddha and Taoist deities were toppled, burned, and beheaded. Temples and monasteries were looted and torched or appropriated for communist use. Monks and priests who objected were imprisoned or killed.

Like the Bolsheviks before them, the Chinese communists also targeted cemeteries and graves they believed were associated with the old ways. Of note was their desecration of the Cemetery of Confucius, which had housed the remains of the philosopher and his family for over two thousand years. In late 1966, the Red Guard descended on the cemetery and laid waste to it for twenty-nine days. Graves were dug up. Corpses were defiled. Thousands of cultural artifacts were looted or destroyed. Statues and monuments were smashed. More than one hundred thousand classical texts were burned or pulped. Shortly after their orgy of destruction, members of the Red Guard sent a telegram to Chairman Mao boasting of their actions. "[W]e have torn down the plaque extolling the 'teacher of ten-thousand generations,'" the message read, "we have leveled Confucius' grave; we have smashed the stelae extolling the virtues of the feudal emperors and kings, and we have obliterated the statues in the Confucius Temple!"

In Cambodia, the Khmer Rouge took great care to wipe out any trace of Buddhism, which had served as a central part of Cambodian identity for centuries. During their reign, statues of Buddha were torn down or used as target practice. Most monks and religious leaders were either murdered or driven into exile, and nearly every Buddhist temple and library was destroyed. After years of destruction, Yun Yat, minister of culture in the Khmer Rouge regime, declared, "Buddhism is dead, and the ground has been cleared for the foundations of a new revolutionary culture."

While these sick displays of hostility toward the faiths of the people may look like efforts to eliminate religion, the truth, as I've already said, is that communism is a religion. As such, communists are not looking to destroy religion, they're looking to monopolize it by erasing the competition.

Don't believe me? Let me illustrate.

In what was arguably the most macabre aspect of their anti-religious campaign, Russian communists disinterred and desecrated the remains of Orthodox saints. Prior to the revolution, it had been common for Orthodox Christians to make pilgrimages to view the remains of the saints, a practice the Bolsheviks viewed as barbaric. After taking power, the party vowed to "fully liquidate the cult of dead bodies."

Ironically, when Lenin died in 1924, his body was preserved and placed within a glass sarcophagus. Every year since, millions have made the pilgrimage to Red Square to catch a glimpse of the corpse of their own communist saint.

## It Began with Columbus

Communists are already doing these things in the United States and other Western nations. You don't have to sit around and wonder when all this will happen here. The onslaught is already started. Fittingly, it started with the man most responsible for the European conquest of the Americas, Christopher Columbus.

In 1925, the small Italian American community in Richmond, Virginia, organized a campaign to erect a statue of Columbus. The statue would be the first of its kind in the South, a celebration of the Italian explorer who discovered the New World. The monument faced immediate opposition. The same year, the Richmond City Council rejected the proposal, in part due to the agitation of members of the Ku Klux Klan. Throughout the 1920s, the nativist Klan had engaged in a coast-to-coast campaign to prevent the honoring of Columbus. The group objected to the explorer's foreign origin and Catholic faith.

Despite the fierce opposition, the community persisted. The

City Council eventually reversed its decision. In 1926 ground was broken and the statue was dedicated the following year. For close to a century, the bronze statue overlooked Richmond's Byrd Park and served as a regular gathering place for Italian Americans on the eve of Columbus Day, where they would eat spaghetti and exchange gold chains (probably).

That all changed in 2020.

In June of that year, following the death of Saint George Floyd, the statue was ripped from its foundations, set on fire, and thrown into a nearby lake. The statue that had overcome the Ku Klux Klan a century earlier had fallen to the destructive forces of communism in a matter of moments.

Richmond wasn't the only city in which a statue of Columbus was toppled. In Boston, St. Paul, Denver, and Baltimore, statues of the explorer were torn down or damaged beyond repair. Many of the statues the communist mobs failed to destroy were removed by local governments. For example, in Columbus, Ohio, which is, ironically, named in honor of the explorer, a statue of him that had stood in City Hall since 1955 was vandalized with the word *rapist* written across its base. The next day, the city's mayor announced it would be removed. Dozens of other cities made the same decision, including Chicago, Trenton, San Antonio, San Francisco, and Philadelphia.

The erasure goes beyond statues. Columbus Day, which has been a national holiday since 1937, is no longer observed in many states. Instead it's been replaced by Indigenous Peoples' Day, which, in October 2021, President Joe Biden became the first president to officially recognize. It's only a matter of time before Columbus Day is removed from the federal calendar completely.

That was the *what*. Now for the *why*. Why tear down statues of Christopher Columbus? Why tear down statues of Teddy Roosevelt or Robert E. Lee? Is the modern American street communist genuinely concerned about what Columbus and his men did to the Indians? Are they worried about Teddy Roosevelt's past? Do they tear out their twelve nose rings at the plight of black people in America's slave era?

Be serious. The communist is unbothered by cruelty and death. Cruelty and death are his life's purpose. The American communist doesn't actually care about *anything* he tells you he cares about. Again, he just wants to destroy. He starts with targets you'll be more likely to accept. These are just an appetizer for him. He'll destroy it all if allowed.

Back to Columbus: they've held a grudge against the explorer for more than a century and a half, beginning with Karl Marx himself. In his book *Capital,* Marx all but blames Columbus's discovery of the New World for the rise of capitalism. He writes:

> The discovery of gold and silver in America, the extirpation, enslavement and entombment in mines of the aboriginal population, the beginning of the conquest and looting of the East Indies, the turning of Africa into a warren for the commercial hunting of black-skins, signalised the rosy dawn of the era of capitalist production.

Their opinion of Columbus hasn't changed much.

The historical reality of Christopher Columbus is complicated, and you can form your own opinions on him. I'll leave that to the historians (if you can find a sane one these days). It really doesn't matter what you think of him. What does matter is that you understand *why* the communist wants him banished from memory. Columbus is part of American history, and you cannot remove that history without removing him. As anti-American Marxist historian Howard Zinn, whose revisionist history book *A People's History of the United States* is required reading for students across the country, said, showing his hand, "Objectivity is impossible and it is also undesirable." Instead, Zinn continued, history should serve a "social aim." In other words, the communist's goal is to replace history with his own mythology.

To that end, Zinn and his comrades remythologized Columbus, transforming him from a revered explorer into a genocidal madman. This new mythology serves as the baseline of evil on which the free world was founded. For the communist, Columbus is a symbol of slavery, exploitation, private property. More broadly, he represents what they consider the worst sin in modern history: the establishment of the United States of America.

## The Slippery Slope

That's enough talk about Italians for one non-mafia book. I already feel like I need some gold chains around my neck and a track suit. Let's get back to the Confederate generals I touched on earlier.

Over the past few years, 270 Confederate statues and tributes have come down, either toppled by mobs or removed by government decree. In addition to the targeting of statues, there is a growing effort to eliminate any commemoration of Confederate military leaders, including street names, and military bases named in their honor. The move to scrub the Confederacy from the public consciousness has been celebrated by the left, and even many on the right, as part of a "historical reckoning" or an effort to establish "racial justice."

"Monuments to men who advocated cruelty and barbarism to achieve such a plainly racist end are a grotesque affront to these ideals," declared then–House Speaker Nancy Pelosi. "Their statues pay homage to hate, not heritage. They must be removed."

Republican senator Mike Rounds of South Dakota agreed with Pelosi. "If we're going to have bases throughout the United States, I think it should be with the names of individuals who fought for our country," Rounds told reporters. "This is the right time for it."

"[I'm] not opposed to it," added then–House minority leader Kevin McCarthy, a Republican.

As was to be expected, anyone who broke with the conventional wisdom was smeared as a racist who must sympathize with the cause of the Confederacy. Even the gentlest of defenses was considered out of bounds.

In 2017, shortly after the events in Charlottesville, Virginia, which had been precipitated by the planned removal of a statue of Confederate general Robert E. Lee, President Donald Trump predicted that the razing of the statue would lead to a slippery slope. "This week it's Robert E. Lee," Trump said at an August press conference. "I wonder, is George Washington next week and is it Thomas Jefferson the week after? You really do have to ask yourself: 'Where does it stop?'"

Trump was immediately dragged for the suggestion.

In the *Atlantic*, writer David Graham called Trump's slippery-slope argument a "canard" that "falls apart under scrutiny."

NBC News published a piece titled "Statues of Washington, Jefferson Aren't 'Next,' but It's Complicated." NPR ran a "fact check" of Trump's statement and arrived at the brilliant conclusion that statues of Washington and Jefferson weren't going to come down because "they are not all the same" as statues of Lee.

As we now know, Trump's critics were all wrong. It soon became clear that the slope wasn't just slippery—it was a sheet of ice covered in ball bearings and baby oil. During the 2020 George Floyd protests and shortly thereafter, the communists went on a rampage. Their targets weren't limited to Confederates this time, but included the founding fathers, national heroes, and religious figures.

- In Portland, Oregon, protesters tore down a statue of George Washington and set fire to its head. They spray-painted the granite pedestal with "BLM" and "Big Floyd."

- Statues of Thomas Jefferson were either toppled by protesters or removed by officials in New York, Oregon, and Georgia.

- In San Francisco's Golden Gate Park, statues of Francis Scott Key and a bust of General Ulysses S. Grant were all toppled.

- In Boston, a copy of the so-called Emancipation Memorial was removed from Park Square. The original statue, which depicted Abraham Lincoln and a black man breaking free of the chains of slavery, had stood in the park for over 140 years.

- In New York City, a statue of Theodore Roosevelt accompanied by a Native American and a black man was removed by the American Museum of Natural History.

Even the nation's capital is no longer safe from the cultural vandals. In 2020, a committee reporting to Washington, D.C., mayor Muriel E. Bowser called on the city to "remove, relocate or contextualize" the Jefferson Memorial and the Washington Monument. The group also recommended removing the names of Jefferson, Benjamin Franklin, and Francis Scott Key from city buildings. The offending monuments, the committee explained, celebrated "persons of concern" who had "disqualifying histories."

"In all instances," the committee wrote, "we believe strongly that all District of Columbia owned public spaces, facilities and commemorative works should only honor those individuals who exemplified those values such as equity, opportunity and diversity that DC residents hold dear." In their place, the committee recommended the city "identify diverse candidates to honor," including "more women, people of color and LGBTQ Washingtonians."

So, how did we go from Robert E. Lee and Stonewall Jackson to George Washington and Thomas Jefferson in the blink of an eye? The answer is easy if you've been paying attention. Confederates were just an appetizer.

The toppling of Confederate monuments was never about racial justice or facing historical truths—it was about opportunity. The communist doesn't care about "racism," and he sure doesn't care about the Civil War. He simply knew most Americans were uncomfortable defending the monuments because of their association with slavery and the communists knew that cowardly politicians and the media class wouldn't dare object. In short, Confederate generals were the easy targets. They were the foot in the door.

So, what is the ultimate target? Well, not to put too fine a point on it, but the ultimate target is everything. The communist wants to destroy absolutely everything. Your foundations, your statues, your history, your values, your books. He wants to destroy it all. Whether it's President Abraham Lincoln or President Jefferson Davis, General Ulysses S. Grant or General Robert E. Lee, the communist hates them all the same because they're all part of the fabric of America. Any reverence paid to these men only serves to enshrine, in the minds of Americans, the system that they are desperate to burn to ash.

## How to Fight Back Against Cultural Destruction

The statues are falling. The names are being changed. The process of uprooting the American people from their culture and history is already under way. If it is allowed to continue unopposed, the tributes to the great men of America's past will be replaced by the ideological totems of the communist—not only in the bronze sculptures that occupy our parks and town squares, but in the hearts and minds of future generations. It's time for the anti-communist to step up and turn back the tide.

Think back to the story I told you at the beginning of this chapter about the communist who wanted to burn down your house. In every room he visited, he used a nugget of truth to alter your perspective of your home. He used your father's strict work ethic and your mother's discipline in your living room. He used your sliced skin and burnt hands in the kitchen. In the backyard, he used your son's broken arm and your daughter's burnt fingers. In the basement, it was all about the termite damage.

These were all things that you already knew about your home, but you never thought to smash the photos of your parents, rip out your oven, or chop down the tree in your backyard. Unpleasant as they may have been, you understood them in their full context. They are as much a part of what makes your home special as are the home-cooked meals and backyard birthday parties. In other words, you came to terms with those things.

Your nation is no different. To preserve your culture and history, you first must come to terms with them. To do that, you must stop fearing history. The communist wants you to be meek in the face of the past. His new mythology declares that the Western world was uniquely founded upon suffering, death, and war. He uses that ugliness to get you to go along with his desecrations. The communist's greatest ally is not his soy-based comrades who help him pull down statues; it's those who hide in fear when someone is needed to defend those monuments.

History is dark. All of it. It's a place filled with bloodshed and conflict. People were killed. Nations were conquered. Cultures were destroyed or subsumed. This is not the history of America, it's the history of mankind. Once you've fixed this reality in your mind, it will act as the most effective suit of armor you can wear against the communist. You should feel no shame in the fact that America was born the same way as every other nation that ever existed. Rather, you should be proud of the fact that what emerged from the storm was the greatest nation to have ever graced God's earth.

You also need to make sure your children accept it as early as possible. Remember, it was the high school and college students of the Red Guard who were the most prolific vandals during Mao's cultural revolution. The communist's most powerful instrument in cultural destruction is not a can of spray paint or a long chain: it's young people. You see the college student as some harmless idiot. Just an ignorant child who will wake from his slumber, wash the pink out of his hair, and become a contributing member of society. The communist has always understood the real truth: that kid is the foot soldier who will wield the guns and pull the trigger.

The communist wants to inspire guilt and contempt for the past. These are the emotions that are in the heart of every man or woman who's ever smashed a monument, whether it honored the czars, Confucius, or Thomas Jefferson. As a parent, you need to inspire appreciation. In appreciating the full picture, your kids will be less likely to be fooled by the one-sided portrait the communist paints for them. While your children are likely to be fed the new mythology in schools and through popular culture, you should be eager to counteract it with a healthy dose of reality. I imagine that conversation would go something like this:

**Son:** Dad, today our teacher taught us about what happened when the Europeans came to America.

**Dad:** Europeans didn't just come to America, son. They conquered it.

**Son:** She told us all about how the Europeans killed indigenous people.

**Dad:** Because they did. That's how conquest works. The Europeans showed up and found several tribes, often at war with each other. The tribes didn't have the technology, the immune system, or the willingness to work together to defeat the Europeans. This same story can be told about every plot of ground on the planet.

See? At no point did Dad run away from reality. Instead he acknowledged it and added context that the peddlers of the new mythology conveniently ignore.

Armoring yourself and your loved ones against the communist mythology is an important first step, but it's not going to prevent the next wave of the American cultural revolution. It's not enough to mutter to yourself, "But those guys weren't too bad" as statues tumble to the ground like Joe Biden climbing a flight of stairs. And there's something critical you have to understand: saying no is not enough. It's necessary, but it's not near enough. That's defense. Play offense. The answer to the communist destruction of your culture is to build even more of it. Feed the communist whatever he hates.

According to a recent count, there are 171 statues or monuments of George Washington, 149 of Christopher Columbus, 59 of Robert E. Lee, and 36 of Thomas Jefferson still standing across the United States. Don't just protect them. Double those numbers. Every single one is a treasure and will eventually become a target for communists. You need to rally your fellow anti-communists in their defense. Know where these statues are in your community. Show up at your city council meetings and demand the protection of current statues and the building of new ones.

The communist is inevitably going to push back against anyone who comes to the defense of a statue they find objectionable. They're going to call you names. They're going to call you a white supremacist or a neo-Confederate, or claim that you sympathize with slavery. This is where you must understand the tactic the communist loves the most: using your values against you. You must understand that that's what he's doing and refuse him that. Laugh at his insults. Would you stress about the opinion of the worm slithering across your sidewalk? No. Then don't worry about the opinion of the communist. His opinion is worth less than the worm.

The communist mob aren't the only cultural vandals. Invertebrate politicians operating in broad daylight arguably represent a greater threat to these monuments than the masked Bolsheviks who work in the dead of night. For every statue that was torn down by chains and hammers, half a dozen more were taken by a vote or decree. These politicians should be put on notice: the protection of our history is always on the ballot. Weakness in the face of the mob will not be tolerated, and their political careers will meet the same fate as those statues they vote to remove from their pedestals.

It should go without saying that George Washington, Thomas Jefferson, and Christopher Columbus should be a fixture in every city, town, and hamlet in America. We should be able to travel from the Atlantic Ocean to the Pacific without losing sight of a monument to one of these historical giants. So, in addition to dedicating new statues of these men in places across the country, I propose we change the name of U.S. Route 20, which stretches from Boston, Massachusetts, to Newport, Oregon, to the George Washington Highway.

In addition, I've drawn up a short list of monuments and tributes I'd like to see pop up in the future:

- A statue of Senator Joseph McCarthy overlooking the Harry S. Truman Building, the headquarters of the U.S. State Department.

- The street in front of the Chinese Embassy in Washington, D.C., should be renamed "Victims of Communism Plaza."

- While we're redecorating the Chinese Embassy, Colonel Lewis "Chesty" Puller—a Marine Corps legend with arguably more Chicom notches on his bayonet than any other American in history— should have a statue facing the front door.

- The Museum of Television & Radio (now Paley Center for Media) should establish a Rush Limbaugh Wing.

- Bill Darden, the founder of Red Lobster, should have a statue in his hometown of Waycross, Georgia, that will hereafter be known as "Cheddar Bay."

Finally, anti-communists need to support and build constant reminders of communism's bloody legacy. "But Jesse," I already hear you asking, "what does anti-communism have to do with American history? Surely that would be more appropriate in the former Soviet states or eastern Germany, right?" Nonsense. Anti-communist history *is* American history. The fight against the communist is as critical a part of our past, present, and future as the overthrow of the British Crown or our role in the defeat of the Third Reich. Our culture needs to reflect our commitment to that fight.

To that end, America should be covered with museums and memorials to the tens of millions of people who died because of communism. While there is only one such monument in the United States, located in Washington, D.C., you can support groups like the Victims of Communism Memorial Foundation, who are fighting to establish more. Anti-communist monuments and museums should be as common as those commemorating the founding fathers. In parks. In town squares. In front of city halls. No man, woman, or child should go without a daily reminder of where communism ultimately leads. The plaque on the pedestal of each statue should read "Dedicated to the millions of souls who were slaughtered at the hands of the communist ideology. You're next if you allow it . . ."

# ANTI-COMMUNIST ACTION ITEMS

- Always remember that although history is a dark place, you should never be ashamed of your nation's past.

- Inoculate your children from the new communist mythology by inspiring an appreciation for history and culture—warts and all.

- Protect the statues and monuments that already stand in your community.

- Punish politicians who acquiesce to the mob.

- Support the building of new monuments, memorials, and museums that forward the cause of anti-communism.

# CHAPTER FOUR

## Red in the Streets:
## The Foot Soldiers of Communism

In the early 1930s, Germany, a nation humiliated by its defeat in the Great War and damaged by the conditions imposed by the Treaty of Versailles, faced the rise of a radical and deadly political movement.

In major cities around the country, the thugs and malcontents who had been seduced by the impassioned words of their leaders laced up their jackboots and took to the streets. Marching under banners bearing the symbol of their movement, they rioted, terrorized their political opponents, and even engaged in cold-blooded murder.

Their mission was simple: bring Germany to its knees, tear it down to its foundations, and remake it in accordance with their own twisted doctrines.

They were known as *Antifaschistische Aktion*, or *Antifa*, the foot soldiers of Germany's communist movement.

Today the heirs of these "red-lacquered doppelgangers of the Nazis" (as one prominent German politician called them) have taken to America's streets. Just like their forebears, they riot, terrorize their political opponents, and engage in cold-blooded murder. Though the battlefield may have changed, their mission remains the same.

And they will succeed if we don't defeat them.

---

The summer of violence that followed the death of George Floyd in 2020 was a wake-up call to America. In cities around the nation, rioters caused mayhem in the streets in what would become the worst civil unrest in American history. According to estimates, the widespread looting, vandalism, and arson cost between $1 billion and $2 billion in damages, not including the long-term impact of neighborhoods stripped of local businesses and buildings that were reduced to piles of rubble. In addition to the damage to property, the riots took a toll in lives. In total, the street violence led to the deaths of at least twenty-five Americans.

Much of the media, of course, treated the ordeal like it was a block party. One of the most memorable moments came when CNN declared the riots in Kenosha, Wisconsin, "mostly peaceful" even as the flames of car fires flickered behind the reporter on the scene. Years later, even after the full scope of carnage has become apparent, the riots are still referred to as "protests" and "demonstrations," obscuring what they truly were.

Despite what the communists in the media would have you believe, these riots were not some historical anomaly—a departure from the left's gentle approach to politics. The campaign of violence was a deliberate act. It was an offensive carried out by and with the approval of communists. This wasn't about one dead criminal in Minneapolis. His death just provided the opportunity. This was organized and purposeful. This was intended to sow chaos and fear in our society, as communists have always sought to do.

How do we know this? All you have to do is take a look at the groups at the heart of the mayhem to figure it out. Two groups in particular stand out: Antifa and Black Lives Matter.

The groups shroud themselves in language that would elicit sympathy from many in the political mainstream. Black Lives Matter, for example, poses itself as a "racial justice" movement. It has the support of celebrities and media outlets and has even raked in millions of dollars in corporate sponsorships. The group's name itself, the statement that "black lives matter," has become a political purity test, a mantra that politicians are required to parrot without question if they want respectability in left-wing circles.

Similarly, Antifa, a ragtag collection of losers scraped off the bottom of the communist political scene, has been defined entirely by what they claim to oppose rather than what they support. "*Antifa* is short for *anti-fascist*," the useful idiots repeat. "How can anyone oppose being anti-fascist? What are you, some kind of Nazi?"

It's all a lie. Both BLM and Antifa are explicitly communist, as I'll get to. They are the Red Guards of the American communist movement—the foot soldiers of the revolution. The language they speak is violence and destruction. The battlefield on which they fight is the streets of your city or hometown. Their goal is no different than that of their comrades in past generations: to destroy everything before them and replace it with their own chaotic hellhole.

We'll take a closer look at these thugs who stalk America's

streets a little later. First let's take a brief look at the historical inspiration for today's communist street fighters.

## Red vs. Brown

At first glance, interwar Germany, the decade-and-a-half time between world wars that history remembers as the Weimar Republic, might seem like a strange place to begin a study of the communist foot soldier. As we know, the communists were ultimately crushed underfoot alongside the rest of the opposition when the Nazi Party took control of Germany in 1933. However, the current crop of commie thugs can draw their lineage straight back to the communist organizations of this era.

Now, let's stop for a moment. I know exactly what you're thinking. "But Jesse," I already hear you asking, "they were against Nazis, so they were the good guys, right?"

Wrong.

Communists are never the good guys. Ever. If you're looking for heroes who fought against the Nazis from within Germany, look elsewhere. There are plenty for you to choose from without turning to the reds. I suggest starting with Lutheran pastor Dietrich Bonhoeffer or Father Alfred Delp, two men of Christian faith who died resisting the Nazis. If you praise the communists, you're just praising one group of evil bastards because they opposed another group of evil bastards. In a perfect world, they both would have lost.

All right, let's jump into these shark-infested waters.

The most active communist street fighters in Weimar Germany operated under several different names. The first major group was organized under the name the *Roter Frontkämpferbund,* or "Red Front Fighters." This group would be succeeded by others, primarily the *Parteiselbstschutz,* or "Party of Self-Defense," and, as I've mentioned, *Antifaschistische Aktion,* better known as *Antifa* (sound familiar?). These groups were the militant wing of the *Kommunistische Partei Deutschlands* (KPD), or Communist Party of Germany, serving the same role that the *Sturmabteilung* (SA) served for the Nazi Party.

Contrary to what many would have you believe, these communist militants were not the polar opposites of their Nazi counterparts. The communists in Germany were not principled opponents of totalitarianism who were standing against political repression and murder. They were authoritarians battling it out on the streets for control of the same radical territory as the Nazis. The communists might have been separated from their brownshirt peers by ideology, but they were all united in their desire to overthrow the German government and establish a dictatorship (the Nazis' based on race, the communists' based on class).

The Nazis and the communists were also unified in the tactics they used. Mobs of communist militants would strap on their jackboots and take to the streets, often carrying flags bearing their official emblems. In the case of the Red Front Fighters, they marched under a banner featuring a raised clenched fist (virtually identical to the emblem of Black Lives Matter). Armed with clubs, knives, and occasionally pistols, the communist hooligans would attack the meetings of rival political groups, assault political opponents, and engage in acts of vandalism.

There was so much overlap between the commies and the Nazis that the two groups occasionally found common ground.

In 1931, the KDP, Germany's primary communist party, and the Nazis joined forces to promote a referendum to dissolve the regional government of Prussia. In the weeks before the vote, the KDP lovingly referred to the Nazis and their SA thugs as "working people's comrades." The campaign even featured a rally at which Nazi propaganda chief Joseph Goebbels shared a stage with prominent KPD figures.

I don't want to overstate any affinity between the reds and the browns in Weimar Germany. The groups fought. A lot. But the communists' primary enemy was not Adolf Hitler's storm troopers, the SA. The communist militants called themselves anti-fascist, but that never meant they were just anti-Nazi. Just like today's communists, they used the term *fascist* to describe pretty much anyone with whom they disagreed. Even fellow socialists, like Germany's dominant Social Democratic Party (SDP), were considered nothing more than the moderate wing of fascism, or "social fascists."

Communist thugs also routinely targeted German police, whom they considered the enforcement arm of the fascist government. Their most notable attack on the police occurred in 1931, when three militants assassinated a pair of police captains in Berlin. Two of the perpetrators escaped punishment, fleeing to the Soviet Union following the murders. In an ironic turn, one of the men who pulled the trigger, Erich Mielke, would return to Germany following World War II and become a police officer himself—serving as the head of the Stasi, communist East Germany's secret police, from 1957 until the fall of the Berlin Wall in 1989.

As we all know, the Weimar Republic would ultimately fall, coming under the control of the brown menace instead of the red one. Once Hitler became chancellor in 1933, the government began a campaign of suppression against the Communist Party. However, that wasn't the end of the communists in Germany. While some die-hard Marxists would take their activities underground or flee into the arms of the Soviet Union, many simply switched their allegiance, finding a home among the Nazi brownshirts. According to the SA itself, a full 55 percent of their ranks were composed of former communists. The phenomenon was so common that they had a term for it: "Beefsteak Nazis"—brown on the outside, red on the inside.

## Antifa 2.0

On June 6, 2020, NPR national political correspondent Mara Liasson tweeted a photograph of American soldiers storming the beaches of Normandy in 1944. It was the seventy-sixth anniversary of the D-Day invasion and many Americans were posting similar images in order to celebrate the U.S. role in the destruction of the Nazi war machine. However, Liasson's tweet was not a touching tribute to the Greatest Generation.

Along with the photo, the NPR correspondent added the telling caption, "Biggest antifa rally in history." By associating Antifa with the legacy of those who liberated France, Liasson revealed whom the tribute was truly intended for: the masked, black-hooded thugs who were, at that very moment, wreaking havoc on American streets.

Media propagandists like Liasson want Americans to believe that Antifa is defined by its moniker. The name itself, which, as we know, was appropriated from the Weimar communist group *Antifaschistische Aktion*, suggests that fighting fascism is their primary motivation. The truth, however, is that just like their German predecessors, these lowlifes, scumbags, and criminals consider everyone to the right of Karl Marx himself to be a fascist. Despite Liasson's claim, Antifa is not carrying on the tradition of the men who ran into machine gun fire on the beaches of France. To the contrary, our grandfathers and great-grandfathers, who proudly wore the American flag on their uniforms while fighting *actual* fascists, would have hated Antifa. Those men represented the best America had to offer, and, as such, would've earned the hatred of Antifa in return.

So, just who are these street thugs whom Mara Liasson loves so much? In a historical sense, there's little connective tissue between the Antifa of interwar Germany and the current American incarnation. However, make no mistake, this is the same group—the modern communist adopting the name, look, and tactics of communists past.

Let's start with the way the group operates, which is more akin to a terrorist organization than a political movement.

Antifa is a decentralized organization with no official national leadership, membership, or organizational structure of which to speak. Instead, the group is organized into small, autonomous cells, a tactic commonly employed by groups like Al Qaeda as a means of evading authorities. While Antifa cells are active in dozens of cities across the country, its decentralized and secretive nature makes the group difficult to infiltrate and prevents law enforcement from keeping track of members.

On the ground level, members evade law enforcement by covering their faces and dressing from head to toe in black during what they call "direct action," the violence, riots, and vandalism that are their hallmarks. The tactic, known as black bloc, helps to ensure that no single individual can be identified and allows them to melt back into an anonymous mass after committing criminal acts.

In their efforts to confound police, Antifa members are instructed to go as far as to make sure they don't leave DNA evidence behind. In an article titled "Fashion Tips for the Brave," published on Antifa-friendly CrimethInc.com, an anonymous author writes:

> Be careful not to leave fingerprints and DNA evidence! Wear cloth gloves—leather and latex can retain fingerprints and even pass them on to objects you touch. Wipe down tools and other items with alcohol in advance, to clean fingerprints off them—you never know what might get lost in the chaos. Don't forget about the batteries inside flashlights!

The article also warns members to cover up tattoos, change their shoes to prevent footprints from being used as evidence, and remove any identifiable insignias. It's hard to tell whether these communist thugs are trying to smash fascism or pull off a bank heist.

In another article, titled "Blocs, Black and Otherwise," a CrimethInc.com author describes the "offensive gear" members should carry during Antifa actions. They list:

> spraypaint, projectiles, slingshots, signs or flags on thick poles (or just plain poles), Molotov cocktails, bright lights (to obscure police or camera vision during night

actions), ladders and/or bolt cutters for scaling or breaching barriers, etc.

According to the author, Antifa's tools of the trade also include "shields," "steel-toed shoes," "body armor," and "gas masks."

While they have no national hierarchy, local cells are often highly organized and frequently coordinate with one another through encrypted messaging apps and social media. The oldest Antifa cell, Portland's Rose City Antifa, maintains a website and active accounts on Facebook and Twitter. The group even has a hotline where people can leave anonymous voice-mail tips about fascist activities in the Pacific Northwest (or where you can leave extensive rants about the evils of communism—not that I would condone such a thing).

Rose City Antifa also gives us some good insight into what constitutes "fascist" activities in the mind of an Antifa member. On its website, the group compiles a handy list of traits for spotting fascists. Those traits include:

- Ultra-nationalism, which defines the "nation" around a shared racial, ethnic, cultural, or historical identity.

- Belief in "patriarchal hierarchies" that place "men over women."

- "Anti-communist" and "anti-liberal" rhetoric.

- Opposition to unions and other organized labor groups.

- Anti-elitist, populist rhetoric that appeals to the "common man."

- Movements that are "revolutionary and tradition-alist."

In short, if you're reading and agreeing with anything in this book, Antifa considers you a fascist. Wear it as a badge of honor.

Although Antifa does not keep official membership rolls, we have good insight into the type of people who would consider themselves part of the team and participate in their direct actions. In addition to communist ideologues, the group tends to attract social misfits, criminals, and, if their mug shots are any indication, the ugliest people on earth. (I'm not joking. If you don't believe me, go to your web browser right now and type "antifa mug shots" into a search engine. It looks like school picture day at the leper colony.)

I think that's a pretty accurate generalization of the model Antifa member, but let's look at some specific examples. The type of person who is drawn to Antifa and its direct actions was perfectly illustrated on August 25, 2020, in Kenosha, Wisconsin. That evening, then-seventeen-year-old Kyle Rittenhouse shot three rioters in self-defense, killing two and removing both inches of another's bicep. Let's leave aside the fact that all three of his attackers were in Kenosha to provoke violence, set fires, and cause havoc. A quick look at their biographies show that they were, to a man, disgusting human beings.

- Anthony Huber: According to a December 2012 Kenosha County criminal complaint, Huber threatened and assaulted his brother and grandmother at their home. According to reports, Huber choked his brother and told him that he would "gut him like a pig" while holding a butcher's knife to his stomach. He pled guilty to strangulation and suffocation, false imprisonment, and domestic abuse. Huber was sentenced to probation, but it was revoked after he was charged with battery against his sister. He wound up spending two years in prison.

- Gaige Grosskreutz: Grosskreutz had a long history of run-ins with law enforcement, including convictions for criminal trespass, damage to property, and operating a firearm while intoxicated.

- Joseph Rosenbaum: We've saved the worst for last. In December 2002, a court in Pima County, Arizona, sentenced Rosenbaum to a decade in prison after he pled guilty to several counts of child molestation. We'll spare you the heinous details, but his victims were several boys between the ages of nine and eleven. At the time of his death, Rosenbaum also had pending charges in Wisconsin for alleged domestic abuse and jumping bail.

Kyle Rittenhouse shot three people who were threatening his life that evening. In doing so, he managed to hit three degenerates, one of whom victimized children and another who menaced his own loved ones. What are the odds? Apparently, they're pretty good if you're firing at the foot soldiers of the communist left.

The facts about Rittenhouse's attackers were already public by the time the teenager's trial began in 2021, but that didn't stop the left from treating them like martyrs. In November 2021, actor Mark Ruffalo tweeted, "We come together to mourn the lives lost to the same racist system that devalues Black lives and devalued the lives of Anthony [Huber] and [Joseph] JoJo [Rosenbaum]." Ruffalo is free to mourn whomever he wants, but I wouldn't expect sympathy cards from any of the children JoJo raped.

Kenosha County assistant district attorney Thomas Binger, who led the prosecution of Rittenhouse, took the martyrdom theme even further. During his closing statement in the trial, Binger described the mob in Kenosha—the same mob that caused tens of millions of dollars in damage to city and private property—as a "crowd full of heroes" who showed "courage" by trying to stop an "active shooter."

Antifa's actions aren't limited to assaulting seventeen-year-olds with good aim. The group has been known to target government buildings and federal law enforcement agencies. In July 2019, motivated by U.S. Immigration and Customs Enforcement raids and images of children behind chain-link fences in immigrant detention centers, a self-proclaimed member of Antifa named Willem Van Spronsen attempted to firebomb the ICE detention facility in Tacoma, Washington. Armed with a rifle, Van Spronsen hurled Molotov cocktails at vehicles and buildings, causing one car fire, and unsuccessfully tried to ignite a propane tank. The militant was killed in a hail of gunfire when he was confronted by police.

Following his attack, Van Spronsen was lionized by his fellow communists. On the Puget Sound Anarchists website, the group memorialized him with a post titled "We Are the Fire That Will Melt ICE—Rest in Power." In a Facebook post, the Seattle Antifascist Action group eulogized Van Spronsen as a "good friend and comrade," adding, "May his death serve as a call to protest and direct action."

While public perception of Antifa is largely based around images of burned-out buildings and vandalized property, less known is the fact that supporters of the group have also engaged in cold-blooded murder. On August 29, 2020, thirty-nine-year-old Aaron Danielson was shot and killed in Portland, Oregon, shortly after attending a pro-Trump rally. The shooter was quickly identified as Michael Reinoehl, a far-left radical from the Portland suburbs. In an Instagram post a few months prior to the shooting, Reinoehl proudly proclaimed, "Every Revolution needs people that are willing and ready to fight. . . . I am 100% ANTIFA all the way! I am willing to fight for my brothers and sisters!"

The forty-eight-year-old Reinoehl was charged with second-degree murder and unlawful use of a weapon shortly after the shooting. After briefly evading law enforcement, Reinoehl was shot to death by federal authorities as they moved to arrest him in early September. At the time of his death, the accused murderer was carrying a .380-caliber handgun and a rifle with the serial number removed.

Among communist agitators, the murder of Aaron Danielson was openly celebrated. In the early morning of August 30, just hours after the shooting, a crowd of BLM activists and Antifa supporters cheered as a speaker proclaimed, "We can take out the trash on our own. I am not sad that a fucking fascist died tonight."

Not long after Danielson's alleged killer, Reinoehl, got unceremoniously dropped into a lake of burning sulfur for all of eternity, he was made into a martyr by Antifa in Portland and beyond. According to journalist Andy Ngo, a spray-painted message that read "Long Live Mike" appeared in the city. The group turned one of the bridge pillars in North Portland into a "memorial" for their fallen comrade, featuring spray-painted eulogies. In December 2020, an Antifa cell in Boston hung a banner on an overpass that read, "Avenge Michael Reinoehl."

The murder of Aaron Danielson was met largely with indifference from the media, and the typical gaslighting from bureaucrats and Democratic politicians. Less than a month after the killing, the FBI was barely willing to acknowledge that Antifa even existed. On September 17, FBI director Christopher Wray, arguably President Donald Trump's most horrendous appointee, told members of Congress that Antifa is "not a group or an organization," but rather a "movement or an ideology." When Joe Biden was asked to condemn the group during a debate with President Trump, he echoed the FBI director's comment, declaring, "Antifa is an idea, not an organization."

Think about that for a moment. The people in the highest levels of your government, who are tasked with keeping you and your family safe, deny the very existence of an organization that is responsible for murder and mayhem in cities across the country. With our own eyes, we've watched them set fires, destroy statues and monuments, and assault innocent people. And yet the head of the federal government's premier law enforcement agency and the president of the United States are bold enough to lie to you and call Antifa "an idea."

Keep this gaslighting and denial in mind the next time they try to tell you that parents demonstrating their anger at their school board are the domestic terrorists or that questioning the results of an election is the gravest threat to democracy America has ever faced.

## Black Is the New Red

The death of George Floyd was the best thing to ever happen to Black Lives Matter.

Founded in 2013 after the shooting of Treyvon Martin, BLM reemerged on the national stage in 2020 as the most visible and potent organization working under the guise of racial justice. Throughout that summer, BLM organized numerous demonstrations around the country. According to the Armed Conflict Location & Event Data Project, more than nine thousand Black Lives Matter demonstrations took place after the death of George Floyd, many of which descended into lawlessness and anarchy. The project estimates that at least twenty-five Americans were killed during protests and political unrest. The summer of BLM is estimated to have caused up to $2 billion in damage nationwide, leading the insurance industry to call it the costliest civil disorder in U.S. history.

It's difficult to overstate the influence the group has had. Millions of Americans changed their social media profile pictures to black squares to signal their support for the group. They received celebrity endorsements and raked in millions in corporate donations. The very name of the group was practically a byword for righteous outrage. Repeating the words *black lives matter* and showing proper deference to BLM became a nationwide social imperative, and not doing so could get you condemned and even fired.

A brief look at just some of the people who were punished

for failing to bend the knee to BLM shows that nobody was absolved from their duty to do so, whether they were popular media figures or anonymous workaday Americans.

- Grant Napear, the TV play-by-play announcer for the Sacramento Kings, was fired by his radio station after tweeting "All Lives Matter."

- Stan Wischnowski, the top editor of the *Philadelphia Inquirer*, was forced to resign because a headline on an article in the paper about buildings destroyed in the riots read "Buildings Matter, Too."

- Several Cisco employees were fired after posting comments including "all lives matter" during a company-wide videoconference.

- Tiffany Riley was fired from her position as principal at the Windsor School in Vermont for making unflattering comments about BLM.

- Heather McVey, a nurse in New Jersey, was fired by health care company AtlantiCare for Facebook posts critical of the Black Lives Matter movement.

While BLM was hailed by the left as champions of racial and social justice, the organization's history is more complicated than a simple slogan. In fact, BLM is an explicitly Marxist organization dedicated to the communist ideology.

Uncovering BLM's underlying doctrine doesn't require sifting through coded language. The group's three cofounders, Alicia Garza, Patrisse Cullors, and Opal Tometi, have all been candid about their communist leanings. When a communist tells you they're a communist, you should believe them.

In a 2015 interview with San Francisco newspaper *SF Weekly*, Alicia Garza boasted that communist doctrine was at the heart of social movements like the one she's leading. "When I trained in sociology, we would read Marx," she told the newspaper. "It never got mentioned in those classes that social movements all over the world have used Marx and Lenin as a foundation to interrupt these systems that are really negatively impacting the majority of people."

That same year, Garza acknowledged that capitalism was the system she was seeking to "interrupt." At a conference of the communist Left Forum, Garza told the audience that it's "not possible for a world to emerge where black lives matter if it's under capitalism, and it's not possible to abolish capitalism without a struggle against national oppression."

Like any good communist, Garza has explicitly stated that her goal is the total dismantling of the nation and a radical reorganization of American life. "We're talking about changing how we've organized this country, so that we actually can achieve the justice that we are fighting for," Garza told a group of Maine progressives in 2019. "I believe we all have work to do to keep dismantling the organizing principle of this society, which creates inequities for everyone, even white people."

Garza's cofounder Patrisse Cullors has been equally open about her dedication to communist ideology, describing herself and Garza as "trained Marxists" in a 2015 video. Cullors acknowledged her ideology again in a 2020 video, creatively titled "Am I a Marxist?" Cullors states, "I do believe in Marxism. It's a philosophy that I learned early on in my organizing career."

Cullors spent her early years as a community organizer at the Labor Community Strategy Center, which she refers to as her "first political home." The Los Angeles–based organization describes itself as a "think tank/act tank" but is really a font of communist agitation. The center's founder, whom Cullors calls her "mentor," is Eric Mann, a veteran of the communist movement of the 1960s and '70s. Mann was a leader of Students for a Democratic Society and would eventually join its terrorist splinter group the Weather Underground. He was arrested in 1969 when he led a group of Weather Underground members in an attack on Harvard University. Mann was charged with five criminal counts, including conspiracy to commit murder. Though the conspiracy charge was ultimately dropped, he served eighteen months in prison for his role in the attack. No doubt Cullors's mentor would be proud of his radical student.

BLM's third cofounder, Opal Tometi, has openly praised communists across the world. In 2015, she penned a letter to express her support for Venezuela's Marxist government after pro-democracy opposition parties defeated the Maduro regime in legislative elections. "We are Black organizations and individuals fighting against U.S. white supremacy and imperialism and for human rights and social justice," Tometi wrote. "We offer this expression of our unwavering solidarity with the progressive and revolutionary Venezuelan people as they reflect, regroup and rectify to defend the Bolivarian Revolution." Tometi went on to denounce "corporate media lies" about the government's corruption and accused Bernie Sanders of "defamation" after the Vermont senator labeled late president Hugo Chavez a dictator. That same year, Tometi met with Nicolas Maduro personally, after BLM invited the Venezuelan dictator to a summit in Harlem, New York City.

The cozy relationship between BLM and the Venezuelan government demonstrates just how little the organization really cares about the causes it claims to champion, namely, its opposition to government brutality. According to Human Rights Watch, police and security forces killed nearly eighteen thousand people in Venezuela in instances of alleged "resistance to authority" between 2016 and 2019. The regime also carried out raids in low-income areas between 2015 and 2017 that resulted in widespread allegations of extrajudicial killings, mass arbitrary detentions, mistreatment of detainees, forced evictions, destruction of homes, and arbitrary deportations.

Tometi and her BLM cofounders had a similar admiration for late Cuban dictator Fidel Castro. Following the death of Castro in 2016, the group published an editorial in which they mourned his loss. "There is an overwhelming sense of loss, complicated by fear and anxiety," the founders wrote. "Although no leader is without their flaws, we must push back against the rhetoric of the right and come to the defense of El Comandante." The group went on to praise Castro for his "integrity" and for his recognition of people's fundamental right to "decent housing, safe communities, quality healthcare, [and] free and quality education." The editorial concludes, "As Fidel ascends to the realm of the ancestors, we summon his guidance, strength, and power as we recommit ourselves to the struggle for universal freedom. Fidel Vive!"

Once again, BLM's praise of Fidel Castro is at odds with its stand against government brutality and racism. Of course,

Castro oversaw thousands of summary executions and the mass incarceration of political dissidents throughout his five decades in power, but what should be even more troubling for so-called anti-racist activists like BLM is the Castro regime's repression of black Cuban activists. After seizing control of the island in 1959, Fidel promised a raceless society, and made class the only acceptable identity. Any discussion of race became taboo, and those who organized based on skin color were often imprisoned.

Ironically, BLM's founders would have likely been thrown in prison or a forced-labor camp if they'd attempted to organize in Castro's Cuba. Carlos Moore, a Cuban-born writer and activist who was imprisoned and exiled after speaking out about racism under Castro, told the *Miami Herald* in 2007 that black activists live under an "unstated threat" from the regime. "Blacks in Cuba know that whenever you raise race in Cuba, you go to jail," Moore told the *Herald*. "There cannot be a civil rights movement. You will have instantly 10,000 black people dead."

Their praise of men like Hugo Chavez, Nicolas Maduro, and Fidel Castro shows that BLM's founders seem fine with government brutality if it's being carried out by Marxists. The abuse of power is not opposed as a matter of principle but seems entirely dependent on who is abusing it. They claim they want to abolish the police in the United States, but they've never seen a communist police state that they didn't like.

Despite its founders' disdain for capitalism, the organization has been raking in cash. In 2020 alone, the Black Lives Matter Global Network Foundation claims to have raised $90 million. Those funds include donations from massive consumer brands like Intel, Unilever, and Nabisco.

So, where has the money gone? Much of the organization's

spending remains shrouded in mystery, but at least a small portion of its funds have gone to its operations on the ground. According to the group's financial disclosures, it committed approximately $21.7 million to thirty local organizations and BLM chapters.

While the organization's finances remain murky, we have learned that the group and its founders are buying up enough expensive real estate to keep RE/MAX in business for the next century.

In October 2020, the group purchased a mansion in Studio City, an upscale neighborhood in Los Angeles, for $6 million in cash. According to real estate listings, the 6,500-square-foot house has more than half a dozen bedrooms and bathrooms, several fireplaces, a soundstage, a pool and bungalow, and parking for more than twenty cars.

In July 2021, the *New York Post* reported that Black Lives Matter transferred millions to a Canadian charity run by the wife of Patrisse Cullors to purchase a 10,000-square-foot house in Toronto. The three-story Victorian mansion had once served as the headquarters of the Communist Party.

The success of BLM has apparently been very good for cofounder Patrisse Cullors's portfolio. According to the *Post*, Cullors went on a multimillion-dollar real estate buying binge, purchasing four high-end homes for $3.2 million. Among those purchases is a $1.4 million compound in Topanga, California, a wealthy suburb of Los Angeles. The 2,370-square-foot property reportedly features "soaring ceilings, skylights and plenty of windows" and is just a short drive from Malibu. According to public records, the compound is just one of three homes Cullors owns in the Los Angeles area.

BLM's seemingly shady financial dealings have led to criticism from the right, but even local BLM chapters are won-
dering how the group is spending its millions. In November
2020, ten chapters of the Black Lives Matter Global Network
Foundation published an open letter denouncing the group
for keeping its finances a secret. "For years there has been inquiry regarding the financial operations of BLMGNF and no
acceptable process of either public or internal transparency
about the unknown millions of dollars donated to BLMGNF,
which has certainly increased during this time of pandemic and
rebellion," the statement read. Who would've thought a group
of communists couldn't be trusted with millions of dollars
they didn't earn?

You might be tempted to believe that BLM's alleged corruption is evidence that they're not real communists, but rather a
group of hustlers looking to benefit personally. However, the
opposite is true. *Real* communism is corrupt to its core. Fidel
Castro, for example, was estimated by *Forbes* magazine to have
had a personal net worth of $900 million, which included luxury
properties throughout the Caribbean and even a private island.
Hugo Chavez is believed to have amassed a similar fortune, with
one organization estimating the Venezuelan dictator was worth
approximately $1 billion by the time he died in 2013.

By snatching up luxury properties and allegedly obscuring
their finances, BLM and its leaders are just carrying on the long
tradition of their communist heroes. In doing so, they have
become America's purest practitioners of the godless religion.

## The Communist Model

So, we've identified who Antifa and BLM are and how they operate, but what do they hope to achieve? Their goal is the same as all American communists': destruction. Fortunately, the two groups have given us some insight into what that revolutionary state would look like.

Arguably, the closest the communist has ever come to setting up its own autonomous territory within the United States came in June 2020 with the establishment of the so-called Capitol Hill Autonomous Zone, or CHAZ. After days of clashes with police, BLM rioters and Antifa thugs barricaded a six-block area in downtown Seattle known as Capitol Hill. The Seattle Police Department, handcuffed by city officials, ceded the area to the mob, abandoning the precinct building located within. Once abandoned by law enforcement, the area became a microcosm of the society the communist would build if he had the power: a lawless, chaotic hellhole.

Not long after walling themselves off from the outside world, the far-left mob set about creating its own utopian society.

Like any society, the citizens of CHAZ first had to figure out how to feed themselves. Food stands lined the sidewalks offering up free meals to all comers. The efforts were bolstered by donations from local restaurants and a Ben & Jerry's ice cream truck that rolled into the area to serve free Cherry Garcia to the communist masses.

The people of CHAZ quickly found out that giving away free food wasn't a sustainable solution. "The homeless people we invited took away all the food at the Capitol Hill Autonomous Zone," tweeted one CHAZ resident. "We need more food to keep the area operational. Please if possible bring vegan meat substitutes, fruits, oats, soy products, etc.—anything to help us eat."

Not to be discouraged, some resourceful CHAZites endeavored to grow their own food. One of the more notable efforts was the establishment of a community garden, which appeared to be little more than potting soil spread over the top of some cardboard boxes. The pile of dirt was accompanied by a sign that read, "This garden is for black and indigenous folks and their plant allies." Of course, the laughable attempt at farming was about as successful as you'd expect, and CHAZ's community garden became just another footnote in communism's long history of failed agricultural reform. Thankfully, it only led to a handful of hungry soy boys instead of millions of corpses like Mao's agricultural reform.

While feeding their population was difficult, the communists' efforts to establish a functioning economy proved to be even more hilarious. Of course, the good residents of CHAZ immediately demanded wealth distribution. One vocal resident demanded that white people simply hand over cash to the zone's black occupants. "I want you to find, by the time you leave this autonomous zone, I want you to give ten dollars to one African American person from this autonomous zone," the man urged. "If that is a challenge for you, I'm not sure you are in the right place." The demand was met with cheers of approval by a gathered crowd.

What couldn't be redistributed voluntarily was redistributed by force. There were numerous reports by CHAZ residents of belongings being stolen, and local businesses tried in vain to summon the police when their shops were burglarized. One business owner, whose car repair shop was burglarized and vandalized, called 911 nineteen times to alert authorities. His pleas went unanswered.

Ultimately, the communists turned to mafia-like tactics to raise money. During a press conference, Assistant Chief of Police Deanna Nollette reported that citizens and businesses were being asked to pay a fee to continue operating in the area; in short, police claimed the locals were being forced to pay protection money.

Efforts to establish public safety failed spectacularly as well. With the area free of police, the streets were patrolled and dominated by armed criminal gangs and untrained anarchist paramilitaries. According to the Seattle Police Department, there were sixty-five reported offenses over the course of twenty-four days, include aggravated assault, larceny-theft, and rape. There were also at least four shooting incidents, resulting in two fatalities. The Seattle Police Department reported a total of thirty-seven offenses during that time in the same area the previous year.

Finally, there was the issue of leadership. Like any good communist nation, CHAZ saw the rise of its own wannabe strongman, a rapper named Raz Simone. In a June 2020 article in the *New York Post*, journalist Andy Ngo, who spent time undercover in the occupied area, described how Simone "patrols the CHAZ on some nights with an armed entourage" carrying a "long semi-auto rifle and sidearm." One member of Simone's entourage can be heard to say in a video shared on social media that "We are the police of this community now . . . we are the leaders of this community now."

Thankfully, the Raz Simone regime didn't last long enough to carry out a five-year plan. On July 1, 2020, the area known as CHAZ was cleared out by the Seattle Police Department. The short-lived communist community left behind graffitied walls, a few tents, and streets covered in human waste.

Of course, the communist sympathizers in the city and state governments did their best to whitewash the chaos. Seattle mayor Jenny Durkan described the area as having "a block party atmosphere" and a "summer of love." Lori Patrick, a spokesperson for the mayor, told CNN that city officials had not interacted with "armed antifa militants" at the site, even though there was already ample photographic and video evidence proving otherwise. Washington governor Jay Inslee described the scene as "unpermitted" but "largely peaceful."

The media did their part to hide the truth as well. At Vox, one reporter claimed the CHAZ had evolved "into a center of peaceful protest, free political speech, co-ops, and community gardens." A reporter for *Rolling Stone* called the zone "a peaceful realm where people build nearly everything on the fly, as they strive to create a world where the notion that black lives matter shifts from being a slogan to an ever-present reality." The *Nation* described the zone as "an anti-capitalist vision of community sovereignty without police."

Some members of the media even heaped praise upon Raz Simone, the wannabe CHAZ strongman whose sole qualification for leadership seems to have been once opening for hip-hop artist Macklemore. *Forbes* magazine writer Jack Kelly described Simone as a man who is "passionate about achieving racial equality and justice" and "wants to stand up for what's right."

So, let's review.

Over the course of its brief existence, CHAZ's achievements included a failed agricultural project, an economic model built on theft, a marked increase in crime and violence, and the rise and fall of a wannabe strongman. In other words, it was the model communist society and a perfect glimpse into what lies in store for America if we continue to allow them to flourish.

## Retaking the Streets

The communists have left the comfort of their colleges and ideological enclaves, and they've taken to the streets. They've descended upon city after city, terrorizing locals and leaving destruction in their wake. It is up to the anti-communist to stop the rampage and deprive these thugs of an atmosphere in which they are allowed to thrive.

Chaos and violence are never a loss for the communist. They are the fertile soil in which he grows and a means by which he attains power. From chaos comes social anxiety. An anxious society will become desperate for peace. In that desperation, they will inevitably turn to the government—the same government already dominated by communists.

Where chaos does not exist, the communist will create it.

We can expose these groups to sunlight and attempt to turn public opinion against them, but this alone won't be enough to bring them to heel. Standing idly and hoping these communists self-destruct is not an option. Anti-communists must go on the offense. To do so, we first need to shut down the money supply that allows these groups to operate.

Although it has tried its best to keep its finances secretive, using a complex network of legal entities through which it filters and distributes cash, BLM's tax-exempt status requires it by law to be somewhat transparent about its sources of funding. In addition to numerous small donations from individuals, BLM is sponsored by massive charitable foundations. Some of these foundations operate as the charitable arms of American corporations, which makes them vulnerable to economic influence.

One of BLM's biggest charitable supporters has been the NoVo Foundation. Funded by Warren Buffett, chairman and CEO of Berkshire Hathaway, and controlled by his son Peter, the foundation contributed $1.5 million to BLM and associated organizations between 2015 and 2018. Berkshire Hathaway owns or controls numerous consumer brands, including Benjamin Moore, Dairy Queen, Fruit of the Loom, and many more. A complete list of companies that are controlled by Berkshire Hathaway is readily available. Avoid them. If you spend your money on these brands, you are indirectly funding the machine that keeps BLM going.

The W. K. Kellogg Foundation has also been cutting checks for BLM. The foundation is funded in large part through its ownership stake in the Kellogg Company. If you want to do your part, stay away from Frosted Flakes and Eggo waffles. Buy generic brands instead.

Still other corporations have donated directly to BLM, proudly announcing their financial support through public statements. In July 2020, Amazon announced that Black Lives Matter was among twelve organizations "working to bring about social justice and improve the lives of Black and African Americans" that would receive $10 million from the online retail company. Cancel your Amazon Prime subscription and buy from local retailers or brick-and-mortar stores.

Other corporations and brands that openly support BLM include DoorDash, Gatorade, Microsoft, and Airbnb. Identify these companies and their products and spend your dollars accordingly. As always, make sure you're not giving money to people who hate you.

In addition to withdrawing your financial support from these companies, write, email, post to social media, and call them to voice your displeasure. They've chosen to prop up an anti-American organization whose agitation has led to death, destruction, and financial ruin for hundreds of small business owners. Let them know how angry you are.

That takes care of BLM, but going after Antifa's money is going to be more difficult. Since they're not a single organization and have no official financial status, little is known about how their activities are funded. Cracking their finances is going to require the involvement of law enforcement (if only we had a competent, nonpartisan FBI to investigate).

To bring the full weight of law enforcement down on Antifa, the group should be designated a terrorist organization. The label would allow the government to use its vast anti-terror resources to track Antifa's members and finances.

Designating Antifa a terrorist organization should be a no-brainer. The FBI defines domestic terrorism as:

> Violent, criminal acts committed by individuals and/or groups to further ideological goals stemming from domestic influences, such as those of a political, religious, social, racial, or environmental nature.

If Antifa doesn't fit that definition, I don't know what does.

But, of course, the feds cannot be relied upon. The FBI is fundamentally broken, and, as we previously discussed, the agency's director, Christopher Wray, has referred to Antifa as an "ideology" and not an "organization." Apparently, America's premier law enforcement agency is too busy investigating parents speaking out at school board meetings to deal with communists burning down major cities.

Efforts to make the designation official by Republican politicians and lawmakers have not been effective, either. In 2020, former president Trump promised the U.S. would designate Antifa a terrorist organization. Although our useless former attorney general Bill Barr indicated he would use the FBI's regional joint terrorism task forces to bring the criminal organizers of the George Floyd riots to justice, Trump's promise went unfulfilled.

Senators Ted Cruz of Texas and Bill Cassidy of Louisiana have been met with similar resistance. In 2019, the pair introduced a resolution to the U.S. Senate condemning the violent acts carried out by members of Antifa and calling for the designation of the group as a domestic terrorist organization. "Antifa is a group of hateful, intolerant radicals who pursue their unhinged agenda through aggressive violence," Senator Cruz said. "Time and time again their actions have demonstrated that their only purpose is to inflict harm on those who oppose their views. The hate and violence they spread must be stopped." The resolution has gone nowhere.

It's no surprise that the federal government won't act. In all likelihood it never will, because they're on the same side. So, when fighting back against communists, our goals are better served by focusing our efforts at the state and local level.

One of the biggest lessons we should take away from Seattle's CHAZ—besides the total inability of communists to organize a society in any meaningful way—is that groups like Antifa and BLM will only operate in places where they can do so free of consequences. The very existence of CHAZ was made possible by a total failure of local government and law enforcement. In many states, these organizations have been allowed to operate with impunity, with local officials paralyzed by fear of the political consequences they might face if they fight back.

Our local governments will only become proactive in taking on these thugs if we stop electing cowards. If we're going to prevent another CHAZ and crack down on violence on our streets, anti-communists need to be elected to local government, and we need to focus specifically on the election of sheriffs and district attorneys.

Anti-communists have a lot of ground to make up in this regard. For the past several years, billionaire George Soros has been openly pumping tens of millions of dollars into numerous district attorney races across the country. With his support, far-left district attorneys have been elected in at least two dozen major cities and counties. Once taking office, Soros-funded DAs like Kim Foxx in Chicago, Kim Gardner in St. Louis, and Alvin Bragg in New York City implement soft-on-crime policies under the guise of "criminal justice reform." They often refuse to seek appropriate prison sentences for crimes such as armed robbery, drug dealing, and burglary, and let violent offenders go free on little to no bail.

Soros expresses no regret for the chaos and violence that he has invited through his funding of weak DAs. In fact, he has promised to do more. He should be arrested, deported, and banned from ever entering the United States again. No sane nation, in the history of the world, would allow a foreign-born rich guy to intentionally cause chaos within its borders.

These rogue prosecutors are Antifa and BLM's greatest allies, allowing them to operate without fear of prosecution. In July 2020, as rioters were still rampaging across the country, Philadelphia district attorney Larry Krasner, whose campaign was bankrolled by Soros to the tune of approximately $1.7 million in 2017, threatened to arrest and criminally prosecute federal law enforcement who targeted Black Lives Matter or Antifa rioters. In a statement, Krasner echoed Antifa propaganda, saying, "It's the least we can do to honor those who fought fascism, including those who are fighting it even now."

Some Soros-backed prosecutors simply refused to bring charges against rioters. In Chicago, more than four hundred people were arrested for violating a curfew that had been imposed during the protests and violence. Cook County state attorney Kim Foxx, whose election campaigns have been supported by the Soros-funded Illinois Justice & Public Safety PAC, declined to charge them, saying the prosecutions wouldn't be worth her office's time.

Anti-communists need to elect law enforcement officials with backbones. We should support the campaigns of prosecutors and sheriffs who promise to crack down on the violence and the recall of those who refuse, as San Francisco did with commie DA Chesa Boudin.

George Soros's millions are going to be difficult to overcome, but if you can afford to do so, you should consider donating to the campaigns of men and women who are running against his preferred candidates. Remember, these officials will have far greater impact on the streets of your city or town than even your congressman or senator. If you must choose, cut a check for your local law enforcement candidates, and tell your legislators to take a hike.

Better law enforcement leadership is important, but if you live in many areas of the country, you may be stuck with weak-kneed officials. If law enforcement fails to act, anti-communists need to exercise their right to defend themselves and their property. Take a page out of the book of the armed Koreans who took to the roofs during the 1992 LA riots. If you live in an area that is likely to be hit by street violence like what we saw in the summer of 2020, you should organize with like-minded business owners to create a last line of defense. Don't wait until the rampage has already begun. Do this now. Have a plan in place.

Don't be deterred by accusations that this is vigilantism. You're not out there dispensing justice like Denzel Washington in *Man on Fire*. Self-defense is freedom in its ultimate form. It's the right from which all other rights are derived and one you should be ready to exercise to protect yourself, and your community, from the communist street fighter.

# ANTI-COMMUNIST ACTION ITEMS

- Shut down the money supply to communist groups like BLM by withholding your support of their corporate sponsors.

- Lobby your federal officials to support measures that would designate Antifa as a domestic terrorist organization.

- Support the campaigns of district attorneys and sheriffs who promise to crack down on violent communists.

- Have a plan to defend your home or business in the event that communists become violent and law enforcement fails to do its job.

CHAPTER FIVE

# American Red-ucation

*Among the elementary measures the American government*
*will adopt to further the cultural revolution are the following:*
*the schools, colleges, and universities will be coordinated and*
*grouped under a National Department of Education and its*
*state and local branches. The studies will be revolutionized,*
*being cleansed of religious, patriotic, and other features*
*of bourgeois ideology.*
William Z. Foster, chairman of the Communist Party USA
*Toward Soviet America*, 1932

The introduction of communism into America's public schools has been a long-term project for the communist movement. Although the ideology is now found inside many of today's classrooms, communists have been trying to take control of American schools since the early twentieth century.

Almost a century later, the communist's goals remain unchanged. He seeks to control schools through national authority. He wants to purge them of God. He wants to banish American patriotism. And he wants to use them to eliminate Western ideals.

I wish I could tell you that there's still time to prevent the communist from achieving his goals, and that your children's schools remain safe from his influence. The truth, however, is that these goals have already been achieved.

---

In an earlier chapter, we discussed the communist takeover of colleges and universities, and explored how that control has given them the ability to manufacture new generations of revolutionaries. While it's true that idealistic young adults make great warriors for the cause, the communist does not limit himself to recruiting college-aged students. No, he wants them younger. He wants obedient, child soldiers.

The earlier the communist ideology is implanted within a young mind, the more deeply rooted it will be. To this end, the communist has made it his mission to inject his poison into the curriculums of schoolchildren. We see it in classrooms across the country, in the school districts of both blue states and red alike: children being initiated into the cult of Critical Theory, radical gender politics, and racial grievance. Marxist ideology now flows from the ivory towers of academia into the playgrounds of primary schools.

The phenomenon is most apparent in America's public school system, which has for decades been dominated by far-left teachers unions, but it is not unique to government-run institutions. Increasingly, we're seeing the ideology worm its way into private schools as well, ensuring that parents and children can no longer escape its influence.

The communist's efforts to wrest control of the education system is in keeping with their ideology. From their earliest days, as I've outlined, they have seen education as yet another means of control. In *The Communist Manifesto*, Marx implored his minions to "replace home education by social" in order to "rescue education from the influence of the ruling class." To do so, the communists called for education to be controlled exclusively by the government.

The domination of education was not a small matter to the communist. It was, and remains, a central component of his overall plan. As Russian dictator Vladimir Lenin is claimed to have said, "Give me four years to teach the children and the seed I have sown will never be uprooted."

For the communist, education is not about reading, writing, and arithmetic. America's dismal reading scores should tell you that much. Graduates today sound less like Thomas Jefferson and more like LeBron James.

Broadly speaking, a communist education is designed to serve and sustain the spread of communism. More specifically, education serves two functions: 1) to indoctrinate children into the communist religion and 2) to sever the relationship between parents and their children.

The first function is the most obvious. For children to be turned into communists, they need to understand the doctrine. Communist education introduces children to fundamental Marxist concepts like class identity and warfare. It "socializes" them, teaching them to identify not as individuals, but primarily as members of a group. It also seeks to undermine national identity by presenting a self-serving version of history that focuses on grievance. In doing so, the communist encourages a deep-seated hatred of traditional, noncommunist culture. The result is young students who are more interested in radically changing the culture than in preserving it.

While indoctrinating children is an important function of

the communist curriculum, the second function is even more critical to his goals. It's not enough for children to accept communism: they must also reject the alternative. To this end, the communist seeks to sever the bond between parent and child.

To most people in the free world, the idea of tearing children away from their parents is so unthinkable, so evil, that we hesitate to think that anyone would ever intend to do so. After all, the relationship between parent and child has always been a sacred one in the eyes of God.

That's exactly why the communist hates it. If the parent-child relationship is the unbroken thread that links the past to the present, then it must be cut.

Getting between a parent and their child, although unthinkable to us, is perfectly acceptable for communists. Remember, your values are not his values. He hates the idea of a "sacred" relationship into which he cannot interpose himself. Marx makes this perfectly clear in *The Communist Manifesto*, dismissing the idea as "the bourgeois clap-trap about the family and education, about the hallowed co-relation of parents and child."

To break the relationship with their parents, children are reeducated—unlearning the traditional morals they've been taught so that they can be rebuilt on communist principles. At the heart of the new communist principles is contempt for the old ones and resentment toward the people by whom they were introduced.

Above all else, the communist has pulled the rug out from morality by removing God from the classroom. Whether or not you personally have a religion is irrelevant. The communist does. Western civilization is built on Christian principles. According to those principles, we're more than material creatures or accidents of nature. We are uniquely created by God. We are wonderful. The last thing the communist can afford is for you to be content and believe you are wonderful. The communist needs you to be bitter and think you're worthless.

We can no longer prevent the communist from taking our schools. They're already his. We've handed them to him like so many of our important institutions. But it doesn't have to stay that way. We can take them back. It all starts by understanding how we lost them in the first place.

## America's Blackboard Bolsheviks

While the indoctrination of children has always been important to the communist, their earliest efforts to introduce a Marxist education in America were not focused on the infiltration of mainstream schools. Instead, they first tried to establish their own parallel system of "workers schools," run by the Communist Party USA. The network of schools focused on educating adults and began popping up in the early 1920s in major cities like Chicago, San Francisco, and New York City. Students at these schools were offered classes based in Marxist theory. Courses included "History of the American Working Class," "Fundamentals of Communism," and "Labor Journalism."

While the workers schools acted as ideological training centers for the American communist movement for adults, the communist eventually turned his attention to a younger demographic. In the 1930s, the Communist Party USA began a concerted effort to infiltrate America's public schools. At that time, the party exerted its influence mainly through organized labor movements and—surprise, surprise—the teachers unions proved to be their most useful vehicle for gaining power. In particular, the American Federation of Teachers, which had been cofounded in 1916 by democratic socialist John Dewey, proved to be the most fertile ground for infiltration.

In 1937, Richard Frank, a member of the Education Commission of the Young Communist League, spelled out the movement's plans for subversion. "The task of the Communist Party must be, first and foremost, to arouse the teachers to class consciousness and to organize them into the American Federation of Teachers, which is the main current of the American labor movement," Frank wrote. "They must take advantage of their positions without exposing themselves to give their students, to the best of their ability, working class education." Pay particular attention to "without exposing themselves" in Frank's statement—subversiveness is standard practice among communist teachers.

With their marching orders in hand, communists set about infiltrating America's schools and wresting control of teachers unions. Their success was limited, as anti-communist feelings were running high at time, but they did manage to take control of several local chapters of the American Federation of Teachers.

The most notable union in which communists gained influence was the American Federation of Teachers Local 5 in New York City. The union claimed to have around six thousand members, the vast majority of whom were teachers in the city's public school system. By the early 1930s, two communist factions within the union became active: the so-called rank-and-file group, which was committed to orthodox communism, and the less radical "progressive" faction. Any effort to oppose the communists were met with charges of "red-baiting" and intimidation.

The communist factions within Local 5 became so aggressive that most noncommunist members were forced to abandon the group in 1935, after which the union fell under the complete control of the radical rank and file. During this period of communist control, the union was accused of silencing opponents, blackmailing critics through the threat of public vilification, and acting as an arm of the Communist Party USA.

Every step of the way, Local 5's political positions mirrored those of the Communist Party and Stalin. For example, the union was staunchly anti-Nazi, publicly supporting collective security against German aggression and the boycott of Nazi goods. However, the union dropped its public stance against Nazi Germany in 1939, immediately after Hitler and Stalin signed a nonaggression pact.

While their public political activities were intended to support Moscow, what Local 5's members and communist teachers nationwide were doing in their classrooms was even worse—that was where the *real* political activity was taking place.

The communist subversives were smart enough to understand that they had to disguise their indoctrination. They wouldn't want to anger parents or raise the suspicions of noncommunist administrators. As Richard Frank explained in 1937, communist teachers would "skillfully inject it into their teachings at the least risk of exposure."

Teachers would silently slip communism into every subject, even those that were not political. In 1936, Professor Howard Langford published *Education and the Social Conflict*, which was virtually a handbook for communist teachers. In it, Langford explains how teachers would abandon traditional methods of teaching their students and replace them with methods designed to introduce children to socialism and class warfare. In doing so, teachers would quietly transform their students into little anti-capitalists.

Let's take Langford's recommendations subject by subject:

- Literature: Children would be encouraged to analyze all of their assigned reading, whether it's a poem, novel, or drama, from a Marxist perspective. Book reports would no longer be graded based solely on issues like comprehension, spelling, or grammar. Instead, students would be rewarded for "clarifying issues between the workers and the ruling class."

- History: Teachers would make sure history would no longer be "a medium for the glorification of national heroes or of a national tradition." Instead, they would teach "a new science of human societies" and enable children to become "decisive participators" in the historical class conflict instead of spectators.

- Geography: Communist teachers would abandon illustrated maps that showed people in traditional clothes or the "animal, vegetable, or mineral" that could be found in certain countries. Students would instead be shown "the worn faces, the bodies prematurely old, the grinding poverty" of peasant laborers. Children would be made to understand that these workers were exploited for "American pockets and American tables."

- Science: Teachers would no longer limit themselves to merely describing the world but would teach children how to transform it. "The workers need to know not simply the classifications of plants and animals," Langford explained, "but their social significance, their role in human life, past and present, and in the building of socialism."

- Mathematics: Teachers would give lessons in "social statistics" so that students could better understand the "socialized economy" of the future. Langford wrote that students "need to know mathematics not simply as a subject to study in school but as an ever-present and essential part of production in all its technical processes and social planning."

Communist indoctrination would not just take the form of in-class instruction, but extracurricular activities as well. Richard Frank explained how the strictness of American schools could be exploited to transform students into communist activists. This "rigorous discipline," he claimed, made children hate school and gave them a revolutionary spirit. "The rebelliousness of school children, directed against a part of the state machinery itself," Frank wrote, "is something that the Communists cannot afford to ignore." Communist teachers and administrators would encourage student's hatred of school and turn them into revolutionary journalists for their student newspapers or push them to join communist youth groups.

While communists planned on carrying out their subversion quietly, they still ran the risk of being exposed. If they were caught, communists were instructed to hide behind the concept of "academic freedom" to defend their indoctrination. Teachers, Langford wrote, "must interpret academic freedom to mean the right to teach the best they know, whatever the subject taught, and whatever the age level of the students." In other word, teachers must claim that it is their right to teach whatever they want to children of any age.

That sounds familiar, doesn't it?

Communist teachers unions were allowed to get away with their subversion for more than a decade. Despite pleas from Local 5's less radical members and the recommendation of its parent organization, the American Federation of Labor, the AFT failed to act. They resisted kicking the group out of the organization until 1941, when, under intense pressure, they finally revoked Local 5's charter.

In July 1949, the National Education Association passed a resolution banning the communist teachers from the organization. "Members of the Communist Party shall not be employed in the American schools," the resolution read. "Such membership involves adherence to doctrines and discipline completely inconsistent with the principles of freedom on which American education depends."

The infiltration by communists was eventually met with pushback from the federal and state governments as well. In 1949, for example, lawmakers in New York State passed the Feinberg

Law, which banned communists from teaching in New York schools. At the same time, the U.S. House and Senate began holding hearings to expose the activities and methods employed by communist educators.

## A New Communist Generation

The Marxists lost the battle in the early half of the twentieth century. One hundred million dead people tends to taint the brand a little. But, as we now know, the war was far from over.

The previous generation had hitched their wagon too tightly to the Soviet Union. But by the time the 1960s rolled around, the failures of communist regimes around the world were coming to light. The dictatorships of the proletariat were repressive nightmares. The workers' paradises were hellish. Worst of all, the global revolution predicted by Karl Marx had never materialized.

The 1960s presented new opportunities. The first generation of American communists may have failed, but their children would learn, adapt, and overcome. The new generation would take a less orthodox approach.

In an earlier chapter, we talked about Critical Theory, the ideology developed by the communists of the Frankfurt School. To refresh your memory, Critical Theory claims that society is made up of categories of oppressors and oppressed. For the oppressed to be liberated, all societal norms need to be dismantled and all systems of power replaced. All that is needed is to find and agitate the malcontents.

Critical Theory would form the ideological bedrock for the new generation. Having grown up during the civil rights movement, the new breed of communists would adapt Critical Theory to America's new race-conscious sensibilities.

Critical Race Theory, or CRT, first emerged in the late 1970s and '80s, just as the children of the radicals of the 1960s were taking control of America's institutions. Whereas Critical Theory claimed society was made up of categories of oppressors and oppressed, CRT went one step further, claiming those categories were racial. Simply put, blacks, Hispanics, and other ethnic minorities were the oppressed, and whites were the oppressors. The eternal struggle between workers and capitalists was out; the eternal struggle between aggrieved racial groups and their white antagonists was in.

If you were white, it didn't matter if you weren't overtly racist; you were simply unconscious of your racism. If you were a member of a minority group, it didn't matter if you didn't consider yourself oppressed: that made you a race traitor and worse than whitey himself.

The oppressors, according to the communist, are infected with an invisible parasite called "whiteness." This parasite works quietly, causing its host to lash out at minorities in ways both seen and unseen, and reinforce the system of oppression, known as "white privilege," on which the United States is built.

The oppressed have a parasite of their own, called "internalized oppression." This parasite causes its host to turn racism inward and accept, or even contribute to, their own oppression.

Communists claim that Critical Race Theory is the only cure for these parasites. In the case of both the oppressors and oppressed, the parasite can only be purged by its victims being made aware of this system and raised to a new level of consciousness. Instead of raising "class consciousness," as the old

THE ANTI-COMMUNIST MANIFESTO   133

communist did, the new communist sees as his mission the raising of "race consciousness."

While CRT is the foundation of the new class grievance for the communist, it isn't the only grievance-based ideology he's peddling. In addition to separating people into racial classes, he also seeks to divide Americans with a multitude of ideologies that create social tension along sex and gender lines. These include:

- *Radical Feminism*: This ideology claims that Western society, which it refers to as "the patriarchy," is built to oppress women and maintain male superiority. Radical feminism seeks to liberate women by reordering society by eliminating all systems of male supremacy and replace it with chicks who drive Subarus.

- *Queer Theory*: According to this ideology, Western society is built on a system that "normalizes" heterosexuality and oppress all people who engage in sexual practices that fall outside of it. Proponents of queer theory work to end "heteronormativity" and liberate queer people by normalizing sexual deviance, including homosexuality, bisexuality, and transgenderism. Extremely damaging to the country, but a huge boon for Navy recruitment.

- *Gender Theory*: This ideology holds that sex and gender are two independent concepts. Gender theorists claim that while sex is determined by biological factors (like chromosomes), gender is

a psychological phenomenon that has been re-
pressed by Western society, which normalizes
a "gender binary." Those who subscribe to gender theory seek to break down those norms by
normalizing gender "nonconformity" and "non-
binary" gender identities. Most of history rightly
called them what they are: insane.

While all of these ideologies appear to have different groups
supporting them, it's important to understand that they are, in
fact, the same group with the same goal.

Think of them as different menu items at the same fast-food
restaurant. McDonald's, for example, offers a good deal of variety
in addition to their burgers. You may not want a Big Mac, so they
also offer Chicken McNuggets, or a Filet-O-Fish. There's even
a salad you can order if you're a weirdo. It's all about appealing
to as many customers as possible.

The communist has many different menu items for the same
reason as Mickey D's. If he only appealed to the feminists by
handing out cat litter and marshmallow cream, he wouldn't have
enough soldiers, because there are only so many bitter women
in America. They'd be lucky to recruit enough people to loot a
Joann Fabrics. The communist needs more malcontents, so he
tries to appeal to as many aggrieved groups as he can. Why do
you think all of these "separate groups" are always arrested at
the same rallies?

These are the brands of communism that infect nearly every
aspect of our society now. These are the brands of communism
that are being passed along like a virus to our children in their
schools.

The ideas may be dressed up in fancy new terms. The classes the communist seeks to "liberate" may have changed. Marx may now dye his beard pink, wear a dress, and identify as Karla—but he's still Marx. The ultimate goal of the communist is the same as it ever was: destruction. The changes they seek to bring about and the principles on which they want to build their new society are no longer called "communism." Most of today's believers don't even know what they are. The new racial, sexual, and gender norms fall under the catchall term "social justice."

So, has the vision of William Foster and communist educators like Richard Frank and Howard Langford been achieved? Without a doubt, the answer is yes.

The communist religion has now been introduced into nearly every aspect of education. While CRT may be decades old, school administrators have taken it up with renewed gusto since the George Floyd riots.

In June 2020, numerous organizations and education associations raced to announce they would work to rapidly inject CRT and its tenets into their schools. The School Superintendents Association promised it would work to implement an "anti-racist curriculum" in history classes and help "dismantle systemic racism." Similarly, the National Council for the Social Studies promised to overhaul content "to stop . . . the systemic pattern of dehumanization." For its part, the National Council of Teachers of English vowed "to apply the power of language and literacy to actively pursue justice and equity" in classrooms.

For every subject, a curriculum has been developed, and in many cases adopted, for delivering the new communist gospel.

For young English students, books are increasingly being chosen, or removed, based on their handling of race and gender issues. Books that were traditionally part of the English curriculum, like *Adventures of Huckleberry Finn*, *The Adventures of Tom Sawyer*, and *Of Mice and Men*, are being pushed out of elementary and high school classrooms because of "problematic" portrayals of race. Even *To Kill a Mockingbird*, a book that explicitly condemns racism, has come under fire. In their place, school libraries are beginning to stock books like *Gender Queer: A Memoir*, which features pornographic illustrations of gay oral sex, or *Lawn Boy*, which has been described by some angry parents as "pedophilic" due to its discussion of sex acts between young children.

But the communist's hostility toward traditional literature isn't limited to banning books or pushing pornography. As Howard Langford recommended, students are being encouraged to analyze everything they read from a communist perspective. One widely used English curriculum, called Units of Study, tells students in seventh through ninth grade to engage with "the politics of race, class, and gender" of contemporary fiction. Activities instruct students to break down "hegemonic masculinity" in the books they're reading. Another builds so-called identity lenses through which students can look at literature.

History, as Langford wanted, is no longer "a medium for the glorification of national heroes or of a national tradition." Instead, it's been replaced by an anti-American grievance-fest that focuses on the oppression and exploitation of aggrieved classes. Columbus was a madman who brought slavery to the New World and butchered the Native Americans. Washington, Jefferson, and Madison were nothing more than racist slave masters. The founding documents were all written to uphold white supremacy and the patriarchy.

Countless schools have adopted "The 1619 Project" as part

of their curriculum, a work of revisionist history that claims America was not founded in 1776 with the Declaration of Independence, but instead came into being in 1619 with the arrival of the first slaves on the continent. Throughout the 1619 Project, its author, Nikole Hannah-Jones, traces everything America has achieved—economically, culturally, and socially—to the legacy of slavery, making it clear that blacks are not just heroes in American history, but the *only* heroes in American history.

Not only is the work deeply anti-American, but it's also filled with factual errors and inaccuracies. It makes ridiculous claims, such as that the patriots fought the American Revolution in large part to preserve slavery in North America. Historian Leslie Harris, who was hired to fact-check the 1619 Project, claims her objections to the errors were ignored. Of course they were. Facts don't matter to communists; the ideology is what's most important.

In science, districts are adopting curriculums that are less about biology or technology and are instead focused on social justice activism.

One such curriculum is the Underrepresentation Curriculum Project, which is "designed to help students critically examine scientific fields and take action for equity, inclusion and justice." Students are taught how to use "tools such as data analysis, hypothesis creation, and investigation" to "look critically at science through the lenses of equity and inclusion." Throughout its lesson plans, teachers are instructed to teach students about the "myth of meritocracy," systemic racism and sexism, racial privilege, and political correctness and micro-aggressions.

In mathematics, many school districts are instructing

teachers to focus on "equity." Officials in several districts in California, for example, have created "equitable math," a curriculum that is described as offering "critical approaches to dismantling white supremacy in math classrooms" for students in grades six through eight. The curriculum's first handbook makes no mention of addition, subtraction, or multiplication. The term *equity* is used 17 times. The term *white supremacy* appears 54 times. The word *racism* appears 100 times.

In Seattle public schools, classrooms have adopted a "Math Ethnic Studies Framework" for K–12 students. This curriculum includes the themes of "power and oppression" and the "history of resistance and liberation." The curriculum is meant to teach students how "Western mathematics" have been used "to disenfranchise people and communities of color" and "erase the historical contributions of people and communities of color." It also teaches "the history of resistance and liberation" through "the stories, places, and people who helped liberate people and communities of color using math."

These curriculums are just the tip of the iceberg, and while they might appear psychotic to you, parents in some parts of the country are fully on board with the communist indoctrination. In many districts, teachers and school officials aren't bothering to disguise it anymore. In districts where parents do raise concerns about this invasive ideology, the communist's favorite vehicle for subversion—the 1.5 million members of the American Federation of Teachers—is ready to fight back.

Just as Howard Langford instructed, they hide behind the concept of academic freedom, or they flat-out lie about what is taught in their classrooms. "Let's be clear: Critical race theory is not taught in elementary schools or high schools," AFT president

Randi Weingarten told her members at a 2021 conference. She added that those pushing to prevent CRT from being taught in schools were "bullying teachers and trying to stop us from teaching kids honest history." Rest assured, Weingarten likely knows this is a lie. The brain that sits underneath that monkey's haircut knows what's being taught.

## Retaking America's Schools

The issue of communism in America's classrooms isn't going to get better anytime soon. The new generation of communist educators being pumped out by the universities is more radical than the generation that preceded it. We see it every day with teachers who are obsessed with sowing contempt between white and minority students, "coming out" to their classes, and insisting children acknowledge their preferred pronouns. Without a radical shift in the way we view education and a concerted effort to take back the minds of our children, America will be doomed in the years to come.

Let me repeat that—doomed. These kids are our destiny, and they're being primed to loathe the nation they will inherit.

Once again, we must start by acknowledging where the communist is right. Yes, education is about literature, math, science, and history, but it's more than that. Education shapes young minds and lays a moral foundation that students will carry for a lifetime. Young minds are the most fertile, so if we're going to produce future citizens who hold our principles and values, the process needs to begin as early as possible.

As anti-communists, we need to start fresh by rejecting the idea of modern, so-called liberal education altogether. For centuries we have been led to believe that the best form of education is one that sets out to produce students who are open-minded and free from ideology. Open-mindedness is useless, and even dangerous, if it ultimately closes around something poisonous. No, we don't want open minds. We want minds that are closed off to communism, godlessness, and other destructive ideas.

With this in mind, we must stop saying that we want to take politics out of schools. That's loser talk. The anti-communist rejects the idea for two reasons:

1. We understand that it's an impossible fantasy. There is no neutrality. Your kids are taught by human beings. Human beings have biases. Those biases will come out in how and what they teach.

2. We understand that politics reflect values. Even if neutrality were possible, it wouldn't be desirable. We don't want our children to be blank slates. We want our values and politics to be written upon them.

The communist's goal is simple: to have *his* values reflected in your children's education. Therefore, our goal must be the opposite: to have *our* values reflected in our children's education. To ensure that happens, we need to take as much control of their education as possible.

If there's one thing I want to stress, it's this: the communists might control the schools for the time being, but this is a battle we can win. You are in total control of the place where your child's education begins—at home. If your kids are attending public school, their teachers have them for a few hours a day. You, on the other hand, have them for their whole life. If you find yourself watching your son or daughter slowly transform into a pint-sized Trotsky as they step off the school bus every day, the failure lies with you. It was, and is, your responsibility to prepare them to reject the poison they may be learning from their instructors.

As it says in Proverbs, "Train up a child in the way he should go: and when he is old, he will not depart from it." If *you* do not fill the role of trainer, it will inevitably be filled by someone else—perhaps someone who doesn't have their best intentions in mind.

Abandon the notion that your child can be apolitical. The communist has no such delusions. You need to make sure your values are in your child's mind before the communist gets his hands on them. You should be reading and having discussions with your child about those values, and make sure that they understand them.

Let me take things one step further: stop treating your children like they're your friends. Friendships come and go. They can be thrown away over petty things and forgotten over time. The relationship between you and your children cannot. It's way more important and sacred than any friendship you will ever have in your life. You must treat it that way.

Your children must understand that you are *the* authority in their lives. From the day they are born to the day they move out of your home, you are in charge. This is your most important role as a parent.

In establishing your relationship with your children on a firm foundation of obedience, they will not only become more pleasant to be around, they will also be less likely to fall under the influence of their teachers.

The most destructive lesson kids learn in today's schools is the idea that the only thing to which they owe obedience is their feelings. In many ways, this is at the heart of the Critical Theory–communist curriculum. For example:

> Do you feel bad because other families have more than yours? Great! You're a victim!

> Do you feel like others treat you differently because of your race? Great! You're oppressed!

> Do you feel like a girl today? Great! You're a girl!

Every step of the way, kids are told that their feelings define their reality and should determine their course of action. A child who understands that they are not the ultimate authority in their life—at least not yet—will naturally be skeptical of this idea and return to their parents for guidance.

It begins with little things. Teach them independence. Teach them toughness. Teach them kindness. They should wash and get dressed by themselves as soon as they're able. You should set small tasks for them. Cleaning their rooms. Washing their own dishes or loading them into the dishwasher. When dining out, have them order their meal themselves, addressing the staff in a clear and polite voice.

Not only will this prepare them for the day when they become responsible for themselves, but it will go a long way toward building an individual identity and preventing socialization.

If you really want to raise an anti-communist, teach your

children the importance of being grateful. There has never been a grateful communist. Ever. There's a reason that they're ingrates. Communists believe that they have been the victims of theft on a societal scale. The wealth of others has been stolen from them and the group to which they belong. This belief carries with it a sense of entitlement. What most normal people would view as an act of generosity, they see as an act of justice.

Children should be made to understand that nothing is owed to them. When they receive something—anything—they should do so with humility and gratitude.

The final point I'll leave you with is this: give your children God.

Of all the ways in which the communist has undermined the education of children, nothing has been more destructive than the removal of scripture and prayer from the classroom. By taking God out of schools, the communist has removed the foundation upon which Western society was built and created the vacuum into which he has poured his own godless religion. If you deny your children God, you are leaving the door wide open.

This applies to every parent, even the ones who are not particularly religious. However, it's especially important for the families of public school students. Since the Supreme Court has all but banned religion in public schools, you must give your children religious instruction at home or at church.

Okay, that's about as far as I'll go with parenting advice for now. After all, this isn't *Jesse Kelly's Guide to Anti-Communist Parenting* (coming in spring 2025). Let's return to the issue of schooling and making sure that our kids aren't being subjected to communist education.

The most effective way to ensure that your kids are learning your values is obviously not to send them to communist schools. If you're going to opt out of the communist school system, then homeschooling is your best option. It gives you the most direct control over what your children are exposed to and puts them beyond the influence of communist educators.

"But Jesse," I already hear you asking, "won't that lead to my kids being socially awkward and weird?" To this, I respond: Have you seen what passes for normal these days? Antisocial behavior, godlessness, and gender confusion have become the norm. So, yes, your children might be a little weird. And that's exactly what we want.

Americans are seeing through the "but your kids will be weird" argument that the public school advocates have been pushing. Over the past few decades, the number of home-schooled students has skyrocketed. In 1999 it was estimated that around 850,000 American students were homeschooled. By the 2020–21 school year, that number had grown to around 3.7 million students. I'd call that a good start, but those are rookie numbers. We've got to pump those up.

Thankfully, the rapid growth in homeschooling has made it easier than ever before. The number of resources available for homeschooling has multiplied, as have the number of groups and co-ops that offer support to parents.

Homeschooling has additional benefits besides keeping your kids away from communist influence. Data consistently shows that homeschooled students perform better than their institutional-school-educated peers. For example, home-schooled kids typically score 15 to 30 points above public school students on standardized academic achievement tests.

Communists aren't the only thing homeschooled students

will avoid. Public schools are the place kids will most likely have their first exposure to tobacco, drug abuse, and other fun stuff (just kidding). As a result, homeschooled students are also less likely to fall prey to these self-destructive behaviors. According to a 2015 study by the journal *Drug and Alcohol Dependence*, homeschoolers are significantly less likely to report the use of tobacco, alcohol, marijuana, and most other illicit drugs than their non-homeschooled counterparts.

The facts are clear. Homeschooling produces better-adjusted, smarter, and healthier kids. It should be the go-to choice for anti-communist parents.

As great as homeschooling is, I understand that it's not a realistic option for many families. In more than half of American households with children under the age of seventeen, both parents are employed. The dual-income household has become increasingly necessary to make ends meet, and to maintain a quality of life that Americans have come to expect.

In cases where homeschooling is not possible, parents should send their children to vetted private schools. Notice I said *vetted*. Private schools have terrible teachers as well; some are no doubt as bad as those in public schools. However, while they're not ideal, private schools offer a level of choice that doesn't exist in the public system, in which students are assigned to schools based on their geographic location.

In addition, fewer private schools are unionized, meaning that bad teachers are more likely to be held accountable. They have a financial incentive to make parents happy and will be more responsive to your individual concerns about your children's education.

Since they are not funded publicly, private schools are not

bound by the same legal requirements as public education. Most importantly, the prohibition on God in the classroom doesn't apply to private schools. Many schools are associated with specific faiths and churches, which will guarantee that your children receive religious instruction. The largest system of private schools in the United States is operated by the Catholic Church, but whether Catholic, Protestant, Orthodox, or Jewish, there's a good chance that you can find a local school that represents your faith.

I understand that going private can be expensive. The average tuition of a private K–12 school in the United States is well over $12,000 per year. That's a lot for most families, but your children's education must be a priority. If it means the difference between that family vacation—especially if it's a trip to Disney World—and keeping your kids out of the public school system, choose the latter every time.

Let me leave you with a warning when it comes to private schools: you must remain vigilant. The communist curriculum is increasingly finding its way into private institutions, especially in blue cities and states. Not even religious institutions are free from its influence. If you send your kids to private school, you need to join with other like-minded parents and demand total transparency from teachers and administrators. Together, you must monitor what your children are being taught every day, and make noise if you see communism creeping in.

If homeschooling is out of the question and private schools are too costly, your only choice is going to be to send your kids to public schools. While the ideal would be the total dismantling of the public school system, the reality is that most American students are currently enrolled in government schools. That's unlikely to change anytime soon.

If your children are going to attend public schools, you need to be active in efforts to shape the school's curriculum. This is going to require state and local government action.

At the state level, you need to rally around governors and lawmakers who are willing to pass laws that prevent teachers from pushing the communist ideology.

Florida has led the way on this with the state government's passage of two laws: the Stop WOKE Act and the Parental Rights in Education Act. The former prohibits the teaching of Critical Race Theory in K–12 schools and forbids Florida school districts, colleges, and universities from hiring CRT consultants. The latter protects students in grades K–3 by prohibiting teachers from discussing sexual orientation or gender identity in the classroom, and requiring schools to notify parents of a changes in student's mental, emotional, or physical health. Similar laws have been proposed in other states and more are likely to follow. You need to find lawmakers who back these laws and support them.

Don't allow yourself to be fooled by the argument that these laws curb the freedom of speech of teachers. Our schools are not "the marketplace of ideas." We don't want their values competing with our values. No matter what they may think, teachers don't have the right to teach your children whatever they want.

In addition to the defensive measure of preventing teachers from indoctrinating students into the communist ideology, we should be pushing state governments to be proactive in mandating anti-communist education in public schools. Here again, Florida has led the way. In 2022, Governor Ron DeSantis signed the "Victims of Communism Day" bill. The law requires that every November 7, high school students:

> [M]ust receive at least 45 minutes of instruction . . . to include topics such as Mao Zedong and the Cultural Revolution, Joseph Stalin and the Soviet System, Fidel Castro and the Cuban Revolution, Vladimir Lenin and the Russian Revolution, Pol Pot and the Khmer Rouge, and Nicolas Maduro and the Chavismo movement, and how victims suffered under these regimes through poverty, starvation, migration, systemic legal violence, and suppression of speech.

Victims of Communism *Week* would have been better, but setting aside one day a year is a good start. Similar bills should be introduced in every state legislature around the country and, ultimately, the day should be recognized nationwide.

State action can be effective, but the most important institution anti-communists need to focus on is their local boards of education. In most states, these committees have direct control over the day-to-day operation of public schools. They are responsible for staffing decisions, developing the curriculum, and school finances. If your local public schools have communist administrators, are indoctrinating young children into gender ideology, and are teaching students to hate their country, the board of education has allowed it to happen.

Organization is going to be key. Find and unite with other anti-communists in your school district. Together you need to audit the curriculum. Scrutinize the syllabus, comb through every homework assignment, and examine every textbook. Question your children regularly to find out what they're learning.

Additionally, learn what you can about your children's teachers. You wouldn't leave your children with anyone for seven hours a day without a background check, right? Teachers are no exception to the rule. I'm not saying that you need to be going through their garbage cans when they put them out to the curb, but you need to know who they are. Do your due diligence. There's a lot you can learn through information that is publicly available. Know their employment history. Find their public statements. Monitor their social media accounts.

Keep in mind, communist indoctrination doesn't have to be overt. A lot of it is subtle. If your kids' history teacher, for example, is spending an hour on the Declaration of Independence, two months on slavery, an hour on World War II, and two months on Jim Crow, your kids are going to hate America.

If you find that your children's curriculum has become infected with communism and Critical Theory, you need to hold the school board accountable. In an ideal world, school boards would be responsive to the voices of the community. However, many of these committees are ideologically motivated. They view the concerns of the parents as an annoyance and will meet them with hostility.

If your local school board ignores your concerns, you must become more assertive. If we've learned anything over the past few years, it's that the most effective way to make your voice heard is by causing a ruckus at school board meetings. The more voices you have, the greater the ruckus. The greater the ruckus, the greater the effect. So, don't be afraid to raise hell.

Go public. Publicize objectionable material through whatever channels you have access to. Alert the media. Get cameras in the room. Name and shame.

In school districts where parents make noise, the effect has been undeniable. The most notable example came in 2021, when parents in Loudoun County, Virginia, launched a highly publicized rebellion over the teaching of Critical Race Theory and the alleged cover-up of a sexual assault on a young girl by a male student in a dress. Parents showed up to school board meetings in force. They were aggressive. They were unrelenting. The father of the young girl who'd been assaulted was even arrested and found guilty of disorderly conduct and resisting arrest when he demanded to speak. Loudoun County became the center of a firestorm, generating headlines and national news coverage. The issues parents raised were incorporated into the campaigns of Republicans across Virginia, leading to a red wave in state elections that year.

That's how it's done. Anti-communists need to follow the example set by the parents of Loudoun County. Show up in force. Be aggressive. Be relentless. Become activists. Anti-communism is activism.

Of course, school boards hate when their power is challenged. You need to be prepared for the inevitable pushback. However, you should know that when they push back, it means they're frightened. And when they're frightened, you attack even harder.

Learn to love their pushback. Learn to love their fear.

Most predictably of all, school board members, teachers, and administrators are going to play the victim by claiming they're scared of your agitation. I say, good. They should be scared.

Anti-communists are done playing when it comes to our schools. We consider the issue to be the most important one we're facing today, and we will go to great lengths to achieve victory. Let them tremble before us. It is preferable that they be guided by fear than by the warped ideology they are feeding to our kids.

Agitation and public protest are good ways to bring about change, but this is still a defensive measure—a reaction to what they're imposing on our children. Ultimately, the only way to alter the system in the long term is to seize control of it. That means anti-communists need to take control of the school boards.

I can't overstate the importance of America's school boards. If the communists were to offer me every school board in the country in exchange for every congressional seat, it would be an easy choice: give me the school boards every time.

Despite their importance, school board elections have been a blind spot for the right. They're not exciting, they don't receive much media attention, and candidates rarely have name recognition. As a result, school boards around the country have become dominated by communist radicals, including many of those found in deep-red states. The impact has been devastating and the indifference needs to end.

Like-minded parents need to seek out candidates who share a commitment to an anti-communist, pro-Western curriculum, and will appoint school administrators who are committed to the same. Again, we don't want school board candidates who preach neutrality. We don't want to prevent children from learning *about* communism. To the contrary, we want them to learn about the multitude of crimes committed by communist governments. We want them to learn about how the ideology represents a grave threat to freedom. We want them to learn why and how they should reject communism. If you can't find an anti-communist candidate, then become one.

Once you've found your candidates, get them funded. Communists will pump money into school board elections if they foresee a threat to their control, so you'll need all the dollars you can get your hands on. In addition to raising funds locally, there are national organizations dedicated to funding candidates who support pro-Western education and oppose Critical Race Theory. Seek the endorsement of these groups and their money.

Once funded, you must actively campaign for your candidates. These are local elections, so it's going to require retail politics. Go door-to-door. Hand out literature in front of your local supermarket. Flyer parking lots. Distribute lawn signs.

I know this all seems like a lot of effort for a local election. We'd all rather slap a bumper sticker on our car for our favorite presidential candidate every four years and call it a day. But that's what losers do. The president isn't going to save your schools. He doesn't care about your child. Only you do. Your child is worth fighting for.

# ANTI-COMMUNIST ACTION ITEMS

- Your child's education begins at home. Teach them your values and be *the* authority in their lives.

- If possible, remove your children from the public school system. Choose homeschooling or vetted private schools.

- Support governors and lawmakers who are willing to pass laws that prevent teachers from pushing the communist ideology.

- Shape the public school curriculum by making your voice heard at school board meetings and, ultimately, electing anti-communist school board members.

# CHAPTER SIX

# Climate Communism:
# Green on the Outside, Red on the Inside

What if I told you that the most genocidal ideology in the history of mankind is currently taking hold in the Western world? This ideology, if it is not stopped, will kill more people than Stalin, Mao, and Hitler combined by an order of magnitude. When I tell you this ideology will kill a billion people, please understand that I'm probably *underselling* it significantly.

You see this ideology everywhere you go. You see it in your movies. Your politicians talk about it often. Your children learn about it in school. Maybe you're a true believer yourself. We refer to this ideology as environmentalism or "going green," and it is the communist's deadliest idea to date.

---

A central theme of this book has been destruction. The communist inevitably destroys everything he claims he will save. The environment is no different.

In the communist's worldview, there is no God in whose image man was created and by whom he was given dominion over nature. Man has no spiritual dimension or soul. There is little that sets men apart from the environment. He's just another accident of the universe, different from other beasts in one way only: he is a curse upon all living things.

Far from being a deviation from communism, environmentalism is its ultimate expression. If the communist believes it is immoral to exploit men for profit, it must, logically, be immoral to exploit all of nature for profit—whether nature takes the form of an animal, vegetable, or mineral. In this sense, the sins of the Western world, whose prosperity is largely built on economic freedom, make it a plague of exploitation on the earth itself. Only through radical transformation can that exploitation be ended. To millions of godless people, the green religion has become the perfect way to attempt to fill the hole in their heart left by atheism.

In 2003, *Jurassic Park* author Michael Crichton gave a speech to the Commonwealth Club in San Francisco in which he explained how environmentalism has replaced traditional Western religion:

> Why do I say it's a religion? Well, just look at the beliefs. If you look carefully, you see that environmentalism is in fact a perfect 21st century remapping of traditional Judeo-Christian beliefs and myths. There's an initial Eden, a paradise, a state of grace and unity with nature, there's a fall from grace into a state of pollution as a result of eating from the tree of knowledge, and as a result of our actions there is a judgment day coming for us all. We are all energy sinners, doomed to die, unless we seek salvation, which is now called sustainability. Sustainability is salvation in the church of the environment.

Just as organic food is its communion, that pesticide-free wafer that the right people with the right beliefs, imbibe.

Like all other religions, environmentalism has its own evangelists, fundamentalists, and fanatics. It has adherents who live, die, and are even willing to kill in the name of the faith.

Environmentalism even has its own version of doomsday. Climate change has become the end-times prophecy of the green movement. Only by cleansing the world of capitalism, the original sin of Western civilization, can mankind be saved. And just like a proper doomsday cult, they have a countdown clock that miraculously resets every time their predictions don't come to pass.

This vision of the end-times is more dangerous than anything found in the book of Revelation. Its most ardent believers are not found at the pulpit or on a street corner screaming "the end is near." The climate change fanatics occupy the halls of power. They write and pass legislation. They control billions of taxpayer dollars. They agree to far-reaching international plans and propose polices on a global scale. They will cleanse mankind of their sins, whether they like it or not.

Whether environmentalists are driven by a sincere concern for nature or a fanatical hatred of capitalism, the green movement is about one thing: destruction. Destruction of industry. Destruction of the economy. Destruction of infrastructure. Destruction of the food we eat and the cars we drive. Destruction of you.

However, their efforts will end in a way that is significantly worse than every communist revolution that has preceded it. Not only will liberties be trampled under the boot of the government and the people be driven into grinding poverty, but it will also be done in total darkness as the environmentalist cuts off the lifeblood of the world: energy.

You see, unless you're walking around naked in the mountains right now, almost everything you see around you required cheap, abundant energy to make. By declaring war on cheap energy, the communist has declared war on everything.

Just as the Marxist claims to love the people he says he wants to liberate—yet mercilessly slaughters them once he takes power—the same is true of the environmentalist. He doesn't believe that people are the solution to the problems of mankind: he believes they're the *cause* of it. While the Marxists of the past have imposed their will by subjecting the masses to firing squads and gulags, the environmentalist will do the same through economic desperation and hunger.

Worse still, the communist will sleep well at night as the people around him suffer because, as we'll see, it's all part of the plan.

## Communism vs. the Environment

While the modern communist claims to be the savior of the environment, history tells a much different story. Indeed, if we look to the past, it's easy to see that there is no pollutant on earth that is worse for nature than his twisted religion. In virtually every nation in which he has taken control, environmental disaster has followed, because the communist will inevitably show just as much concern for nature as they do for human rights—which is to say, none.

The Soviet Union offers the most striking example of the communist's brutalization of nature. When Lenin and the Bolsheviks took power, all forest, animal, water, mineral, and plant resources became the property of the state. Throughout the communists' seventy-year rule, the government oversaw some of the worst environmental disasters in human history. When the Iron Curtain was lifted in 1990, it revealed noxious air, poisoned soil, and polluted lakes and rivers.

The Soviet Union didn't usually set out to trash the environment on purpose. All of the worst disasters that occurred in the Soviet era stemmed from the government's nationalization of agriculture and industry. Their destruction of nature was simply the result of their efforts to carry out "the plan."

So, how bad was it? Let's start with the fact that the Soviet Union made one of the largest lakes on earth disappear. I'm not making that up. There was a gigantic lake and it's gone now.

In 1946, the Soviet Union was hit by a massive drought that devastated farmlands throughout the country's breadbasket. The drought was one of the main factors in a widespread famine that claimed the lives of an estimated 2 million Soviet citizens. With the country's agriculture in shambles, the government in Moscow needed to figure out how to prevent similar famines in the future.

Don't worry, the communists had a plan.

In late 1948, Stalin proposed the appropriately named "Great Plan for the Transformation of Nature." The massive undertaking involved the creation of artificial canals and reservoirs throughout the Soviet Union to transform unproductive land into fertile farmland. The plan would come to include the area surrounding the Aral Sea, which communist planners decided would make perfect farmland.

Straddling the border between Kazakhstan to the north and Uzbekistan to the south, the Aral Sea was the world's fourth-largest freshwater lake, measuring more than 26,000 square miles by area. For comparison, it was larger than Lake Huron, Lake Michigan, and more than three times the size of Lake Ontario. The area around the Aral Sea hosted a thriving fishing industry and contributed to the livelihoods of countless people. At its peak in 1957, the lake produced more than 48,000 tons of fish, roughly 13 percent of the Soviet Union's fish stocks.

In the 1960, they began cutting canals into the Syr Darya and the Amu Darya, the two rivers that fed the Aral Sea. Unfortunately, the geniuses in Moscow gave little thought to the impact the diversion of the rivers would have on the huge body of water that they fed. In addition, the irrigation canals that were built were typical of communist engineering. Huge amounts of water went to waste through leakage and evaporation. Without the water needed to replenish it, the Aral Sea began to starve. Starting in the 1960s, the water level began to drop. By 1992, right around the time the Soviet Union fell, the Aral Sea was roughly 13,000 square miles, or half the size it had been in the early 1960s.

Today, little remains of the Aral Sea. As it dried up, it broke into two smaller bodies of water that are puddles compared to what the lake once was. Most of the area that it once occupied has become a barren salt flat. The communities that surrounded the lake have disappeared, as has the fishing industry that relied upon it. The communists promised thriving agriculture. What they delivered was a monument to their own stupidity.

As terrible as their efforts to control agriculture were for the environment, the Soviet government's efforts to control the energy industry resulted in a disaster that threatened to wipe out half of Europe.

Before the Bolsheviks took power in the early twentieth century, Russia was the backwater of Europe. The country was largely rural, had a low level of industrialization, and had very little technical infrastructure. With the country lagging behind the West in its efforts to modernize, the government in Moscow needed to figure out how to catch up.

Don't worry, the communists had a plan.

In the 1920s, Bolshevik leader Vladimir Lenin had declared that "Communism is Soviet power plus the electrification of the whole country." Under communist rule, the nation would rapidly modernize, bringing light into Soviet homes and electrifying the country's transit system. In the decades that followed, the Soviet Union would dot the landscape with power plants. They built coal, hydroelectric, and eventually nuclear plants, and they did so with their typical concern for safety and quality engineering.

With Lenin's vision for an electrified Soviet Union being carried out, it's fitting then that the worst nuclear disaster in human history would occur at a plant in Ukraine that bore his name: the Vladimir Lenin Nuclear Power Plant, better known as Chernobyl.

In April 1986, workers at the plant carried out a poorly designed safety test on one of the station's four reactors. I'll spare you the technical details of what happened, but, as with most communist disasters, the cause can be chalked up to incompetence and poor engineering. At 1:23 a.m. on April 26, Chernobyl's reactor unit 4 exploded, exposing the nuclear core and sending a massive amount of radioactive smoke and steam into the atmosphere. Fearful of the reaction from Moscow, officials at the nuclear power plant were slow to react, informing the government that the incident posed no real threat.

They were wrong.

In addition to the two plant workers killed by the explosion itself, the incident irradiated the surrounding area, including the neighboring city of Pripyat. Of course, nobody bothered to inform local inhabitants, because communists hate people.

Worse yet, the explosion had resulted in a partial nuclear meltdown. If left unchecked, a full meltdown could have spread fallout across half of Europe, potentially killing countless millions and leaving much of the continent uninhabitable.

Thankfully, the plant operators couldn't keep the disaster under wraps for long, and the meltdown was eventually brought under control.

While the worst outcome was narrowly avoided, the delayed response took its toll. Within weeks, a further twenty-eight people, including firefighters and plant operators, died horrible deaths from acute radiation syndrome. People who lived in the surrounding area, most of whom were eventually evacuated, suffered from radiation sickness and cataracts. Later effects included increased instances of thyroid cancer, especially in children, and leukemia among exposed workers.

In addition to the human toll, the damage to the environment was catastrophic. The Chernobyl exclusion zone, an area of more than a thousand square miles around the site of the plant, is among the most radioactively contaminated regions in the world, with some experts claiming it will remain uninhabitable by humans for as many as three thousand years. The fallout had a major impact on both agricultural and natural ecosystems in several European countries, including Belarus, Russia, and Ukraine. Radioactive material was absorbed by plants and wildlife in the region. In some areas, radioactivity was found in milk, meat, food products, freshwater fish, and wood.

To this day, Chernobyl remains the worst nuclear disaster in history. The meltdown is often cited by the green movement as a way of stoking fear and preventing the construction of new power plants. In other words, communists hate nuclear energy because *communists* can't be trusted to safely operate a nuclear reactor. Are you getting that?

The meltdown at Chernobyl is the most infamous nuclear disaster to have occurred in the Soviet Union, but it wasn't an isolated incident. Although less well known, a second devastating nuclear incident also took place on the communists' watch, the so-called Mayak disaster.

In 1942, the Soviets caught wind of the fact that Germans and Americans were secretly working on a superweapon, the atomic bomb. Faced with the prospect of atomic-armed enemies and already behind in research and development, the government in Moscow needed to figure out how to develop their own atomic bomb.

Don't worry, the communists had a plan.

In 1944, Stalin placed Lavrentiy Beria, the head of the Soviet secret police and a man who raped so many children he could have been a Hollywood producer, in charge of the country's atomic bomb program, giving Beria five years in which to develop and test the nation's first bomb. Beria hastily ordered the construction of the Mayak plutonium plant in the southern Urals, where five nuclear reactors were built to produce plutonium that was refined and weaponized. Eventually the plant ran out of space in which to store the radioactive waste it produced, so, rather than taking the time to construct new storage capacity, workers simply dumped the waste into the nearby Techa River. Of course, nobody bothered to inform local inhabitants, because communists hate people.

Over the course of several years, the Mayak plant flushed the shallow river with the equivalent to half the fallout from the bomb that was dropped on Hiroshima.

In 1957, an underground tank of radioactive waste exploded. The explosion released radioactive dust and materials high up into the air, contaminating an area stretching approximately 12,000 square miles. The fallout led to the evacuation of thousands of area residents, and hundreds received fatal doses of radiation from the dust and debris.

It wasn't until after the fall of the Soviet Union that the Mayak disaster become public knowledge. The consequences of the incident remain to this very day. Those living near the Techa River suffer cancer rates 3.6 times higher than Russia's national average and birth defects 25 times more frequently than in other parts of the country. Residents living in the irradiated zone receive additional benefits from the Russian government for medicine. A study carried out in 1993 found nearby "Lake Karachay" to be the most contaminated place on earth, and it has since been filled in and concreted over.

The Aral Sea and the nuclear disasters at Chernobyl and Mayak are the starkest examples of the Soviet desecration of nature, but they were far from isolated incidents. Communist control of industry and central planning guaranteed a poisonous environment throughout the Soviet Union.

In 1990, journalist James Ridgeway described the levels of pollution caused by Soviet policies:

40% of the Soviet people live in areas where air pol-
lutants are three to four times the maximum allowable
levels. Sanitation is primitive. Where it exists, for example in Moscow, it doesn't work properly. Half of all
industrial wastewater in the capital city goes untreated.
In Leningrad, nearly half of the children have intestinal
disorders caused by drinking contaminated water from
what was once Europe's most pristine supply.

The pollution caused by the Soviet planners should clearly
bring the tree-huggers to tears, but the animal rights activists
should be downright horrified by what the communists did—
especially the "save the whales" crowd.

Between 1948 and 1973, the Soviet whaling industry engaged in what some marine biologists have called "arguably
one of the greatest environmental crimes of the 20th century."
Over the course of a quarter century, Soviet whalers illegally
killed some 180,000 whales, driving several species onto the
endangered list. Although they made a good showing during
the 2017 Women's March in Washington, D.C., the whale population is still struggling to recover.

To a hard-hearted guy like me, this is all somewhat forgivable.
Whales provide all sorts of useful products, from oil made of
whale blubber to perfume made of sperm whale vomit. (I'm serious, look it up.) Of course, we don't want to drive animals into
extinction—*especially* the useful ones—and the Soviets appear
to have done it for no reason whatsoever, needlessly wasting the
whale carcasses after they'd been killed.

Writer Charles Homans described the senselessness in
*Pacific Standard* magazine:

[T]he Soviet Union had little real demand for whale products. Once the blubber was cut away for conversion into oil, the rest of the animal, as often as not, was left in the sea to rot or was thrown into a furnace and reduced to bone meal—a low-value material used for agricultural fertilizer, made from the few animal byproducts that slaughterhouses and fish canneries can't put to more profitable use. . . .

Why would a country that had no use for whale products needlessly slaughter them to the brink of extinction? You guessed it—because the communists had a plan.

Homans continues:

The Soviet whalers . . . had been sent forth to kill whales for little reason other than to say they had killed them. They were motivated by an obligation to satisfy obscure line items in the five-year plans that drove the Soviet economy, which had been set with little regard for the Soviet Union's actual demand for whale products.

Alfred Berzin, a Soviet-era fisheries scientist who spent much of his career with the communist nation's whaling fleets, explained it this way in his memoir, titled *The Truth About Soviet Whaling*:

Whalers knew that no matter what, the plan must be met! Looking for whales they would go farther and farther from the islands and bring rotten baleen whales to the stations, those which could not be used for food. This was not regarded as a problem by anybody. The plan—at any price! And whalers were killing everything.

Berzin's description of the Soviet whalers' motivation perfectly captures the communist mindset. Once set in motion, the plan is all that matters, and he will destroy anything that stands in its way. He will dry up lakes, poison the air, contaminate the soil and rivers, and needlessly slaughter animals to see it through. What chance do the people have?

So, what does the new "environmentally conscious" communist have in store for the United States? Don't worry, he has a plan.

## From the Little Red Book to the Little Green Book

As the Soviets were busy destroying their own environment, the communists were busy agitating for their own revolution here in America. By the late 1960s, the radicals had consolidated around the anti–Vietnam War movement. Young communists like Tom Hayden, founder of Students for a Democratic Society, were organizing protests on college campuses and making pilgrimages to Hanoi. Demonstrators were taking to the streets, many carrying communist flags and waving around Chairman Mao's Little Red Book.

The war in Vietnam had been a boon for the radicals, giving them an issue around which to unite. However, at the same time another movement began animating the communists as well: environmentalism. Just as their opposition to the Vietnam War grew out of a desire to fight American's military-industrial complex and political dominance overseas, the communists enthusiastically embraced environmentalism as a means of fighting American capitalism here at home.

The origins of the modern environmental movement can be traced back to 1962, when biologist Rachel Carson published the book *Silent Spring*. Carson argued that the widespread use of the pesticide dichloro-diphenyl-trichloroethane, better known as DDT, was poisoning the environment. Even though the U.S. National Academy of Sciences estimated DDT had saved 500 million lives from malaria by 1970, *Silent Spring* claimed that the pesticide was threatening many species of birds and other wildlife with extinction. Carson also argued that DDT was affecting humans in "sinister and often deadly ways," causing a "threat of chronic poisoning and degenerative changes of the liver and other organs." The book stoked fear with chapter titles such as "Elixirs of Death" and "Rivers of Death," and argued that Western civilization was waging a "relentless war on life."

Carson's book was a massive success. *Silent Spring* ended up selling more than 2 million copies and popularized environmentalism. Others saw something more sinister at work. Agriculture secretary Ezra Taft Benson, for example, said Carson was "probably a communist" and wondered why a "childless spinster" should be worried about how pesticides might affect future generations.

Whatever Carson's political leanings were, *Silent Spring* would have a major impact on future generations—just not in the way she had intended. The book, it turned out, was full of pseudoscience and unfounded fearmongering. In the years that followed its publication, studies showed that many of the key claims made by Carson were false. DDT's effect on the wildlife population was overstated at best, and there remains little evidence that its use carries an elevated risk of cancer or death in humans.

In 1972, ten years after *Silent Spring* hit bookshelves, the newly established Environmental Protection Agency banned the use of DDT. Other nations followed suit, including those where insect-borne diseases continued to plague the population. The bans were largely a result of the hysteria Carson had stoked.

As a result, tens of millions of people died from malaria unnecessarily, a large majority of whom were children under the age of five years old.

You read that right: *millions of children*. Remember when I told you that the environmental communist will kill a billion people? The body count has already begun. That count includes millions of children who, racked with fever, died in their own vomit and diarrhea.

And they died for nothing.

Despite *Silent Spring*'s flaws, the book was perfect for communists. It confirmed all their beliefs about capitalism's destruction of nature and the need for radical change. In the years following its publication, many would exchange Mao's *Little Red Book* for Carson's little green one.

The new movement's coming-out party took place on the first Earth Day. On April 22, 1970, environmental activists took to the stage in cities across the country, issuing dire warnings about the dangers of pollution and the imminent crisis facing humanity. The date also happened to be the hundred-year anniversary of the birth of Vladimir Lenin. Whether the day was chosen on purpose or not, the significance was not lost on many in the crowd.

One of the most prominent faces of the first Earth Day was Ira Einhorn. Einhorn was a prominent antiwar and counterculture activist who served as master of ceremonies at the event in Philadelphia. In later years, he claimed to have been instrumental in creating and launching Earth Day, a claim that event organizers deny for reasons that are about to become obvious.

In 1977, seven years after the first Earth Day, Einhorn's ex-girlfriend Holly Maddux disappeared after showing up at his Philadelphia apartment to collect her belongings. When questioned by police, Einhorn claimed to have no knowledge of her whereabouts. However, the building's landlord became suspicious after neighbors began to complain of a rancid odor emanating from Einhorn's apartment.

In March 1979, eighteen months after Maddox's disappearance, police raided Einhorn's apartment. Inside, they found her partially mummified body in a steamer trunk, buried beneath layers of air fresheners, plastic bags, foam peanuts, newspapers, insects, and larvae. Einhorn died in prison in 2020, claiming until his final days that he had been framed by the CIA.

The role of John Wayne Gacy notwithstanding, the environmental movement became a haven for communist radicals. Deprived of the issue that had united them when the Vietnam War ended in 1975, many turned to environmentalism as a new vehicle for their anticapitalist crusade.

Arguably the most prominent communist-turned-environmentalist was SDS founder Tom Hayden. Hayden, whose group spawned the terrorist Weather Underground in the 1960s, found a new respectability among the California elite, serving for nearly two decades in the Golden State's Assembly and Senate.

He became part of a new breed of environmentalist that fused together environmental concerns with their Marxist class and racial struggle.

Environmental justice, as the movement would come to be known, gained steam throughout the 1980s. It championed not only more government regulation to address environmental concerns, but socialist policies to address inequality, which they claimed was a result of the disparate impact of pollution on poor and marginalized communities.

The concept of environmental justice now infects every single department and agency in the executive branch of the federal government. Here are just a few examples:

- In 1992, the Environmental Protection Agency established an Office of Environmental Justice, which promises "fair treatment and meaningful involvement of all people regardless of race, color, national origin, or income, with respect to the development, implementation, and enforcement of environmental laws, regulations, and policies."

- The United States Department of Commerce has an "environmental justice strategy" in which it takes steps to "integrate environmental justice into its programs, policies, and activities."

- In 2016, the U.S. Department of Agriculture announced its plan "to institutionalize environmental justice principles at USDA."

- In 2022, the U.S. Department of Justice established the Office of Environmental Justice to "engage all Justice Department bureaus, components
and offices in the collective pursuit of environmental justice."

- The U.S. Department of Energy proudly pro-
claims on its website that it is "committed to
promoting environmental justice . . . [by] iden-
tifying and addressing, as appropriate, disproportionately high and adverse human health or
environmental effects of its programs, policies,
and activities on minority populations and low-
income populations, American Indian Tribes,
and Alaska Natives."

- On the U.S. Department of Health and Human
Services website, the department states that their
"priority is to improve the well-being of under-
served communities, including low-income communities and communities of color, who continue
to bear the brunt of pollution from industrial
development, agricultural practices, cumulative
impacts of land use decisions, transportation, and
trade corridors."

- In his first week in office, President Joe Biden
established the White House Environmental Justice Interagency Council to "develop a strategy to

address current and historic environmental injustice."

The environmental justice virus isn't limited to civilian agencies. In 2021, the U.S. Department of Defense (yes . . . the military) announced its own environmental justice strategy, which "includes environmental equity and justice in department organizational structures, policies and implementation guidance through inclusive and equitable climate adaptation and resilience as well as in agile mission assurance." The United States military, the institution whose job it is to kill people and destroy things in defense of our nation, is now dedicating resources and adjusting its strategies to satisfy the communist religion. So, instead of investing in more effective body armor and deadly munitions, I suppose our military is now pouring cash into developing soy-based tanks and fighter jets that run on unicorn farts.

(Side note: As I've said before—we're going to lose a major war. And when I say major, I don't mean some twenty-year global-war-on-terror debacle. I mean a military disaster that will see tens of thousands of our bravest killed in an afternoon.)

This isn't just a federal issue. States have also embraced environmental justice dogma. The majority of state governments across the U.S. have now established environmental justice offices, agencies, or initiatives.

And it's not just the blue states.

In 2021, the Texas Commission on Environmental Quality announced its first environmental justice initiative. The Lone Star State established a quasi–task force to "protect people of color and low-income residents who often live in communities

near sources of pollution" by "better understanding the environmental justice concerns of Texans."

Through environmentalism, the communist has carved out
a space for himself at all levels of the government from which he
can exert influence. Even in the face of the horrors his plans have
wrought on the natural world throughout history, the modern
communist marches on singing his favorite refrain, "This time
it'll be different."

## The Doomsday Cult of Climate Change

If the environmental religion has an ultimate form, it has arrived
under the name "man-made climate change." This is the religion's
doomsday cult, which believes that all human activity is leading
the species toward environmental Armageddon. Under the cloak
of preventing the end of the world, the belief in man-made climate change has become the perfect excuse for regulating and
controlling the world population.

The concept of man-made climate change was conceived in
the 1970s. Though the term may be new, the idea that humans
must be controlled to prevent the apocalypse has a long history.
At the turn of the nineteenth century, an English scholar named
Thomas Malthus became the first prophet of the population
control cult. In his 1798 book, titled *An Essay on the Principle of
Population*, Malthus claimed that the population of England was
growing at a faster pace than the nation's ability to feed itself. As a
result, he claimed, the people would eventually suffer from mass
starvation due to food shortages, inevitably leading to universal
suffering and death.

Malthus didn't believe that human beings would voluntarily

practice restraint in order to prevent the worst from happening. They were too stupid to resist their base urges. He was also an Anglican cleric, and believed that all forms of birth control, besides abstinence, were immoral. To solve the problem, Malthus proposed a novel way of controlling the population: if we can't stop them from reproducing, we'll encourage people to die more quickly.

It makes sense, right? If too many human beings are the problem, fewer human beings must be the solution. If we're trying to prevent the end of the world, then who cares how we arrive at the solution?

So, who would have to suffer? Not Thomas Malthus, of course; he was too intelligent. Not the wealthy, either; they were too important. The elites would be spared. Malthus concluded that the poor, ignorant rubes would have to die.

To decrease life spans, Malthus made a modest proposal:

[W]e should facilitate . . . the operations of nature in producing this mortality. . . . Instead of recommending cleanliness to the poor, we should encourage contrary habits. In our towns we should make the streets narrower, crowd more people into the houses, and court the return of the plague. In the country we should build our villages near stagnant pools, and particularly encourage settlements in all marshy and unwholesome situations.

After that, Malthus and the rest of the elites would just sit back and watch nature take its course. The rubes would suffer and die miserable, disease-ridden deaths, guaranteeing a continued abundance for Malthus and his powerful pals.

It all sounds very cruel, but Malthus and many of the English elite convinced themselves that it was an act of compassion. They believed it was better that the poor die of disease than everyone be subjected to the risk of starvation.

Malthus's prophecy never came to pass. As the population grew, so did its capacity to feed itself. His anti-humanist ideas, however, lived on, and are now at the heart of the environmental religion.

In 1968, a new prophet emerged. Stanford University biologist and environmental activist Paul R. Ehrlich picked up where Malthus had left off, publishing his bestselling book *The Population Bomb: Population Control or Race to Oblivion?*

Ehrlich was not subtle. The cover of the book featured an image of a bomb, and text that read, "While you are reading these words, four people will have died of starvation." The contents of the book were no less alarmist.

"The battle to feed all of humanity is over," reads the book's first line. He goes on to say, "we must have population control at home, hopefully through changes in our value system, but by compulsion if voluntary methods fail." Ehrlich concludes his opening remarks, writing, "We can no longer afford merely to treat the symptoms of the cancer of population growth; the cancer itself must be cut out."

Ehrlich predicted that in the 1970s and '80s hundreds of millions of people would starve to death unless Americans radically changed their way of living to minimize their impact on the environment and a worldwide program of population control was instituted. "Sometime in the next fifteen years, the end will come," Ehrlich told CBS News in 1970. "And by 'the end' I mean an utter breakdown of the capacity of the planet to support humanity."

Like their predecessors, the new population control crusaders set their sights on the poor. However, unlike the religious Malthus, the new cultists had no objection to birth control. They advocated for large-scale sterilization programs and argued that the United States should pressure developing nations to institute vasectomy campaigns. Numerous organizations, including the International Planned Parenthood Federation, the World Bank, and the United Nations Population Fund, promoted and funded programs to reduce fertility in poor nations.

Developing nations heeded Ehrlich's warning. Population control programs were launched worldwide. By 1970, a total of twenty-seven countries had announced that they aimed to cut birth rates, including South Korea, Taiwan, Malaysia, Pakistan, and India. While the means of population control were sometimes innocuous (through the distribution of contraception and birth control pills), millions were sterilized, often through coercion and in unsafe conditions.

Few world leaders embraced population control hysterics more than India's prime minister Indira Gandhi. In the 1970s, Gandhi, with the assistance of her son Sanjay, carried out a nationwide campaign of forced sterilization.

In his book *Merchants of Despair*, author Robert Zubrin describes the brutal methods the Indian government employed:

Overt coercion became the rule: sterilization was a condition for land allotments, water, electricity, ration cards, medical care, pay raises, and rickshaw licenses. Policemen were given quotas to nab individuals for sterilization. Demolition squads were sent into slums to bulldoze houses—sometimes whole neighborhoods—so that armed police platoons could drag off their flushed-out occupants to forced-sterilization camps. In Delhi alone, 700,000 people were driven from their homes. Many of those who escaped the immediate roundup were denied new housing until they accepted sterilization.

In 1976 alone, more than 6.2 million men were sterilized by the Indian government. For comparison, the Nazis sterilized an estimated total of 400,000 people during the entirety of their reign over Germany.

The mass sterilization campaign was supported by international financial institutions. Notably, the World Bank bankrolled the sterilization efforts with tens of millions of dollars in loans to the Indian government. "At long last," World Bank president Robert McNamara proclaimed in 1976, "India is moving effectively to address its population problem."

As we now know, *The Population Bomb* was another swing and a miss for the population doomsayers. The widespread famine that drove the hysteria of the 1970s and '80s never came to pass. Today, fewer people die of hunger than when *The Population Bomb* was first published. Despite the failure of Ehrlich's prophecy, the book sold millions of copies and became highly influential among environmentalists.

Today, the legacies of Malthus and Ehrlich live on in the doomsday cult of climate change. The new prophecy holds that all human activity that expels $CO_2$ and other greenhouse gases into the atmosphere is causing catastrophic changes to the global climate. According to the climate change cult, the release of $CO_2$ is responsible for:

- Changes in temperature and precipitation

- The increase in ocean temperatures and sea levels

- The melting of glaciers and sea ice

- Changes in the frequency, intensity, and duration of extreme weather events

There is nothing that the true believers won't attribute to climate change. Every single observable phenomenon in nature is now considered that the prophecy is coming to pass.

Is too much rain causing floods? Climate change. Is a lack of rain causing droughts? Climate change.

Busy hurricane season? Climate change. Quiet hurricane season? Climate change.

Hot as heck? Climate change. Cold as Hillary Clinton's heart? Climate change.

The weather is terrible? Climate change. The weather is perfect . . . ?

Well, weather isn't climate.

With all climate-related events now blamed on climate change, the environmental religion has found the perfect basis for control. And since everything human beings do expels $CO_2$, they can control *everything*. Since cars, trucks, ships, and planes use gasoline and diesel, they can control transportation. Since electricity production uses coal and natural gas, they can control energy. Since processing raw materials and manufacturing goods requires energy, they can control industry. Since livestock, soil management, and cultivation cause $CO_2$ emissions, they can control agriculture. Since our homes and businesses require all of the above, they can control us.

There is nothing that the climate change fanatics don't want to destroy. To them, even the simple act of breathing expels a deadly poison that threatens to end the world.

Like all doomsday cults, the climate change fanatics are not interested in debate. There's no time for that. The end is always right around the corner. The clock is ticking, and action is needed now.

So, who are this cult's most ardent followers? They don't meet in secret, wear ceremonial robes, and dance around giant totems to please their angry gods. They meet in public, wear expensive suits, and occupy positions of extraordinary influence and power. They're the global elite, looking to preserve their comfortable lifestyles and maintain government expense accounts. Today's cultists may be flying in private jets to international conferences in Davos, Switzerland, and wearing Gucci shoes, but, just like their predecessors, they are more than willing to engage in human sacrifice.

And who will be sacrificed? The answer is the same as it ever was. The poor, ignorant rubes who are too stupid to resist their base urges. The cancer on this planet who endlessly consume, exhale their poison into the atmosphere, and produce future generations that will continue this destructive cycle, condemning the world to a hot, brutal death.

You, of course.

When I tell you that they're in the highest positions of power,

I'm not exaggerating. The climate change cult operates a tangled web of money and influence in the U.S. government, U.S. universities, and beyond.

In 2009, for example, President Barack Obama appointed Harvard scientist John Holdren as director of the White House Office of Science and Technology Policy and chief science advisor to the president. Holdren was well-known for his expertise in climate change, but he also had a long history of advocating for population control. In 1969, Holdren coauthored an article in which he warned, "if the population control measures are not initiated immediately, and effectively, all the technology man can bring to bear will not fend off the misery to come." The coauthor of the article was none other than Holdren's mentor, Paul R. Ehrlich.

Before and after his tenure in the Obama White House, Holdren was a respected faculty member at Harvard University. As the Teresa and John Heinz Research Professor of Environmental Policy, his work was supported financially by an endowment from the wife of another familiar face in the climate change cult, the first-ever U.S. special presidential envoy for climate, John Kerry. In his role, Kerry acts as the ambassador to the globalist climate change cult, spreading around billions of American dollars and helping to concoct new international schemes to regulate greenhouse gas emissions.

While the high priests of the climate cult sip champagne and fly around the world in their private jets, its acolytes infect every corner of the U.S. government. When the cult exercises its power, it uses a new, more socially acceptable vocabulary. Since terms like "population control" and "sterilization" have fallen out of favor, they talk of "reproductive rights," "sexual health services," and "family planning."

The cultists in the federal bureaucracy design and implement ever-expanding regulatory rules. The rules are meant to curb carbon emissions, which ultimately make agriculture, industry, commerce, and transportation—all the things that are necessary to our daily lives—more difficult and expensive.

In Congress, they propose legislation like "The Green New Deal," which proponents claim would eliminate U.S. carbon emissions. The plan would phase out all nonrenewable forms of energy, including coal, natural gas, and nuclear power plants. It would also remake the American economy, building millions of affordable housing units, instituting universal health care, and guaranteeing high-paying jobs for all Americans.

And that's just the first few pages.

In truth, it's little more than a means to bring America to its knees. With an impossibly high price tag of close to $100 trillion, it would plunge the U.S. further into debt and unleash an army of new regulators to beat down our doors.

In the end, the climate change cultists make you poorer, more miserable, and less healthy. They will do it all with a smile, comfortable in the belief that they are doing it all to save the world.

In short, they're the perfect communists.

## Defeating the Green Communists

The environmental communist has found his ultimate means of control. With climate change at the heart of his plan for radical transformation, he now sits at the levers of power and pulls without regard for the lives of the average, carbon-spewing American. He has taken power because we've allowed him to. It's well past time for anti-communists to take it back.

The key to defeating the green communist is to first reject his religion. Too many of us have accepted that we need environmentalism to protect nature. It's been beaten into our minds since elementary school. Annual Earth Day assemblies. Tree plantings on Arbor Day. Bright blue recycling bins in our classrooms. It all seems innocent at first glance, but it just reinforces the idea that the green movement is a force for good, while we ignore the red that lies beneath the surface.

"But Jesse," I already hear you asking, "don't we want conservation for hunting, and fishing, and camping?"

Yes, we all want a clean environment. But this isn't about picking up litter around your local park or not dumping motor oil into the storm drain. The green communist is not a conservationist. He doesn't care about the animal population, pristine waters, or unspoiled campgrounds. In truth, he doesn't care about the environment.

If you need any evidence of this, just look at the 2016–17 protest of the Dakota Access oil pipeline. For months, thousands of protesters camped out near the Standing Rock Tribal Reservation in North Dakota. They paid lip service to protecting the environment and justice for the Standing Rock Sioux, but when the protesters were cleared out in February 2017, they left behind what one county official referred to as an "environmental tragedy." The once-pristine area was covered in 4.8 million pounds of garbage. The Army Corps of Engineers had to close fifty acres of land for fear that trash and toxic sludge caused by the protests could contaminate nearby rivers—the same rivers those protesters claimed they were trying to protect.

So, no. I don't believe for a second that this is about the environment, and neither should you. This is about destruction.

The most important tenet of the environmentalist religion we need to reject is the one found at the heart of the climate change doomsday cult: that $CO_2$ is poisoning the earth. It has become the green communist's source of his power. Once it became unquestioningly accepted that $CO_2$ was a poison that must be controlled, we invited the communist in to control everything. If we surrender on $CO_2$, we've already lost.

I'm not going to debate the merits (or lack thereof) of the science behind the theory, but ask yourself this question: If it wasn't true, who would tell you? The scientists and academics whose livelihoods depend on billions of dollars in grants to research the causes and impacts of climate change? The government bureaucrats whose budgets have been padded by billions of dollars to tackle the "climate crisis"? The politicians who use climate change to fearmonger their way into elected office? Few, if any, people in positions of authority would be motivated to tell you the truth, and those who do offer an alternative viewpoint are certain to become pariahs in scientific and academic circles.

While man-made climate change may be fiction, the government's response to it is very real and will destroy this nation if it's not stopped.

The anti-$CO_2$ propaganda is all around us. We're fed a consistent diet of doomsday predictions and urgent calls to action. It's in the news we read, the ads we see, and even the entertainment we consume. Children are especially vulnerable to the propaganda. The term "climate anxiety" has been coined to describe the damaging psychological effects. According to a 2021 study, more than 50 percent of children reported feeling sad, anxious, angry, powerless, helpless, and guilty about climate change. It also found that 75 percent think the future is frightening and 83 percent believe people have failed to take care of the planet.

These are cult beliefs being passed on to your children. You need to deprogram them. Assure them that the world is not coming to an end until God is good and ready to end it. Teach them that $CO_2$ is not poison, but rather a necessary element that sustains all life on this planet and without which human beings would not even be able to breathe.

Another belief of the climate cult that must be rejected is its anti-humanism. The idea that the earth is overpopulated or that the growth of the human population will lead to an environmental catastrophe is nonsense. It only serves to feed the idea that human beings are the problem and validates the communist's desire to control them.

The thing the anti-humanists always get wrong is that they underestimate people's ability to innovate, solve problems, and create ways to overcome. Of course, this is only true if they're allowed to do so. The communist prefers to face challenges by placing restrictions on people and relying on bureaucrats and government agencies to carry out "a plan." These plans always fail, and the people end up bearing the brunt of the consequences. Human beings are not the cause of the earth's problems, communists are.

Government agencies are infested with communists and they need to be aggressively rooted out.

Anti-communists can start by bringing an end to all environmental justice initiatives and shuttering environmental justice offices in the federal government. These offices are communists' beachhead into every department of the executive branch. They were first mandated in 1994 when then-president Bill Clinton signed Executive Order 12898, which ordered that "each Federal agency shall make achieving environmental justice part of its mission."

If these initiatives were created by executive order, they can be eliminated in a similar fashion. The ease with which this can be achieved highlights the failure of previous Republican administrations. Even though America has had two Republican presidents since 1994, neither has seen fit to overturn the order, which would have required nothing more than the stroke of a pen. Revoking Executive Order 12898 should be a day-one promise from anyone seeking the presidency.

Once the executive order is revoked, departments will no longer be obligated to integrate environmental justice into their activities. However, it's unlikely that the permanent bureaucrats who control the day-to-day operations will voluntarily make the necessary changes. They hate closing offices, losing staff, and having their budgets cut. To force this change, an anti-communist president needs to appoint cabinet secretaries who are tasked with slashing and burning environmental justice weeds wherever they grow.

The same must be done at the state level. Offices whose mission it is to promote environmental justice must be closed and environmental justice initiatives must be defunded.

Cutting out the environmental justice cancer from the bureaucracies is a good start, but we can take things a step further.

The Environmental Protection Agency was founded in 1970, in part due to the environmental hysteria brought about by Rachel Carson's *Silent Spring*. The agency proudly boasts on its website that the "EPA today may be said without exaggeration to be the extended shadow of Rachel Carson." In 1972, the agency turned that hysteria into action by banning the use of DDT. In that moment, by banning the use of a chemical that has saved millions of lives, it proved that it was an agency unworthy of existence.

The abolition of the EPA should be on the agenda of every anti-communist. How to protect the environment should be the responsibility of individual states. There's no reason why money should flow through unelected bureaucrats in Washington, D.C., to address environmental issues that are best handled at the state or local level. The EPA is also a source of regulations that disproportionately fall on small businesses.

After dealing with the bureaucracy, it's time to shut down the money flow by ending subsidies and incentives for renewable energy. Between 1979 and 2018, the U.S. government spent more than $100 billion to subsidize renewable energy, primarily wind and solar. A large portion of those subsidies ended up in the pockets of foreign companies. If you think $100 billion is a lot, it's nothing compared to what the communists have in store now that trillion-dollar legislation has become the norm. These incentives increase costs for taxpayers, distort electricity markets, leading to blackouts, and ultimately benefit large corporations.

While we're on the subject of large corporations, let's talk about Big Oil. These companies are not our friends. They are just as guilty of perpetuating the "$CO_2$ is poison" narrative as the government and the green communists, and they're doing it at our expense. For example, ExxonMobil, the United States' biggest oil- and gas-producing company, announced in 2021 that it would invest more than $15 billion on lower greenhouse gas emission initiatives, including a "carbon capture and storage" project. Meanwhile, federal direct subsidies to the fossil fuel industry are estimated at $14.7 billion a year.

This is how they're spending our money? Party time is over. It's time to cut off the taxpayer cash to Big Oil.

While the anti-communist must focus his fight on the home front, we must understand that this sick movement has finally achieved what the original bearers of the communist torch only dreamed of: global domination.

World leaders and wealthy elites travel on their private jets to a conference in some European city. While there, they stay at luxury hotels, dine at swanky restaurants, and likely provide a boost to the local high-end escort industry. Between their soup and appetizer courses, they negotiate a framework, an agreement, or an agreement to agree at some point in the future. Once they agree on the agreement, they pat each other on the back for the amazing breakthrough they've achieved and mug for an awkward group photo. After a champagne toast they pack their bags, give the Eurotrash a double kiss on the cheek goodbye, and hop aboard their private jets for the long ride home.

If it all stinks of hypocrisy to you, understand that to them it's all perfectly normal. Remember, these people believe they're your superiors. They're not just leaders, but a new royalty. The king simply has access to things the peasant does not.

If the communists are obsessed with making plans, these ones are the biggest, most ambitious of them all. The agreements that come out of these conferences commit nations to economy-wide $CO_2$ emission reductions and wealth transfer schemes. These plans are destined to fail and will inevitably create catastrophic results. The burden of that failure will not be carried by the people who negotiate the plans, but by you. Instead of draining the Aral Sea, they're going to drain your pockets.

There is no reason for us to participate in this globalist game.

The position of Special Presidential Envoy for Climate should be eliminated. It's a useless office that was specially created for John Kerry, a useless individual.

The United States should withdraw from all climate-related treaties and agreements. Foremost among these treaties is the Paris Agreement, which requires the U.S. and close to two hundred other nations to cut their carbon emissions every five years. Since it was entered into by President Obama without the approval of the United States Senate, the U.S. can withdraw from it in a similar fashion. The U.S. actually did withdraw from the agreement under President Trump, but quickly rejoined once President Biden took office. Future presidential candidates must commit to withdrawing from the treaty once again.

Rooting out the environmental communists is going to be a long-term project. However, purging the government bureaucracies, shutting off the money supply to green initiatives, and disrupting the plans of globalists will go a long way toward stopping the movement in its tracks and reversing the damage it has done.

# ANTI-COMMUNIST ACTION ITEMS

- Reject the religion of environmentalism, especially man-made climate change.

- Deprogram your children. Assure them that the world is not coming to an end.

- Bring an end to all environmental justice initiatives and shutter environmental justice offices within the federal bureaucracy.

- Eliminate the Environmental Protection Agency.

- Cut off taxpayer dollars to big oil companies.

- Withdraw the United States from all climate-related treaties and agreements.

# CHAPTER SEVEN

# Communist Gun Control:

# Disarming the Victims

*Political power grows out of the barrel of a gun.*
—Mao Zedong

The communist is obsessed with power. If he has power, he will fight like the devil to keep it. If someone else has it, he will scheme to take it. It's for this reason that the issue of guns is so important.

In the United States, debates about firearm ownership have become clouded. When we talk about guns or gun control, the conversation almost always devolves into arguments about constitutional rights, violent crime, mass shootings, or even hunting. In reality, the right to own firearms isn't about any of that.

When we discuss firearm ownership, we are really talking about one thing and one thing only: power—who has it and who doesn't. If people have guns, they have power. If they don't have guns, they are powerless.

This isn't an insight revealed by an ancient philosopher or some ideological leap of faith. It's just common sense. If someone can hurt you and you don't have the means to hurt them back, they can force you to do anything.

It's a very simple dynamic: free people are armed, and slaves are not. We've watched this dynamic repeatedly play out through history:

- The Helots were the slaves of the Spartans. The Spartans were armed. The Helots were not.

- The thralls were the slaves of the Vikings. The Vikings were armed. The thralls were not.

- The Russian serfs were the slaves of the land-owners. The landowners were armed. The serfs were not.

For the United States, this simple dynamic was at the heart of our revolution. The British wanted to disarm the colonists; the colonists refused. As George Mason, the father of the Bill of Rights, noted, "when the resolution to enslaving America was formed in Great Britain, the British parliament was advised . . . to disarm the people. That it was the best and most effectual way to enslave them." So, when the British came for their guns, the colonists responded with musket fire.

The writings of America's founders are filled with acknowledgments that keeping people armed was the best way to ensure they would remain free. President of the Continental Congress Richard Henry Lee wrote, "To preserve liberty, it is essential that the whole body of the people always possess arms, and be taught alike, especially when young, how to use them." There can be no mistake about the intention of the founding fathers. The right to keep and bear arms was included in the Bill of Rights to guarantee that an armed populace would act as a check against an oppressive government.

The founders weren't the only ones who understood this. The communists knew it, too.

In 1850, Karl Marx delivered an address to the Central Committee of the Communist League in England. In the address, Marx proclaimed, "Under no pretext should arms and ammunition be surrendered; any attempt to disarm the workers must be frustrated, by force if necessary."

I can already hear you yelling, "Finally! A place where I agree with Karl Marx!"

Not so fast, you commie! If we look a little closer at what Marx said, things are not so simple. Consider whom he was addressing and about whom he was talking. He was addressing his fellow communists and he was talking about workers he hoped would join the communist cause. Of course, he was opposed to disarming *them*. The communist revolution would involve the violent overthrow of the government, so naturally the communist revolutionaries would need to be armed.

But what about the enemies of communism? And what happens once the revolution is over?

This is where we differ from the communists on the issue of guns. We believe all free individuals should have power, so we want *the individual* to be armed. Communists believe they should have power, so they want only people they approve of to be armed. To the communists, guns are a means to achieve the goals of *their* religion and preserve *their* power.

Chairman Mao summarized the communist position in 1938

best when he said, "Every Communist must grasp the truth, 'Political power grows out of the barrel of a gun.' Our principle is that the Party commands the gun, and the gun must never be allowed to command the Party." In other words, if the communists were to have total control over political power, he would have total control of the guns from which it grew. Anyone who posed a challenge to that power would have to be disarmed.

Today's communist plays dumb—dismissing the idea that guns are a means by which liberty is preserved for the people—but he understands the political power that they represent. And, just like Chairman Mao, he knows that if that power is not his, he must seize it.

So, why is the American communist so obsessed with disarming everybody, even, seemingly, himself? If we look back at what Marx said, he looked at the revolution as a distant event that would be achieved some time in a violent future. To the American communist, on the other hand, the revolution is already under way. Its goals are being achieved at the ballot box and through quiet subversion. As far as he's concerned, the government, and the power of its guns, are already his.

Don't let this fool you, though. Ultimately, his reason for disarming you is the same as the communists of the past: he wants your guns so he has the power to hurt you. He might believe that the power of the government is already in his hands, but he now seeks to monopolize that power and guarantee that it can't be challenged.

As he's shown us time and again, the communist will use every tool at his disposal to disarm you. He'll limit your ability to purchase guns. He'll limit when and where you can have them. He'll ban certain types of arms and ammunition. He'll attack firearms manufacturers and disrupt their ability to do business. Finally, he'll call for total confiscation and send other men with guns to take them from you.

All the while, he'll attempt to bully you into complacency. He'll call his new laws "common sense." He'll use the bodies of dead innocents to appeal to your emotions. He'll attempt to turn your neighbors against you by calling you a monster and blaming you for any gun-related tragedy that occurs.

We must fight back against the communist religion by adopting the attitude of its founder: under no pretext should arms and ammunition be surrendered. Ever. Not a single gun, a single bullet, or a single grain of powder.

In many ways, our right to keep and bear arms is the bright line that separates America from the communist's quest for total domination. He can take our schools. He can pervert our culture. He can infiltrate our government. He's done all of these things already, but there's one thing he wants the most and he has yet to achieve it: he has yet to disarm the American public. He must never be allowed to take our means of resistance. On this, there can be no compromise. The right must endure.

Failure to protect our ability to remain armed is the unmistakable final step in the long road to tyranny. As the past clearly demonstrates, it is one that the communist has every intention of taking.

## Disarming the Populace

Over the course of the twentieth century, communist governments always used "public safety" as an excuse to disarm their citizens. In some nations, the people were told gun control was needed to neutralize counterrevolutionaries. In others, it was said to be a tool for fighting crime. But while the reasons for gun control may have varied from country to country, the outcome was always the same.

To better understand the consequences of allowing communists to disarm the public, we should look back at a few examples. As is so often the case, the Soviet Union provides the perfect illustration, and the standard by which future communist countries would operate.

Before the Bolsheviks seized power, Russia had a strong tradition of individual gun ownership. Firearms were imported for civilian use from all over the world. Hunting was popular among all the classes, including peasants, factory workers, and Russian nobility. Firearms dealers circulated mail-order catalogs that offered shotguns and shooting supplies. While some restrictions were introduced in the early 1900s requiring Russians looking to purchase rifles or pistols to obtain a purchase permit from a local police chief, these permits were not difficult to procure so long as the applicant didn't have a lengthy criminal record and was not a known political radical.

That tradition would ultimately come to an end with the rise of the communists, but in March 1917, shortly before the Bolshevik Revolution, Vladimir Lenin could have been mistaken for one of America's founding fathers. "What kind of militia do we need, the proletariat, all the toiling people?" Lenin asked in a 1917 letter. "A genuine people's militia . . . one that, first, consists of the entire population, of all adult citizens." Unfortunately for the Russian people, Lenin would quickly change his mind.

In January 1918, two months after Lenin took total control of the Russian government, the Bolsheviks adopted the so-called

Declaration of Rights of the Working and Exploited People. The declaration read, in part:

> To ensure the sovereign power of the working people, and to eliminate all possibility of the restoration of the power of the exploiters, the arming of the working people, the creation of a socialist Red Army of workers and peasants and the complete disarming of the propertied classes are hereby decreed.

Later that year, the Bolsheviks began the large-scale confiscation of firearms. While the declaration referred only to the disarming of "propertied classes," the order to hand over weapons to the government applied to people of all classes. The regime decreed that "all serviceable and faulty rifles, machine guns and revolvers of all types, including cartridges and ammunition of any pattern," would be turned over to authorities. Anyone caught disobeying the mandate risked being imprisoned for up to ten years.

Of course, members of the Communist Party were exempt from the strict mandate, with members being allowed to own one rifle and one revolver apiece.

The same year the Bolsheviks began the mass confiscation of firearms, they launched the Red Terror, a brutal campaign of executions and political repression. Lenin's government decreed, "it is necessary to secure the Soviet Republic from class enemies by isolating them in concentration camps; that all persons connected with the White Guard organizations, conspiracies and rebellions are subject to execution." An article in the communist-controlled newspaper *Pravda* read, "the anthem of the working class will be a song of hatred and revenge!" Over the next four years, the communists would unleash hell on the Russian people. An estimated 50,000–200,000 people were executed. Many more were sent to concentration camps, where they were tortured and forced to perform manual labor.

The Red Terror was no act of self-defense by the working class or a newly installed government simply attempting to maintain power. It was wholesale slaughter in the name of the communist religion. No evidence of a crime or proof of being an opponent of the revolution was necessary to seal a person's fate. As Martyn Latsis, the head of the Cheka, the Bolshevik secret police that carried out the Red Terror, explained:

> We are not carrying out war against individuals. We are exterminating the bourgeoisie as a class. We are not looking for evidence or witnesses to reveal deeds or words against the Soviet power. The first question we ask is—to what class does he belong, what are his origins, upbringing, education, or profession? These questions define the fate of the accused. This is the essence of the Red Terror.

As bad as Latsis's description sounds, it actually understates the extent of the communist's thirst for blood. In addition to targeting the upper classes and opponents of the revolution, the Bolsheviks killed or imprisoned their political enemies on the left. Anarchists, socialists, and even heretic communists faced Bolshevik firing squads or lifetimes of hard labor (as a side note, BLM and Antifa should know that the same fate awaits them— the revolution always ends up devouring its own).

The Red Terror was just the beginning. The violence became

institutionalized. Lenin would be replaced by Stalin, who killed millions in the "Great Terror" of the 1930s. The concentration camps became the gulag system, which would come to enslave millions of Russians in subsequent decades. The Cheka became the NKVD, and then the KGB, which would use violence, intimidation, and murder to maintain communist rule.

Using the USSR as a model, similar confiscation campaigns and bans on gun ownership were implemented throughout the communist Eastern Bloc:

- Privately owned guns were immediately confiscated in Bulgaria after the communists took power in 1944.

- Private gun ownership was outlawed in East Germany, with few exceptions.

- Following World War II, Hungary's communist minister of the interior László Rajk ordered all pistol and hunting clubs be dissolved to, as he explained at the time, "more efficiently protect the democratic system of the state."

- Romania prohibited gun ownership shortly after communists took power. The prohibition was strictly enforced for decades under the dictatorship of Nicolai Ceauşescu.

With the people disarmed, Eastern Bloc nations carried out some of the most notorious crimes against humanity in history with free hands.

The Soviets and their Eastern Bloc puppets made it clear that the communists' key to taking and consolidating power is disarming the population they intend to terrorize. But what about the so-called commonsense measures we hear about so often? No matter how well intended, those measures will become tools of the communist as well, a fact best illustrated by the communist takeover of Cuba.

The revolution in Cuba did not start as a communist revolution. As a matter of fact, when the fight against Cuban president Fulgencio Batista began, Fidel Castro, the revolution's most prominent voice, vehemently denied being a communist altogether. At the outset, Castro led only one of several groups that were trying to overthrow the Batista regime, including a group of anti-communist students called the Revolutionary Directorate (RD). Unlike the left-wing Castro and his lieutenant Che Guevara, the RD were fighting for liberty and economic freedom.

Following the fall of the Batista regime, Castro told the people that they would be allowed to keep their firearms. At a 1960 rally in Havana, he explained, "This is how democracy works: it gives rifles to farmers, to students, to women, to Negroes, to the poor, and to every citizen who is ready to defend a just cause."

Despite his denial of communist sympathies and his promise to allow the Cuban people to own guns, Castro's true nature was eventually revealed. The political reforms he had promised, including democratic elections, were soon abandoned. Seeing the danger posed by Castro's leadership, the RD and other anti-communist forces prepared for a showdown. Dr. Miguel Faria Jr., a retired neurosurgeon and member of the Cuban exile community, described what happened next:

Fidel Castro defused the situation and neutralized the defiance of the RD. Shortly thereafter, Castro commenced his long-term campaign to disarm not only his confreres in the Revolutionary Directorate who had not joined him, but also, in due time, all Cubans. A 100,000-member "militia" was organized to seek out the political opposition and actively disarm it.

Unfortunately for the Cuban people, Castro had some help in his efforts to disarm the island. The previous government under Batista had established firearm registration lists. Using the lists as their guide, Castro's militia went door-to-door seizing the guns of his political opponents. Before long, the Castro regime was confiscating all firearms. The island's state-run radio station Radio Havana warned that "[a]ll citizens must turn in their combat weapons," adding that the "struggle against our enemies requires a rigorous control of all combat weapons." Those who failed to turn in their weapons would be judged by the so-called Revolutionary Tribunals, Cuba's notorious kangaroo courts.

Like the dictators who came before him, Castro unleashed communism's full fury once the population was disarmed. According to *The Black Book of Communism*, from 1959 through the late 1990s, 15,000 to 17,000 people were executed by Castro's thugs. Thousands more rotted in prisons for speaking out against the regime. Still more died attempting to flee the hellhole the communists created on the island.

And it was all done with the help of a firearm registry—a "commonsense" measure many advocate for today. (As an aside, credit card companies are already creating a de facto gun registry by flagging your firearms purchases. This will undoubtedly end up in the hands of the government.)

When disarming society, the communist's first targets are usually his ideological enemies who are the most immediate threat to his hold on power. In the case of the Bolsheviks, it was the upper class. In the case of Castro, it was other revolutionary factions. However, communists will also use less openly political justifications to disarm the population if the opportunity presents itself. He'll speak of crime prevention or protecting the population from "weapons of war," to institute draconian laws that ultimately serve the same goal: insulating himself from threats of popular uprisings. The most recent example of this can be found in Venezuela.

Venezuela was once one of the most prosperous nations in Latin America. The country possesses the world's largest crude oil reserves, and the inflow of petrodollars made it one of the fastest-growing economies throughout the early 2000s. By 2010, that all began to change, largely because of the influence of Venezuela's authoritarian president, Hugo Chavez.

Chavez first came to power in 1999 after winning the nation's presidential election on a socialist platform. With his country's economy bolstered by sky-high oil prices in the early years of his presidency, Chavez began spending money like a madman. He massively expanded the nation's welfare state, opened free health care clinics, built low-income housing, and offered subsidized food and other consumer goods to the Venezuelan people. The programs earned him the loyalty of Venezuela's poor and praise from the typical communist sympathizers. But, like all communist plans, it ended in ruin.

At the same time Chavez was taking social calls from

Hollywood scumbags such as Sean Penn and Kevin Spacey, he was consolidating power. His government took over many of Venezuela's industries and companies. He nationalized the nation's most important resource, its oil fields, ejecting the companies that had been running them for decades. He seized political power, openly violated the nation's constitution, appointed people to key positions based on personal loyalty, and suppressed political opposition.

In addition to setting the country on a road to economic ruin, he and his government were robbing the people blind. It's estimated that between $11 and $300 billion was looted from Venezuela's national oil company during Chavez's reign, much of which ended up in Swiss bank accounts belonging to cronies and corrupt ministers.

The combination of spending, nationalization, and widespread theft ruined Venezuela's economy. Before long, the petrodollars stopped flowing, the Venezuelan people began facing food shortages, and violent crime started to spiral out of control. The number of murders, kidnappings, and armed robberies skyrocketed across the country. Gun battles between rival gangs became routine in the poor barrios of the capital, Caracas. In response to the chaos, the Venezuelan government implemented a ban on the private purchase of firearms and ammo.

The ban had no impact on crime. According to the Venezuelan Violence Observatory's statistics, Venezuela's murder rate increased from 73 murders per 100,000 people in 2012 to 91.8 murders per 100,000 people in 2016. But fighting crime was never the goal; the goal was power.

After his death in 2013, Chavez's handpicked successor, President Nicolas Maduro, continued in his footsteps. The communist policies ultimately led to out-of-control inflation and food short-ages. When the people took to the streets to protest their gov-ernment, however, they were defenseless. Since 2014, numerous efforts have been made to reform the government, but they've all been violently crushed. In addition to police and armed forces, demonstrators and reformers are attacked so-called *colectivos*, communist militias that are sponsored and armed by the Ma-duro regime. The militias engage in arbitrary arrests, carry out extrajudicial killings, and torture dissidents.

Venezuela, a nation sitting above an ocean of oil, is now one of the poorest countries in Latin America. Three out of four Ven-ezuelans live in extreme poverty and the nation has the highest crime rate in the world. The communist government responsible for the misery has total control, and the Venezuelan people are powerless to stop them.

And it was all done in the name of fighting crime.

## American Gun Control

For generations, America's tradition of civilian gun ownership proved to be an effective obstacle for any efforts to disarm the populace. That tradition predates the United States, stretching back to the first colonists, for whom, in the face of untamed wilderness and hostile natives, owning firearms was an absolute necessity.

When the United States won its independence, that tradition was enshrined in the Bill of Rights. In the earliest days of the republic, civilian gun ownership was not only protected by the Constitution, it was also required as a matter of law. A year after the Second Amendment was ratified, Congress passed the Militia

Act of 1792. The law mandated that every eligible man between the ages of eighteen and forty-five own a musket, bayonet, and ammunition.

So, how did we go from a nation that *required* its citizens to be armed to one that is increasingly and openly hostile to private gun ownership? It would be impossible to catalog the full history of gun control laws here, but by looking at the broad strokes and big wins of gun control advocates, we can arrive at a simple answer as to how they operate: little by little, law by law, and always through fear.

Over the course of American history, states have passed and implemented a patchwork of laws regulating, and sometimes banning outright, the ownership and use of firearms. Laws against carrying guns were the most common, the first being enacted by New Jersey in 1686 because, it was claimed, guns induced "great Fear and Quarrels." Numerous states enacted similar laws in the centuries that followed, with Alabama even passing an 1839 law titled "An Act to Suppress the Evil Practice of Carrying Weapons Secretly." As a general rule, if you find your state following New Jersey in any respect, it's time to start asking serious questions.

Following the Civil War, at least six states banned the sale or exchange of certain types of pistols. The laws were primarily concerned with weapons that could be easily concealed. In Arkansas, for example, an 1881 law banned pocket pistols, Bowie knives, metal knuckles, and sword canes. According to an 1882 Arkansas Supreme Court ruling, the statute was aimed at ending "the pernicious habit of wearing such dangerous or deadly weapons" to prevent "crimes and calamities." The court held that Tennessee residents only had a constitutional right to "such arms that are useful in warfare" (ironic considering that the left now explicitly claims military weapons are not covered by the Second Amendment).

In subsequent years, states would take things further, banning whole categories of firearms, like machine guns. The definitions of these weapons were rarely uniform. In 1927, for example, Rhode Island passed a law defining a machine gun as "any weapon which shoots automatically and any weapon which shoots more than twelve shots semiautomatically without reloading." The same year, a Massachusetts law declared, "Any gun or small arm caliber designed for rapid fire and operated by a mechanism, or any gun which operates automatically after the first shot has been fired . . . shall be deemed a machine gun."

Slowly but surely, the states whittled away at the ability for citizens to keep and bear arms. However, it wasn't until 1934 that the modern era of gun control was ushered in with the passage of the National Firearms Act (NFA), the first major piece of federal gun control legislation.

The passage of the NFA would provide the blueprint for all future gun control legislation. In the same way that modern gun control advocates use school shooters to push their legislation, proponents of the NFA did the same using the mass shooters of their day.

The NFA, which was known informally as the "Anti-Machine Gun Bill," targeted the weapons most associated with the notorious gangsters making headlines in the 1930s: Bonnie Parker and Clyde Barrow, John Dillinger, Arthur "Pretty Boy" Floyd, and George "Machine Gun" Kelly (no relation to the current-day version).

"For some time this country has been at the mercy of the gangsters, racketeers, and professional criminals," Congressman

Robert Lee Doughton of North Carolina declared when he introduced the final bill. He added that the weapons in question and the ease with which they crossed state lines had become "a real menace to the law-abiding people of this country."

The bill limited the ownership of short-barreled shotguns and rifles, machine guns, and suppressors, by levying massive taxes on their importation, sale, and manufacture. In addition, citizens who could afford to own these weapons were required to register them with the U.S. Treasury Department. The feds could then supply the information to state authorities who could then use it to prosecute people whose possession violated state laws.

Advocates for the NFA used arguments that should sound familiar to anyone paying attention to the current gun control debate. "A machine gun, of course, ought never to be in the hands of any private individual," Attorney General Homer Cummings said at a House hearing. "There is not the slightest excuse for it, not the least in the world, and we must, if we are going to be successful in this effort to suppress crime in America, take these machine guns out of the hands of the criminal class." Cummings ramped up the fear factor, declaring the gangsters were "a very serious national emergency" who are "warring against society." He estimated that there were half a million well-armed criminals stalking America's streets, twice the manpower of the Army and Navy combined.

It's worth noting that the NFA would not have prevented most of these notorious gangsters from acquiring the machine guns used in their crimes. Clyde Barrow, for example, famously used an M1918 Browning Automatic Rifle that had been stolen from a National Guard armory. Bank robber John Dillinger used a Thompson submachine gun that had been stolen from the Peru,

Indiana, police department. Similarly, Pretty Boy Floyd carried out the infamous Kansas City Massacre using a machine gun that had been stolen from a Missouri sheriff. The only outlaw who may have been deprived of his gun by the NFA was Machine Gun Kelly, whose Thompson submachine gun was purchased by his wife, Kathryn—proving, once again, that behind every terrible man there might be an even more terrible woman.

The NFA quickly gained widespread support. Even the National Rifle Association, which opposed an initial draft of the bill that included pistols and revolvers, voiced its approval for the final product. "I do not believe in the general promiscuous toting of guns," testified NRA president Karl Frederick. "I think it should be sharply restricted and only under licenses."

The NFA was passed by the House and Senate in June 1934 and was immediately signed into law by President Franklin Roosevelt. While there's little evidence to suggest that the law did anything to curb organized crime or reduce violent crime, it did succeed in bringing sales of machine guns and short-barreled shotguns to a quick halt. With the federal government having taken its first step on the path toward disarmament, the NFA served as a benchmark for future gun control efforts. Just four years later, Congress would pass the Federal Firearms Act of 1938, which required that gun manufacturers, importers, and other businesses selling firearms have a Federal Firearms License.

The next major piece of federal legislation, the Gun Control Act (GCA), came in 1968. The bill banned mail-order sales of rifles and shotguns, limited the importation of firearms from abroad, imposed stricter licensing and regulation on the firearms industry, and established new categories of firearms offenses.

With the assassinations of President John F. Kennedy,

Attorney General Robert Kennedy, and Dr. Martin Luther King Jr. still fresh in the public consciousness, gun control proponents, once again, used fear to sell the new law. Once again, the National Rifle Association bent the knee, with NRA executive vice president Franklin Orth writing that "the measure as a whole appears to be one that the sportsmen of America can live with."

When the GCA was signed into law in October 1968, President Lyndon Johnson complained that the bill hadn't gone far enough:

> I asked for the national registration of all guns and the licensing of those who carry those guns. For the fact of life is that there are over 160 million guns in this country—more firearms than families. If guns are to be kept out of the hands of the criminal, out of the hands of the insane, and out of the hands of the irresponsible, then we just must have licensing.

Johnson blamed the "powerful gun lobby" for the failure to pass more restrictive measures, and asked Americans to work harder to pass new laws that "most civilized nations have long ago adopted."

The persistence of gun control advocates paid off in 1993 with the passage of the Brady Handgun Violence Prevention Act, or Brady Bill, so named for White House press secretary James S. Brady, who'd been paralyzed during the 1981 assassination attempt on President Ronald Reagan. The bill imposed a temporary seven-day waiting period before dealers could sell, deliver, or transfer a handgun to an unlicensed individual, expanded the list of people who would be prohibited from owning firearms, and established America's federal background check system for gun sales.

The Brady Bill took several years to pass, but by the end, advocates even included Ronald Reagan, who publicly supported the bill with an op-ed in the *New York Times*. To this day, the National Rifle Association takes pride in its efforts to implement the bill's background check system. "The best kept secret is that the national instant check system wouldn't exist at all if it weren't for the NRA," bragged NRA executive vice president and CEO Wayne LaPierre in a 2016 video.

Like his predecessors, President Bill Clinton believed the bill didn't go far enough. "[W]e all know there is more to be done," Clinton said during the Brady Bill's signing ceremony in November 1993. "This is a good beginning. And there will be more to be done after that."

It will never be enough. The appetite of the communist will not be satisfied until civilian ownership of firearms is a thing of the past and Americans are at the complete mercy of the government.

America has become a nation bound up in gun laws by allowing itself to be worn down by the persistence of gun control's champions. Under no circumstance can those champions be allowed to wear us down any further. America can and must remain a nation of armed citizens.

## Keeping America Armed

The communist is coming for your guns.

For now, he has settled for a piecemeal approach. He will ban certain guns based on how they look. He will stifle your ability to buy and sell. He will establish firearms registration laws. He will do it all in the name of public safety. In the end, his goal is the same as it ever was: a ban and confiscation of all firearms so that he can hurt you.

As we've shown, gun control laws have found support from all corners of the political spectrum. They've gained support from Democrats and Republicans. They've been helped along by liberals and conservatives. They've been publicly supported by gun grabbers as well as those who hold themselves up as the defenders of the right to keep and bear arms. In truth, there are only two sides to this debate. Anyone who wants to disarm you or make it more difficult for you to arm yourself is a communist or a communist-enabler.

Fighting back begins with adjusting our understanding of the gun control debate. We can no longer allow our opponents to frame it as a hunting issue, as former New York governor Andrew Cuomo did when he proclaimed that "you don't need ten bullets to kill a deer." Nor can we allow it to be framed as a debate over Americans' right to go target shooting or shoot clay pigeons. Rather, we must accept that the right to keep and bear arms is about one thing: people being able to defend themselves against an out-of-control government that wants to strip them of their rights. Period.

The communist has come up with all manner of arguments to obscure this fact. Every one of these arguments should be dismissed. If you find yourself in a debate about gun control, the conversation should go something like this:

**Communist:** Why do you need a thirty-round magazine to hunt a deer?

**Anti-communist:** I don't. I need it to defend myself against a tyrannical government.

**Communist:** So, you own guns because you fantasize about fighting against the government?

**Anti-communist:** Do you own a fire extinguisher because you fantasize about house fires?

**Communist:** Do you really think you can defeat the world's most powerful army with an AR-15?

**Anti-communist:** Yes. If the Vietnamese and Afghans did it with AK-47s, Americans can do it with AR-15s.

**Communist:** AR-15s are useless because, as Congressman Eric Swalwell noted, "the government has nukes."

**Anti-communist:** If you really think the American government is capable of dropping nukes on its own cities, that's all the more reason for us to be armed against it.

The anti-communist must understand that the right to keep and bear arms is not just a constitutional issue. We could sit here and dissect the historical meaning of a "militia" or what the term "well regulated" means, but ultimately none of that matters. Even if the founding fathers had intended to limit the ownership of firearms to trained militiamen who are under direct control of the government, which they didn't, it wouldn't change a thing. The right to keep and bear arms belongs to the individual and we, as anti-communists, intend on exercising that right.

Always keep in mind that a constitution is only as good as

the government's intention to abide by it, and nobody cares less about constitutions than communists.

If you don't believe me, just look at all the rights guaranteed in the constitutions of communist countries. The 1936 constitution of the USSR, for example, expressly guaranteed citizens "freedom of speech" and "freedom of the press." The 1968 constitution of East Germany declared that "every citizen of the German Democratic Republic has the right . . . to express his opinion freely and publicly" and guaranteed the "freedom of the press, radio and television." Similar rights could be found in the constitutions of the Socialist Republic of Romania, the People's Socialist Republic of Albania, and the People's Republic of Hungary. It all sounds great, but in practice these constitutional rights were nonexistent. All speech that was critical of the communist ideology or challenged the authority of the ruling party was censored. If you did manage to publish anything that was forbidden by the state, you could be arrested, imprisoned, or worse.

A constitution is nothing more than worthless pieces of paper if a government is willing to ignore it, and the American government has, on numerous occasions, already demonstrated its willingness to do so. It's great that the right to keep and bear arms is found in the United States Constitution, but, as you're reading this, there are forces at work that would make the Second Amendment as worthless as the Nineteenth Amendment. Writing long social media posts about the true meaning of "a well-regulated militia" or wearing a T-shirt that says "Come and Take It" will not deter them.

So, how do we defend the right to keep and bear arms?

The single most effective thing you can do to defend any

right is to exercise it. If you don't exercise your rights, you have no personal stake in them, and they will ultimately be lost. Therefore, as an anti-communist, you need to own guns.

According to one estimate, there are more than 393 million civilian-owned firearms in the United States, and a 2021 Pew Research survey found that 30 percent of Americans say they personally own one. The communist will tell you that's too many guns. Don't listen to them. You need numbers.

Owning a firearm is good but owning more than one is better. And ammunition. Buy lots of it.

You should *never* be without ammo. A gun without ammo is just taking up space. Replace what you use on the range and restock regularly.

"But Jesse," I already hear you asking, "what if I feel uncomfortable around guns?"

Get over it. Get to a range. Take classes. Then buy one, learn how to operate it, and regularly put rounds downrange. Learn how to strip it. Keep it clean, oiled, and in good working order. Not only will you eventually stop feeling uncomfortable around guns, but owning one will become a source of pride, and you'll feel safe with it.

Furthermore, *bearing arms* is just as important as *keeping arms*. A pistol at your side should be your constant companion. If you live in a state where carrying a firearm is allowed by law, you should do so, even if the permitting process feels like submitting to a rectal exam. There are organizations in every state that will help guide you through the process. Seek them out and get your permit.

Now, you're probably expecting me to tell you about the virtues of gun safety and how you should keep them out of the hands of your children. Quite the opposite. I can't think of anything worse for gun safety than keeping them out of the hands of your children. The only way to learn gun safety is to practice gun safety. Familiarize your children with firearms as young as possible. There are plenty of weapons that are perfect for kids. I'm not going to tell you exactly when they should start joining you at the range or on a hunt, but you should get them going as soon as you feel they are mature enough. Personally, I was accompanying my father on rabbit hunts by age seven. He allowed me to carry my own toy gun and used it to instruct me in how to safely handle the real thing.

(*LEGAL DISCLAIMER: I'm sure I don't need to tell you this, but make sure to be familiar with and comply with all applicable laws.*)

In addition to familiarizing or kids with firearms in our homes, we should push for gun safety and use to be part of our children's education. High school rifle clubs were once extremely common across the country. Even in New York City, virtually every public high school had a shooting club up until 1969. Many schools even had gun ranges on their premises. There's no reason why American schools shouldn't return to this tradition.

Familiarizing kids with firearms will have the benefit of promoting responsible use and will destigmatize guns for the next generation. This is the best way to combat the fear that drives much of the communist's gun control efforts. A kid who regularly handles firearms is less likely to grow up to be an adult who fears or mishandles them.

Once you and your family are properly armed, you need to

become organized. Get to know your neighbors. Go shooting regularly with them. You just might find yourself having fun and creating a community while you train.

Next, we must not only fight against efforts to impose gun control laws at all levels of government, but we must also retake ground. To do this, we must, again, adopt the mindset of our enemy.

Let me ask you a question: Do radical pro-abortion advocates compromise in their support for killing the unborn? Are they willing to settle for limiting abortions to the first trimester? Of course not. They advocate for abortion from the moment of conception up until the moment of birth, no exceptions. They're unflinching and remorseless, like they're fighting to protect a holy sacrament.

Anti-communists must fight with the same level of conviction, so here's our guiding principle when it comes to gun control laws: don't give an inch.

Military-style assault weapons ban? No.

Bump stock ban? No.

3-D printed gun ban? No.

Seven-day waiting period? No.

Stop letting them use your emotions against you, especially in the wake of mass shootings. It's hard to look at these tragedies and not feel a desire to do something—anything—to make it stop. That's how the communist gets you. He appeals to your emotions to override your logic. The public screaming "Somebody do *something*" is music to his ears. He intends to do *something*. He intends to disarm you. That's why he hardly even hides the fact that he celebrates every mass shooting and, frankly, looks forward to the next one. He knows that those dead people will, in the end, bring him one step closer to leaving you defenseless against him.

Don't play his game.

Although fear has been the prime motivator for gun control, it's not the only tool in the communist's arsenal. The most powerful weapon the gun-grabbing communist has against lawful gun owners is not fear, but guilt. In attacking gun owners after every tragic shooting, he is trying to make you feel like an accomplice in the shooting itself. He wants you to believe that by opposing his laws—most of which would have had no impact on the tragedy anyway—you are playing a silent role in enabling the next one.

You have nothing to be ashamed of for exercising your rights and believing that others should be allowed to do the same. Always remind yourself that the consequences of disarming a population have been more tragic than the latest mall shooting, by orders of magnitude.

Ignore their pleas for "commonsense gun laws." The use of that phrase alone should act as a huge red flag. There's no such thing as "commonsense gun laws." It's just an empty term the communist applies to his latest attempt to limit your rights.

In addition to fighting against new gun control laws, we must go on the offensive and be active in rolling back those laws that are already in place. That includes laws that prevent Americans from owning all the "scary" stuff, like fully automatic machine guns and suppressors. On the federal level, that means repealing the National Firearms Act of 1934. On the state level, it means repealing statewide assault weapons bans, limits on magazine capacities, and onerous permitting requirements.

When it comes to bearing arms, there should be no laws or

permits that prevent a law-abiding citizen from exercising the right to carry a firearm. Half of the states in the U.S. already allow for permitless or constitutional carry. Find the organizations in your state that are working to eliminate the requirement to obtain a permit to carry a handgun and donate your time or money to the effort. Maine and Vermont are constitutional carry jurisdictions, so living in a blue state is no excuse.

My last word on gun control is this: remain vigilant and vocal. We are blessed to live in a nation with a long tradition of gun ownership, but that tradition, like so many others, is under constant threat. The ownership of firearms is our final means of defense. It's the line in the sand that separates a free people from subjects. It's not enough to simply push the enemy back from that line—he must fear crossing it.

# ANTI-COMMUNIST ACTION ITEMS

- Buy guns, stock up on ammunition, and become proficient in their use.

- Familiarize your children with firearms. Teach them the basics of firearm use and safety.

- Organize. Find neighbors and friends who are as enthusiastic about gun ownership as you are.

- Fight back against all infringements upon your right to keep and bear arms, no matter how insignificant they may appear. There is no such thing as a "commonsense" gun law.

- If you live in a state where carrying a firearm is allowed by law, do so. In states where carrying is forbidden, fight for permitless or constitutional carry.

# CHAPTER EIGHT

# Corporate Communism:
# The Devil's Alliance

In October 1947, film producer and animation pioneer Walt Disney sat before a hearing of the House Un-American Activities Committee. During the hearing, Disney testified that communists within the labor movement had infiltrated his company, engaged in a campaign of agitation, and attempted to take control of his workforce.

When HUAC investigator H. A. Smith asked if he had ever permitted films that contained communist propaganda to be made at his studio, Disney responded:

> We watch so that nothing gets into the films that would be harmful in any way to any group or any country. We have large audiences of children and different groups, and we try to keep them as free from anything that would offend anybody as possible. We work hard to see that nothing of that sort creeps in.

Decades later, the Walt Disney Company, the corporation that still bears the name of its anti-communist founder, would be unrecognizable to the legendary producer, having been infiltrated and co-opted by the very forces he sought to keep out. While the company was once a reliable source of child-friendly content, it now churns out what many would consider propaganda that celebrates sexual deviance, publicly supports woke political causes, and has turned its back on American families.

A once-iconic American company—one that embodied the entrepreneurial and innovative spirits—is now just another trophy of corporate communism.

---

If controlling the minds of America's youth has been the communist's greatest achievement, then dominating the country's corporations comes in a close second. The alliance he has forged with corporate interests has provided a gateway through which he is able to influence everything and everyone.

At first glance, corporations and communists would appear to mix like oil and water. After all, the abolition of private property, the stated goal of the communist, is totally incompatible with the existence of corporations, most of which are owned privatively or by public shareholders.

According to Marx, the means of production (that is, the technology, machines, and tools used by workers to produce goods and services) would be controlled exclusively by the government. However, he was smart enough to understand that it wasn't likely to happen overnight—at least, not everywhere. In most advanced countries, Marx predicted, the communist takeover of the economy would occur gradually through what he called "despotic inroads on the rights of property, and on the conditions of bourgeois production." In other words, the communists would slowly chip away at private property and businesses, wresting control of everything by degrees using his political power.

Marx laid out several key goals, often referred to as the "planks" of *The Communist Manifesto*, that communists would pursue to gradually concentrate power in his hands. Among those goals are: ***Extension of factories and instruments of production owned by the state.*** The communists would increase their control over factories and the means of producing the commodities people consume. ***Centralisation of the means of communication.*** Telegraphs, telephones, radio, printing presses, and all methods of communication would be under the control of the communist and used to spread his religion. ***Centralisation of credit in the hands of the state, by means of a national bank with State capital and an exclusive monopoly.*** All private banks would be shuttered. The communists alone would control money and make investments.

Control of production. Control of communication. Control of money and investment. Remember these; we're going to come back to them a little later in the chapter.

As you can clearly see, there's no room in there for corporations under communist rule. Once he attained political power, private businesses would be eliminated.

So, how did these opposing forces eventually become allies?

Well, as we already know, Marx's dream of a political takeover by the workers of the world failed to materialize. The worker did not become an increasingly destitute victim of big business as he had predicted. To the contrary, the lives of the working class steadily improved. Anyone can make it here in

America. Even losers can make it. Just look at all the CNN hosts. In the United States, for example, wages rose steadily between 1919 and the 1960s. As a result, the working class had no need to rise up. Instead of turning against the corporations that signed the front of their paychecks, most workers approved of their employers.

The communist had to pivot.

Since they were unable to openly seize the private property through the "despotic inroads" of a disgruntled working class, they found another way: they would seize the corporations that owned the means of production from within. The goals were the same, but the strategy had shifted. The communist would no longer reject big business; he would embrace it and turn it to his own use.

This union of communism and the corporation is what I refer to as the devil's alliance.

So, the communist began waging a covert campaign to infiltrate and wrest control of American business. In doing so, he took control of everything.

And I mean *everything*.

The shift took decades, but it is now undeniable. It's in the commercials the corporations use to sell you their products. It's in the daily news that informs you. It's in the television shows you watch while sitting on your couch. It's in the cartoons your children view on Saturday mornings. It's in the endless stream of emails from your favorite brands declaring their commitments to equity, diversity, and inclusion. It's in the freaking nature documentaries. You cannot escape it.

In short, the influence of the devil's alliance is everywhere.

By allowing the communist to seize the corporations, we handed him the keys to the kingdom. The engines that once drove American prosperity are now the engines that power the spread of his religion.

So, we now know why the devil's alliance came to pass. Let's dive further into how it all went down.

## The Red Media vs. Corporate America

To understand today's corporate-communist alliance, we first need to understand the role corporations have played in America's past.

American corporations first came to prominence during the latter half of the nineteenth century in an era that is often referred to as the "Gilded Age," and were key to the U.S. becoming a bastion of innovation and one of the world's leading economic powers.

America possessed a unique combination of shrewd businessmen and an abundance of hardworking folks eager and willing to man the factory floors. This combination brought about the rise of "industrialists." Together, men like John D. Rockefeller, Andrew Carnegie, Cornelius Vanderbilt, J. P. Morgan, and Samuel Colt forged a young nation into the modern United States. Combined with the sweat of American workers, these men created a period of unbridled prosperity compared to a century earlier.

As the wealth of the industrialist grew, so too did the nation's. Factories sprang up in towns and cities across the nation offering new employment opportunities to millions of Americans. Railroad tracks began crisscrossing the map. Roads and bridges were constructed to accommodate cars and buses. Still others lived on family-owned farms, worked small businesses, and lived a life of relative prosperity.

All of that changed with the Great Depression.

Americans' opinions of corporations crashed along with the stock market in 1929. Billions of dollars were lost, thousands of businesses went under, countless Americans saw their entire life savings gone in minutes. The United States and the rest of the industrialized world plunged into a decade of the deepest and longest-lasting economic downturn in the history of Western civilization.

To some, big business, industrialists, and the robber barons became convenient scapegoats. While they weren't responsible for the crash or Great Depression that followed, the economic misery was a perfect opportunity for communists and their sympathizers to sow discontent and class envy among the American people.

There was one class of people who, among all others, worked the most tirelessly to nurture this discontent and class envy. I'm talking about the dregs of society. The worst of the worst. I'm speaking, of course, about journalists—a profession that draws losers like moths to a flame.

One of the most prominent critics was journalist Matthew Josephson, whose influential 1934 book, *The Robber Barons*, placed responsibility for America's misfortunes squarely on the greed of men like Rockefeller, Carnegie, and Vanderbilt. In it, he painted a portrait of immoral capitalists whose only interest was exploiting American workers.

"They were aggressive men, as were the first feudal barons," Josephson wrote. "Sometimes they were lawless; in important crises, nearly all of them tended to act without those established moral principles which fixed more or less the conduct of the common people of the community."

With Americans desperate for someone to blame, *The Robber Barons* became one of the most popular books of its time, holding on as the number one bestselling nonfiction book in the U.S. for six months. The book was especially embraced by the radical left, for whom Josephson's version of events became the gospel.

So, what was the solution to evil corporations and the greed of the robber barons? Communism, of course. Although he frequently denied it, Josephson's actions suggest he was a dyed-in-the-wool communist.

In 1932, Josephson publicly supported communist candidates in the national elections. "We believe," Josephson said in a letter he coauthored during the campaign, "that the only effective way to protest against the chaos, the appalling wastefulness, and the indescribable misery inherent in the present economic system is to vote for the Communist candidates."

Josephson's support for the cause went beyond supporting a few communist candidates in the U.S. elections. Like most of his ilk, the anticorporate crusader became a mouthpiece for the Soviet Union—praising the revolution and ignoring the campaigns of terror and murder it carried out. The Soviet Union, Josephson said, "seemed like the hope of the world—the only large nation run by men of reason."

In 1934, just as his bestselling book was hitting the shelves, Josephson was in the Soviet Union getting a firsthand look at the communist experiment. He toured factories and steel mills and was delighted by what he saw.

"Before people pass judgment on Comrade Stalin,"

Josephson wrote, "they ought to come here and see his Works, his Opus Major, in many volumes with their own eyes. It is very impressive; and few other statesmen in all history have so much to show."

Despite being a total shill for the communist religion, Josephson's *The Robber Barons* became a foundation of America's anticorporate mythology, being embraced by communists and far-left historians alike.

Josephson, of course, was not alone. The American media had become lousy with communists whose goal it was to undermine Americans' trust in free markets and elevate the red alternative.

There was very little these typewriter Bolsheviks were not willing to overlook when it came to protecting their newfound religion. Reporting on the communist government in Russia, investigative journalist Lincoln Steffens dismissed the widespread violence, calling the misery that had been wrought "a temporary condition of evil, which is made tolerable by hope and a plan." Upon returning to the United States from the Soviet Union, he told a friend, "I have seen the future, and it works."

Walter Duranty, the *New York Times'* Moscow bureau chief, regurgitated Soviet propaganda and constantly downplayed Stalin's brutality. Reporting on Stalin's Five-Year Plan to industrialize the Soviet Union, Duranty said, "Stalin didn't look upon himself as a dictator, but as a 'guardian of a sacred flame' that he called Stalinism for lack of a better name." Duranty would go on to cover up millions of deaths in Ukraine brought about by Stalin's forced collectivization policies. He won the Pulitzer Prize for his work (a prize they refuse to rescind to this day despite evidence that he was a puppet of Moscow).

It wasn't just the reds in Moscow who managed to seduce American journalists. In 1937, author Edgar Snow published *Red Star Over China*, his personal account of the Chinese Communist Party. Snow salivated over communist leader Mao Zedong, declaring that he "appears to be quite free from symptoms of megalomania, but he has a deep sense of personal dignity, and something about him suggests a power of ruthless decision when he deems it necessary." Power of ruthless decision? That's one way to put it. Mao would make many ruthless decisions during more than two and a half decades as the dictator of China. History will remember him as mankind's most prolific mass murderer.

It wasn't just the pages of American newspapers that had become infested with propaganda. In Hollywood, the communist was hard at work producing films in support of the cause.

In 1943, Samuel Goldwyn Productions released *The North Star*, a film about members of a Ukrainian farming collective fighting off a Nazi invasion. It was an unabashedly pro-Soviet picture. The fact that the U.S. was allied with the Soviet Union at the time complicated matters, as it would only be natural that American films would portray our allies' fight against Nazi invasion in a sympathetic light. However, the film also incorporated official Soviet propaganda. When Sam Goldwyn sent a copy of the film to newspaper publisher William Randolph Hearst for review, Hearst responded: "You are a very great producer Sam but I think a good American like yourself ought to be producing pro-American propaganda instead of pro-Russian propaganda." *The North Star* would go on to be nominated for six Academy Awards.

Behind the scenes, screenwriters and directors were taking up the cause of Stalinism, many taking their orders straight from the Kremlin. The Hollywood Ten, a group of writers and filmmakers who would be blacklisted from the industry in the late 1940s, were all card-carrying members of the Communist Party. I'm not making that up. We know their card numbers.

In case you have any doubts, let me demonstrate just how committed these men were to the Soviet Union. When initiated into the Communist Party of the USA, members were required to take a pledge that read, in part:

> I pledge myself to rally the masses to defend the Soviet Union, the land of victorious Socialism. I pledge myself to remain at all times a vigilant and firm defender of the Leninist line of the Party, the only line that insures the triumph of Soviet Power in the United States.

The Hollywood Ten were honor-bound to their masters in Moscow (though, in their defense, honor is not a virtue the communist tends often to exhibit anyway). Today, those same men who proudly read that pledge are celebrated as martyrs. Never mind that every one of them was a traitor and an agent of a hostile foreign government.

However, as effective as the communist propaganda churned out by the likes of Matthew Josephson and his comrades might have been, the events of World War II would lead to a shift in the public's view of corporate America. The stock market began its long recovery. Investments in mining, the military, energy, and agriculture led to a revival of the job market. By 1945, the United States was manufacturing more than half of the produced goods in the world.

The era of American dominance had begun and the

communist, no longer able to exploit the economic misery of the American workingman, needed a new plan.

## The Rise of the Woke Corporation

In the 1960s, the communist's strategy had changed. If the American worker was too satisfied to rise up and seize the means of production, the communist would seize the corporations that controlled them. Instead of being socialized from outside forces, they would become "socially responsible" from within.

The idea of corporate social responsibility (CSR) was first popularized by economist Howard Bowen's 1953 book, *Social Responsibilities of the Businessman*. In it, Bowen emphasized the responsibility businesses have to society over the pursuit of profits, explaining that they were obliged "to pursue those policies, to make those decisions, or to follow those lines of action that are desirable in terms of the objectives and values of our society."

CSR was hailed by progressives and academics to soften the effects of capitalism. Corporations could make a profit—but not too much. Companies could compete—but not too hard. CEOs could make good salaries—but they shouldn't be flashy about it.

However, not everyone was convinced. Economist Milton Friedman blew the whistle on this new guiding ethos of corporate America, calling it a "fundamentally subversive doctrine" in a free society and warning that it would ultimately politicize every aspect of American life. In a 1970 article, Friedman wrote:

> [T]he doctrine of "social responsibility" taken seriously
> would extend the scope of the political mechanism to
> every human activity. It does not differ in philosophy

from the most explicitly collective doctrine. It differs only by professing to believe that collectivist ends can be attained without collectivist means.

Today, Friedman's worst nightmare has come to pass. CSR became the springboard from which the communist conquered corporate America—the glue that holds the devil's alliance together.

As communists entered the corporate world through the second half of the nineteenth century, they were the ones who would ultimately determine what constituted social responsibility. For this reason, the guiding principles of modern corporations completely align with the communist's goals: social, racial, and environmental justice.

Today, the corporation is your enemy.

They have contempt for their American customers because they see Americans as the problem. Just as the communist believes that America is a nation of racists, sexists, and homophobes, so too do corporations. And with the power they wield—whether through the products they make, the services they render, or the media they produce—they believe it's their social responsibility to change you, even at the expense of their bottom line.

Few brands, big or small, have proven to be immune from this destructive disease. It infects the most classic of American companies like Disney and Coca-Cola. Professional sports leagues like the National Football League and Major League Baseball. Energy giants like ExxonMobil and Chevron. Finance giants like Bank of America and Morgan Stanley.

Earlier, I talked about the "planks" of *The Communist*

*Manifesto*, the goals laid out by Karl Marx that would allow the communist to take total control of the economy and, in turn, a nation. Let's return to each of those goals and demonstrate the devil's alliance that has allowed him to achieve them.

## Control of Production

The corporations that produce or sell most of the goods we consume—from the shirts on our backs to the food we eat— have fallen under the communist's influence. Sure, they want you to buy their product, but that's not all they're selling to you and your family. Today, everything comes with a side order of social justice.

Want to buy some new threads? Walk into your local big-box store during Pride Month and you'll find rack upon rack of rainbow clothes. If you're lucky enough to live near a Target store, your children can even purchase gender-affirming clothing. Your daughter, for example, can pick up her first chest binder, which will allow her to look more like a boy and test out the waters before having her breasts removed. She can also pick up "packing underwear," which allows her to wear a phallic object or padding to create the appearance of having a bulge at the front of their pants. It's not enough to sell you coffee and toilet paper. Corporations like Target now encourage your daughter to pretend she has a penis.

Need a jolt of caffeine in the morning? Buy yourself a venti racial equity latte at Starbucks. You'll be happy in the knowledge that a portion of the four dollars you spend will go to funding Starbucks's $100 million pledge to "advance racial equity and environmental resilience."

Hungry for dinner? Pick up a Black Lives Matter burger at your local McDonald's, Burger King, or Wendy's, all of which signaled their support for the organization as their competitors were being burned down during the 2020 George Floyd riots.

Looking for a quick snack? Take pride and have yourself an Oreo cookie. In 2022, the brand released a two-and-a-half-minute advertisement in which a gay teenager comes out to his grandmother. Of course, the actual product that's being sold, which appears for only a few seconds, takes a backseat to the woke messaging. The ad ends with the message "Be a Lifelong Ally." (Reminder: We're talking about a cookie advertisement. Some sweet cream sandwiched between a pair of chocolate wafers. A product consumed primarily by children.)

## Control of Communication

Marx may have had telegraph wires and newspapers in mind, but today it's all about television, movies, and the internet. If a company is piping it into your living room, projecting it on a screen, or serving it up to you on a laptop or tablet, there's a good chance it's tainted by the communist agenda.

Now, I could write a whole book about Hollywood and the corporations that are bankrolling woke film and television productions. However, I think we'd be best served by looking at one company that has come to embody all the worst qualities of the devil's alliance: the aforementioned Walt Disney Company.

The fall of Disney is a unique tragedy because the company's current incarnation represents a complete reversal of the intentions and beliefs of its anti-communist founder.

While Walt Disney worked to prevent communist messages from creeping into his films—as he noted to the House Un-American Activities Committee in 1947—his animated features were by no means devoid of messages. He fully understood the power that movies had over young minds.

Earlier in this book I told you that there is no neutrality when it comes to teachers and what they teach your children. Well, the same thing goes for entertainment. The films and television programs your children watch are created by human beings. Human beings have biases. Those biases will inevitably appear in what they create.

Walt Disney was fully aware of this.

"Movies can and do have tremendous influence in shaping the lives in the realm of entertainment toward the ideals and objectives of moral adulthood," Disney once said. The question is never *if* movies teach ideals and objectives, but *whose* ideals and objectives are being taught.

For Walt Disney, those ideals and objectives never strayed far from tradition. Overt sexuality, for example, was nonexistent in Disney's original feature films. Sure, the prince gave the princess a kiss, but it always served the story and that was about as racy as things got. Movies like *Snow White*, *Cinderella*, and *Sleeping Beauty* featured men and women in traditional gender roles.

So, what is Disney up to these days? Let's just say we could wrap Walt's headless body in copper wire, place him next to a magnet, and he would generate enough electricity to power a small city.

Today's Walt Disney Company pumps out movies that serve cultural Marxist ideals and objectives. Its films present overtly sexual themes to children. They include gratuitous homosexuality to undermine "heteronormativity," as Marxist Queer Theory commands. They even include subtle salutes to Black Lives Matter.

Let's take a look:

*Turning Red*, a story of a thirteen-year-old who turns into a panda when she gets excited. It also happens to be an explicit allegory about the female menstrual cycle and teenage sexuality.

*Lightyear*, featuring the popular character from the Toy Story franchise. It also features a same-sex couple and same-sex kiss.

*Star Wars: The Rise of Skywalker*. The ninth and final film in the Star Wars Skywalker saga. Again, the good folks at Disney were nice enough to shoehorn a same-sex kiss into the movie.

*Eternals*, a superhero film about a diverse group of immortal aliens. In this movie, the Marvel Cinematic Universe got its first gay couple.

A woke remake of the classic *Cheaper by the Dozen*, which features a Black Lives Matter sign in the opening credits.

And if you don't like any of those, you can always turn on *The View* on Disney-owned ABC.

Of course, none of this is by accident. Behind the scenes, producers openly brag about the inclusion of sexual themes and

Queer Theory in Disney programming, and executives give their approval.

During a 2022 Disney staff meeting, executive producer and director of the cartoon series *The Proud Family: Louder and Prouder* Latoya Raveneau said she was advancing a "not-at-all-secret gay agenda" by adding queerness into the show. "In my little pocket of Proud Family Disney TVA [Disney Television Animation], the showrunners were super welcoming . . . to my not-at-all-secret gay agenda," Raveneau explained. "Maybe it was that way in the past, but I guess something must have happened . . . and then like all that momentum that I felt, that sense of 'I don't have to be afraid to have these two characters kiss in the background.'"

"I was just, wherever I could, adding queerness," Raveneau added. "No one would stop me, and no one was trying to stop me." It's worth noting that *The Proud Family: Louder and Prouder* airs on Disney XD, which, according to Disney, is programmed for kids ages six to eleven.

The wokeness goes beyond Disney's film and televisions programming and extends to their theme parks. Disney diversity and inclusion manager Vivian Ware admitted in March 2022 that the company had adopted gender-neutral language in its parks. "Last summer we removed all gendered greetings in relationship to our live spiels," Ware said. "So, we no longer say ladies and gentlemen, boys and girls. . . . It's hello everyone or hello friends."

Disney is using its economic clout to wade into Florida's political debates in support of woke causes. Shortly after the passage of Florida's Parental Rights in Education bill, which prohibits classroom instruction about sexual orientation or gender identity for students from kindergarten to third grade, the corporation condemned the new law. In a statement released on the company's corporate Twitter account, the company declared:

> [The Parental Rights in Education] bill should never have passed and should never have been signed into law. Our goal as a company is for this law to be repealed by the legislature or struck down in the courts, and we remain committed to supporting the national and state organizations working to achieve that. We are dedicated to standing up for the rights and safety of LGBTQ+ members of the Disney family, as well as the LGBTQ+ community in Florida and across the country.

You hear that?

A corporation that was once explicitly dedicated to family-friendly movies and programming is now outraged that teachers will no longer be allowed to instruct children ages six to nine about how they too can swap their gender with cross-sex hormones and life-altering surgeries.

This is what the devil's alliance has wrought. A once-great American corporation stripped of any sense of morality, decency, or dedication to the customers it once served. Today, it only serves communism.

## Control of Money and Investment

The corporate-communist alliance is most visible in the products we buy and the media we consume, but it's also quietly operating in the financial sector. The communist may not have seized the banks, but he has taken command of billions of dollars in their assets and is funneling that money into his causes. At the heart of this control is something called Environmental, Social, and Corporate Governance, or ESG for short.

Without getting into the weeds, ESG is a set of criteria that investment funds are using when selecting investment, rather than traditional criteria like the ability to turn and sustain a profit. The ESG criteria include environmental factors like impact on climate change, social factors like diversity and inclusion, and the ethics of its corporate governance.

Let me put it another way. If you look at the financial sector as a giant game of poker, funds will traditionally invest in players that have demonstrated their ability to win. Do they know which hands to play and which to fold? Are they raising at the right time? Can they read their opponents? ESG, on the other hand, allows funds to invest in players based on social factors. Are they a woman, minority, or member of the indigenous community? Are they underrepresented among poker players? Were they the victims of oppression?

Advocates of ESG investing claim it's a way to promote socially responsible business. In reality, it's a scam designed to direct investment dollars into far-left activism and incentivize corporations to comply with the communist agenda.

And the scam is working.

All of the world's largest asset managers, including companies like BlackRock, Morgan Stanley, and JPMorgan Chase, have all incorporated ESG into their investment strategies. It affects the investment options on most people's 401(k)s. Public money, including public sector pensions and sovereign wealth funds, are also being invested using ESG policies.

As of November 2020, one-third of all investment assets in

the United States are managed using ESG criteria, according to MarketWatch.

That's *trillions* of dollars.

All of those investment dollars are a giant carrot for corporations to elevate the communist agenda over any obligation they may have to shareholders—and woke CEOs are more than willing to play along with the scam in order to receive a share of those dollars.

The impact of ESG is massive. You see it in corporate statements supporting Black Lives Matter and marketing strategies that promote the trans agenda. It's the reason your inbox is filled with emails from mayonnaise brands and clothing retailers about their commitment to social justice. It's why corporate giants like Procter & Gamble and Hewlett-Packard sign on to meaningless pledges to net-zero carbon emissions by 2040.

Ultimately, however, the data shows that all of the statements, pledges, and virtue signaling are meaningless. In 2022, researchers at Columbia University and the London School of Economics compared the record of U.S. companies in 147 ESG fund portfolios and that of U.S. companies in 2,428 non-ESG portfolios. They found that the companies in the ESG portfolios had worse compliance records for both labor and environmental rules. In other words, corporations appear more than willing to shove gender theory down your throat and publicly extoll the virtues of social justice, but when it comes to their own policies, they fail to deliver.

Even worse, the same researchers discovered that ESG funds underperformed financially relative to non-ESG funds (I know. I too was shocked to discover that companies that don't prioritize making a profit ended up making less profit.)

Ultimately, ESG is the communist's version of the Nigerian prince who urgently needs you to send him money in exchange for a piece of his family's fortune. It sounds great on paper, but there's no chance you're going to see a return on that investment. Meanwhile, the money you send is going into the pockets of people who hate you, and toward causes that seek to undermine and destroy American society.

## Breaking the Alliance

The corporate-communist alliance has turned big businesses into nests of communist activity and a bullhorn for his propaganda. Whereas corporations once powered American prosperity, they are now actively undermining it at every turn.

It is up to anti-communists to break the devil's alliance.

Let's start with the most obvious thing we can do. To make corporate America hear us, we must speak in a language they understand: dollars and cents. Withhold them from woke companies and spend them with companies that share your values.

"But Jesse," I already hear you asking, "don't the communists always threaten to boycott corporations they disagree with?"

Oh, you mean the people who've gone from a tiny minority to full ownership of every cultural institution? Those communists? Yes, that's what I mean. That's exactly why we should be doing it, too. Learn to get comfortable with being an activist. Preserving freedom and pacifism are incompatible.

The communists put their money where their morals are. When they say they're going to boycott Chick-fil-A, they make good on their promise. The right can't even turn off the NFL. That has to change.

The most potent weapon the communist has used against corporate America has been fear. Fear that their brand will become toxic. Fear that they'll lose customers. Fear that they'll lose money. Fear is the reason corporations display the rainbow flag during Pride Month on their U.S. social media accounts, while they *don't* display it on their accounts in Muslim countries.

Corporate America should fear us like they fear the communist. Our side needs to use its numbers and, thankfully, we have them.

Take, for example, Disney's public opposition to Florida's legislation banning the teaching of sexual orientation and gender identity to kindergartners. When the right began making noise, Disney's stock lost $50 billion in value within six weeks. The corporation essentially went quiet after their war with DeSantis, leading one Florida state senator to say Disney had been silenced by "shock and awe from the governor."

To win, we must commit to withholding our dollars and make good on that commitment. I don't care if little Johnny is into Star Wars and little Jane is into princesses—you'll dump Disney+ if you care about their future.

Of course, there are countless companies that shouldn't get a penny of your hard-earned money. You must become an anti-communist household. Everything, from your car to your cupboard to your credit card statement, should reflect your values.

While not spending your money with woke corporations is the first step, where you *do* choose to spend your money is equally important. One of the best ways to avoid funding corporate communism is to shop locally with retailers and service providers you trust. Sure, it's tough when everything on Amazon is just a click away, but I never said anti-communism would be convenient. Keeping your money within your community means keeping your money with people who are more likely to share your values.

With personal spending under control, let's turn to what you can do in your place of work and business.

The most important thing I can say to you if you're a business owner is this: don't hire communists. Do a thorough background check on all your job candidates. There's plenty of publicly available information that will help you determine whether you're about to let Che Guevara into your workplace.

If they're posting on social media about intersectional feminism, don't hire them.

If they majored in "Justice and Peace Studies" in college, don't hire them.

If they ask you about your "diversity policies," don't hire them.

By screening out the communist, not only will you be saving yourself a major headache, but you'll also be preventing him from using your resources and any authority you give him, no matter how small, to push his poison on your customers, patrons, and the people your business serves.

(Side note: Don't ever feel sorry for keeping a communist on the unemployment line. That's exactly where he belongs.)

Next, we must talk about the digital side of your business. Now, I'm no tech genius. I know how to plug in a laptop and hit the power button to turn it on. That's about it. But I'm smart enough to know how important cyberspace is to the bottom line and have observed enough to understand how quickly tech companies like Apple, Google, Amazon, Facebook, and PayPal can demolish a business in an instant if they don't like what they're saying or selling.

Apple and Google can refuse to carry your app in their app store. Amazon can suspend you from their web hosting service. Facebook can shut down your business page. PayPal can cancel payment processing services. And they can do it all with impunity. Although your livelihood may be at stake, it means nothing to them. They would sooner see you stomped into the ground than risk confrontation with the woke mob or negative press from the media.

Upstart social media platform Parler provides a perfect cautionary tale. Parler was launched in 2018 as an alternative to Twitter, which had shown a bias against conservative users and views. By 2021, the platform had attracted 20 million users. However, it was demolished in January of that year in the wake of the Capitol riot.

Google and Apple dropped the Parler app from their respective app stores. According to Google, the decision was made in light of an "ongoing and urgent public safety threat." In fact, the decision was based on dubious reports that the event had been planned primarily on Parler. Critics claimed that the social network's failure to moderate its users led to their extremism to manifest itself on January 6.

The move made the Parler app virtually inaccessible to anyone looking to download it. Twenty-four hours after Google and Apple booted Parler from their app stores, Amazon announced it would remove Parler from its web hosting service, effectively shutting the social network down for over a month.

Months later, it was revealed that the accusations leveled against Parler were false. According to a report in Reuters, the

FBI found "scant evidence" that the Capitol riot was the result of a preplanned, organized plot. In other words, Parler was just a convenient scapegoat, a digital patsy for tech giants like Facebook and Twitter to deflect from their own culpability.

Learn from Parler's experience. Do not rely on big-tech corporations for digital services. Host your website with companies that won't kick you off their servers the moment they sense trouble. Find alternative ways to make your app available to customers. Use payment processing services that won't shut down your digital payments if they disagree with your politics. In short, insulate yourself from woke tech.

Okay, let's move on to the government's role in fighting the devil's alliance.

First off, I don't want to hear "get government out of business" anymore. I don't want government involved with business. You don't want government involved with business. But government is already involved in business. It's inevitable, whether we like it or not. Politicians regulate, create tax laws, and court companies to set up shop in their states and districts. We can't ignore reality; we need to use it to our advantage.

State governments need to use the leverage they have to bring woke corporations to heel. When megacorporations decide to wade into politics in support of the communist agenda, they should face consequences. Ending tax breaks, eliminating subsidies, and revoking special privileges should all be on the table. Again, Florida governor Ron DeSantis and the Florida Legislature have set a great example in this regard.

In fiscal year 2021, the Walt Disney Company paid more than $780 million in state and local taxes to the Sunshine State. As you would expect, Florida has, for decades, worked to keep the company happy. One of the special privileges Disney has enjoyed for more than half a century is the Reedy Creek Improvement District. This 38.5-square-mile area of land, created by Florida state law in 1967, is the home of Walt Disney World and is, for all intents and purposes, governed by the Disney Company. The law was a boon for Disney, allowing the company to act autonomously. It could levy taxes, write building codes, develop its own infrastructure, and build anything it wants, including an airport or nuclear power plant.

However, shortly after the Disney Company decided to join the debate over the Parental Rights in Education bill, Governor DeSantis and the Florida Legislature passed a law revoking the Reedy Creek Improvement District.

It was a masterstroke by the Florida government. After all, what was Disney going to do, pull up stakes and roll that giant golf ball from EPCOT to Vermont? Of course they wouldn't. Disney needs Florida as much as Florida needs Disney. Not only was the move punitive, a punishment for the Disney Company's meddling in the debate, it also served as a warning to other corporations: if it could happen to Disney, arguably the most powerful corporation in Florida, it could happen to *you*.

Next, politicians need to stop inviting communist corporations to set up shop in their states and districts. Elected officials love to brag about the companies they've seduced into bringing jobs and economic activity into their states. It always sounds good (and it looks great in their political ads), but as we've seen, it's far less exciting when these companies begin bankrolling efforts to allow teachers to tell your kids that cutting off their private parts will magically transform them into a different gender.

A communist company moving to a red state is no different than a California liberal moving to Oklahoma. He's going to bring his awful religion with him—only this time, he'll also bring billions of dollars in influence. Therefore, state and local governments should court companies that share their values. Red states should become bastions for anti-communist corporations.

Finally, we need to shut off the flow of woke capital by fighting back against ESG.

States and local governments must adopt rules that prevent their funds from being handled by asset managers that use ESG as an investment criterion. A state's pension fund should not be used to bankroll companies that hate America or value social justice over earning returns for their investors.

Several states are already in the process of implementing such rules. Texas, for example, has blacklisted numerous financial firms and hundreds of funds that have attacked fossil fuels. Firms that find themselves on that list are banned from doing business with local and state government entities. Similar steps are being taken in Florida, where the state's $186 billion pension fund is legally barred from considering ESG factors when making investment decisions, and may only invest in funds based on financial factors.

Corporations that push the communist agenda need to suffer the financial consequences and ultimately be forced to shutter their doors. However, we must work to make it a reality, and it begins with being conscious of the decisions we make with our dollars. Starve the beast and enjoy watching it die.

# ANTI-COMMUNIST ACTION ITEMS

- Withhold your money from woke companies and spend them with companies that share your values.

- Screen communists out of your own place of work or business.

- Insulate your business from big-tech companies that can destroy you in an instant.

- Support efforts by local and state governments to punish communist corporations that insert themselves into politics.

- Stop supporting government officials who invite communist corporations to set up shop in your states and communities. Instead, officials should be encouraged to court corporations that share your values.

- Stop the flow of woke capital by supporting rules that prevent Environmental, Social, and Governance criteria from being used to invest state funds.

# CHAPTER NINE

# Political Correctness:
# Euphemisms for Horrors

*"Comrade, your statement is factually incorrect."*
*"Yes, it is. But it is politically correct."*
—old Soviet joke

A s history has shown, the communist will use any means at his disposal to control the people around him. He will threaten them with personal destruction. He will imprison them. He will line them up, stick a gun in their face, and put a bullet in their brains. However, as effective as the boot-on-the-neck approach may be, it is not the most important tool in his box.

In this book, we've focused on the communist's control of America's institutions: schools, corporations, and our government. But there's one institution that unites all other institutions, and influences all of us, regardless of age, class, race, or sex—our common language. Therefore, the most effective method of control the communist has at his disposal is through the manipulation of the words and phrases we use. The primary way in which he carries out that manipulation is *political correctness.*

In the U.S., political correctness is so widespread that most of us have seamlessly incorporated it into the language we use without giving it a second thought. Illegal aliens have become "undocumented workers." Wives and husbands have become "partners." Fat people have become "people of size." It's all so mundane at this point that political correctness feels like nothing more than a punch line. The truth, however, is that political correctness is not only destructive to American society, but also the key to the communist's efforts to control us.

Political correctness boils down to a very simple idea: if the communist can control what people can say, he can influence the way they think—and if he can influence the way they think, he can ultimately influence what they do.

When we speak under normal circumstances, we choose words that most accurately describe reality. Politically correct language, on the other hand, is not chosen for accuracy, but for its political utility or its consistency with a higher "political truth." It bears no relationship to undeniable facts, objective reality, or universal truth because those things are obstacles to the communist, especially if they contradict his worldview. By repeating these words and phrases and making them part of the common language, people will come to believe *his* facts, live in *his* reality, accept *his* truth, and remain loyal to *him*.

Let me give you a simple example of how politically correct language works. If most of us saw a Honduran national crossing over the Rio Grande River into the United States, we would use the following sentence:

The illegal alien crossed the border.

The words we chose accurately describe what happened. The Honduran is a foreigner who crossed into the United States illegally. However, a person adhering to the principle of political correctness would describe the incident like this:

> The worker lacking permanent legal status migrated to the United States.

Unlike the first sentence, the words and phrasing chosen here are completely in line with the agenda of the communist. The word *worker* paints him in a sympathetic light by assuming he is simply coming to work (whether he is or is not). The communist knows you're much more likely to turn a blind eye to a "worker" than you are an "alien." Furthermore, the Honduran does not lack a *legal status*—he lacks citizenship or a residency. This language is used to obscure his *actual* legal status, which, considering he crossed the border without authorization, is criminal in nature.

By manipulating the language, the communist has changed the way you view the incident, and the way in which you're likely to respond to it.

Before you start believing that the communist is just some poor deluded fool who wants to share his delusions with you, you need to understand that political correctness is far more nefarious than that. A delusional person can be forgiven for telling you the sky is green. The communist, however, does not believe the sky is green any more than you do. He does not want you to repeat lies he believes are the truth, he wants you to repeat lies you both know are lies. By getting you to *say* the sky is green, he is exerting dominance over you.

Political correctness is not just a way for the communist to shape perception. It is also a powerful weapon. By classifying words as "correct" or "incorrect," the communist is limiting the scope of acceptable speech. If he doesn't want you to say something, he will forbid you from using the words needed to say it. He's building walls around you and boxing you in. For example, it becomes much more difficult to oppose illegal immigration if you can't use the term *illegal*.

The consequences for failing to use politically correct language can be devastating. In doing so, the offenders are marked as enemies and expose themselves to retribution. They can be turned into social outcasts, become alienated from their friends and family, and lose their jobs. In addition to the social consequences, communists are hard at work trying to criminalize using the wrong language. In Canada, for example, a tribunal has found that failing to use someone's correct pronouns violates their human rights.

The fact that politically correct language does not need to be grounded in reality makes it all the more dangerous. If there's no underlying truth to language, it can be changed on a whim. A word or phrase that is correct today can be considered incorrect tomorrow. Worse still, the correctness of a word can vary from person to person. Using the right words at the right time becomes like hitting a moving target. The communist can keep his enemies walking a verbal tightrope until, ultimately, the safest thing for them to do is to not speak at all.

This is where we find ourselves today. We live in a country where the language we are being told to use no longer has any basis in objective reality. Where media companies constantly alter their standards to meet the political needs of the moment. Where government officials repeat pleasant-sounding platitudes that hide dark political motives. Where a person's individual pronouns can change with their mood. In short, a country where the communist has seized total control of the language. To take back control, we must first understand where political correctness came from and how the communist has employed it in the past.

## Enforcing the Party Line

Let's start by making a distinction. There are two forms of political correctness that I like to refer to as "old political correctness" and "new political correctness." Old political correctness was a blunt instrument. It was like a hammer, enforcing approved political positions by means of intimidation and force. New political correctness, like the one we're experiencing in America and throughout the West, is a much more refined instrument. It's like a scalpel, enforcing approved political positions by slicing up the language. Ultimately, both old and new political correctness are built on lies and seek to achieve the same ends: total control of the beliefs people are allowed to hold and express.

If political correctness is a disease, the Soviet Union was patient zero. It was there, in the cradle of communist civilization, that old political correctness was first developed and employed.

The concept finds its beginnings with Bolshevik leader Vladimir Lenin. In 1894, Lenin coined the term *partiinost'*, which roughly translates to "party-mindedness." The idea held that there was no objective truth, but rather that the truth was a product of a person's class. The very idea of objectivity was rejected as part of the capitalist plot to control society. There were two truths: the capitalist's truth, and the communist's truth. Of course, the communist's truth was the only truth that was acceptable, and Lenin and the Bolsheviks would decide what that truth was.

This idea was reflected in the name of the official newspaper of the Communist Party of the Soviet Union, *Pravda*. The common English translation of the Russian word *pravda* is "truth," but it means more than that. For Russian speakers, *pravda* is both "truth" and "justice" or a higher, morally righteous truth. It didn't matter that *Pravda* was filled with lies, because the lies were morally righteous as they served the Communist Party.

Shortly before the start of the 1917 October Revolution, Lenin made it clear that only communist truth would be allowed when he and his cadre took control, claiming that freedom of the press was just another capitalist plot to maintain power. "The capitalists . . . call freedom of the press that situation in which censorship is abolished and all parties freely publish any paper they please," Lenin wrote. "In reality this is not freedom of the press, but freedom for the rich, for the bourgeoisie to mislead the oppressed and exploited masses."

Lenin was as good as his word. After the October Revolution, the Bolsheviks seized the facilities, paper, and presses of major newspapers and turned them over to Soviet publications. Editors and journalists who did not toe the party line were arrested and forced to submit to revolutionary tribunals. Those who managed to escape the tribunals could expect a visit by the Cheka. By the second half of 1918, all non-communist newspapers had been shuttered.

Lenin's idea mutated over time. It became one of the central tenets of communist rule, and eventually come to be known in Russian as *politicheskaya pravil'nost'*, or political correctness.

Political correctness in the Soviet Union was not limited to the press. Since class struggle supposedly informed every aspect of people's lives, it was applied to politics, medicine, education, literature, history, legal practices, culture, and economics. Nothing, no matter where it was said or in what context, was allowed to contradict the party.

The desire to remain politically correct even applied to the naming of children. In the 1920s and '30s, Soviet babies were given "revolutionary" names. For example, boys were named "Mels" (short for Marx-Engels-Lenin-Stalin) or Vilen (a shortened version of V. I. Lenin), while girls were given names like Lenina or Stalina (hey, I didn't say they were creative).

In addition to the more aggressive methods of silencing politically incorrect thoughts, the Soviets enforced political correctness with *kritika i samokritika*, or "criticism and self-criticism" sessions. If political incorrectness was the communist's version of sin, these sessions were their version of confession. During these sessions, which were essentially show trials, individuals would be publicly subjected to harsh questioning and forced to acknowledge their sins against the party, either real or imagined. According to Stalin, the purpose of criticism and self-criticism sessions was to "disclose and eliminate our errors and weaknesses." In truth, it was a way for communists to publicly humiliate people suspected of being insufficiently loyal and keep potential dissenters in line.

As they tended to do, the Chinese Communist Party took a terrible idea from the Soviet Union and somehow managed to make it worse. The CCP seized on Lenin's concept of *partiinost'* and developed their own version of party-mindedness, called *dangxing*. Just like its Soviet counterpart, the idea of *dangxing* demanded total obedience to communism in every aspect of life. Chairman Mao was even more ruthless in enforcing correctness than Lenin or Stalin. In 1957, the chairman told the Chinese people that "not to have a correct political point of view is like having no soul." To gain their soul, the people would have to submit to the communist religion—a religion that would be totally defined by Mao and the Chinese Communist Party.

Mao and his minions employed the typical means of shutting down politically incorrect speech. Newspapers were shut down. Books were burned. Dissenters were imprisoned or murdered. As terrible as this was, the most terrifying weapon the Chinese Communist Party used against political incorrectness was "denunciation rallies," which were also known as "struggle sessions."

The idea behind struggle sessions was similar to Soviet criticism and self-criticism sessions. Individuals who were suspected of non-communist thought were subjected to public questioning and forced to admit their own guilt. However, the Chinese communists brought it to a whole new level, turning these events into morbid religious rituals. Struggle sessions became public spectacles and would often draw massive crowds packed into workplaces, onto university sports fields, or communal farms. During these events, which could last for days, the accused would be paraded out in front of a jeering audience, subjected to questioning and verbal abuse, and sometimes tortured and killed.

In her 1987 book, *Enemies of the People*, historian Anne

Thurston described the struggle session of You Xiaoli, a professor at a prestigious Chinese university:

> You Xiaoli was standing, precariously balanced, on a stool. Her body was bent over from the waist into a right angle, and her arms, elbows stiff and straight, were behind her back, one hand grasping the other at the wrist. It was the position known as "doing the airplane."
>
> Around her neck was a heavy chain, and attached to the chain was a blackboard, a real blackboard, one that had been removed from a classroom at the university where You Xiaoli, for more than ten years, had served as a full professor. On both sides of the blackboard were chalked her name and the myriad crimes she was alleged to have committed.
>
> ... In the audience were You Xiaoli's students and colleagues and former friends. Workers from local factories and peasants from nearby communes had been bused in for the spectacle. From the audience came repeated, rhythmic chants ... "Down with You Xiaoli! Down with You Xiaoli!"
>
> ... After doing the airplane for several hours, listening to the endless taunts and jeers and the repeated chants calling for her downfall, the chair on which You Xiaoli had been balancing was suddenly kicked from under her and she tumbled from the stool, hitting the table, and onto the ground. Blood flowed from her nose and from her mouth and from her neck where the chain had dug into the flesh. As the fascinated, gawking audience looked on, You Xiaoli lost consciousness and was still.
>
> They left her there to die.

The barbarity of struggle sessions reached its peak during China's Cultural Revolution of the 1960s. "There were beheadings, beatings, live burials, stonings, drownings, boilings, group slaughters, disembowellings, digging out hearts, livers, genitals, slicing off flesh, blowing up with dynamite, and more, with no method unused," read one account of events in Wuxuan County. In some circumstances, victims would be killed, mutilated, and eaten (and if they were lucky, it happened in that order). These "flesh banquets" were not the result of starvation or desperation; they were expressions of pure communist hatred and rage. "This was not cannibalism because of economic difficulties, like during famine," X. L. Ding, a Cultural Revolution expert at the Hong Kong University of Science and Technology, told Agence France-Presse in 2016. "It was not caused by economic reasons, it was caused by political events, political hatred, political ideologies, political rituals."

Although they were not always as violent as those that took place in China, struggle sessions became a hallmark of communist rule in a number of countries. Under the Khmer Rouge in Cambodia, these sessions were called *rein sot*, or "religious education." Under the Kim dynasty in North Korea, they are known as *saenghwal ch'onghwa*, or "daily life review meetings." In each country, struggle sessions were used by the ruling party to enforce orthodoxy and as a means of surveilling the population.

Wherever he goes, the communist's demand for and enforcement of political correctness is sure to follow. Marx is his gospel. The whole world is his temple. The people will worship correctly, mouth the appropriate prayers, and never stray from the path toward his earthly salvation. Heresy will not be tolerated.

## Political Correctness: An Evolving Standard

The United States' experience with political correctness stretches back to the early twentieth century and the influence of the Communist Party USA. The term was most often used to describe CPUSA members who never wavered from the official party line, which was dictated by the Communist International (Comintern), the Moscow-based congress of international communist parties that was under the direct control of the Soviet Union.

Just as it is today, political correctness was constantly evolving. Something that was considered politically correct one day could easily be incorrect the next. There was no moral standard that determined right and wrong. The only standard that mattered was the needs of communism.

The most striking example of political correctness's evolving nature was the constant flip-flopping of the CPUSA on the subject of fascism before and during World War II. In 1935, the Comintern declared that communists and left-wing parties around the world needed to unite to prevent the rise of fascism. The declaration came shortly before Russia began its involvement in the Spanish Civil War, which pitted Mussolini and Hitler-backed Generalissimo Francisco Franco against Soviet-backed Republicans, a group primarily made up of communist, socialist, and anarchist groups.

The CPUSA and its leaders dutifully obeyed the orders of the Comintern. War against fascism became the politically correct position for all its members. "The fascist menace has grown on its easy victories," wrote CPUSA general secretary Earl Browder. "If this course is not stopped, the fascist war aggression will soon be on American soil itself." The party called for boycotts of goods from fascist countries, harshly criticized Western appeasement of the Nazis, and even helped to organize American volunteer battalions to fight against Spanish nationalists.

CPUSA efforts against fascism lasted through the end of the Spanish Civil War. With the Soviet-backed Republicans defeated, Stalin decided that cooperation with fascists was more beneficial than war. In 1939, the Molotov-Ribbentrop Pact was signed, a nonaggression agreement between the Soviet Union and Nazi Germany. The signing of the pact was followed by Nazi Germany and the Soviet Union's joint invasion of Poland, and the start of World War II. The Comintern declared that communist parties around the world needed to seek peace with fascist nations.

The CPUSA and its leaders dutifully obeyed the orders of the Comintern. Peace with fascism became the politically correct position for all its members. "The American government cannot take sides in the imperialist rivalries which directly led up to the invasion of Poland," wrote Browder. "But it can, and must, intervene jointly with the Soviet Union on behalf of peace." The party called for an end to anti-fascist boycotts, publicly attacked Great Britain and France as imperialists, and organized antiwar demonstrations.

CPUSA kept up its "peace" campaign until 1941. On June 22, Nazi Germany violated the Molotov-Ribbentrop Pact by launching Operation Barbarossa, its invasion of the Soviet Union. After enabling Hitler for two years, Moscow changed course again, calling on communist parties around the world to redirect their efforts to fighting fascism.

The CPUSA and its leaders dutifully obeyed the orders of the Comintern. Total war against fascism became the politically correct position for all its members. "For us in the United States, as for the peoples of the whole world, this war has become a Peoples' War of National Liberation," wrote Browder. "Our very existence is at stake. That is why the obligatory slogan is: 'Everything to win the war! Everything for victory over the Axis!'" The party called for military aid to Great Britain and the Soviet Union, supported the immediate opening of a second front in Western Europe, and called for the extension of the military draft they had once opposed.

The constant reversals of official policy struck a major blow against the credibility of the Comintern. In 1943, Stalin disbanded the organization, claiming that doing so would "[strengthen] the United Front of the Allies and other united nations in their fight for victory over Hitlerite tyranny." In truth, the cynicism had simply become so apparent that even a liar as seasoned as Stalin could no longer deny it to allied nations.

But no matter how obvious the lie had become, there was one group that could always be counted upon to believe it: the communist faithful—who would have marched into battle behind Satan himself if they believed it would demonstrate their political correctness and help to usher in their warped vision of America.

## The Birth of a New Political Correctness

By end of the 1940s, the original brand of political correctness was all but dead. In America, the communists had been exposed as useful idiots working in service of their masters in Moscow. However, the red-diaper babies picked up where their parents left off. Just as the communist doctrine would change to suit the radical new left, so too would political correctness.

The new generation largely rejected the international ambitions of the Soviet Union, choosing instead to model themselves after the homespun communism of Mao. In the 1960s, as the Chinese Communist Party was launching its Cultural Revolution in China, the American communists were preparing a revolution of their own. Cultural Marxism, based on racial, ethnic, and sexual grievances, was taking hold on America's university and college campuses.

As it advanced through the institutions, cultural Marxism developed its own language. The new political correctness was born. America's most prominent communist terror organization, the Maoist Weather Underground, even dedicated a chapter of their 1974 manifesto, *Prairie Fire*, to the practice of self-criticism, writing, "Criticism and self-criticism are our tools for this struggle."

The new political correctness is more nuanced than its previous incarnation. It's not imposed by brute strength—not at first, anyway—but through manipulation of the language. Adopting the Critical Theory of the Marxist Frankfurt School, the new left believed that language was not just a means of communication, but also a tool of control. Capitalism, class oppression, and racial injustice were all embedded in the words we spoke. To liberate themselves from oppression, the new communist needs to change the language people use.

The new political correctness is often subtle, taking traditional concepts that are familiar to Americans and altering the language around them. Oftentimes, the new words will have the opposite meaning of the originals. In normalizing this new language, the communist is replacing fundamental Western ideas with ones that are aligned with his goals.

Let's look at some of the most common examples of new political correctness:

- *Equality*, the idea that all people are born with the same value, becomes *Equity*, the idea that everyone should be made materially equal through government intervention.

- *Equal Justice*, the idea that all people should be treated impartially under the law, becomes *Social* or *Racial Justice*, the idea that oppressed groups should be treated differently than others.

- *Truth*, an idea that is grounded in objective reality, becomes *his/her/their truth*, the idea that reality is grounded in personal or class experience.

While the change in *words* may be subtle, the change in *meaning* is anything but. In each case, we can clearly see that ideas that have served as the bedrocks of the Western world have been replaced with ones that are ripped straight out of the communist playbook: the redistribution of wealth, class warfare, and subjective truth.

In addition to shifting people away from traditional ideas, the new political correctness is used to disguise the truth using soft language. By using this verbal camouflage, the communist normalizes absolute horrors.

In no place is this effort more apparent than in the language surrounding the medicalization of the transgender movement—the radical spawn of gender theory. Medical procedures that would have rightly been considered abominable a short time ago have now received new, innocuous-sounding names.

- *Gender Affirmation Care*: Chemical castration using pharmaceutical "puberty blockers"

- *Top Surgery*: The removal of a physically healthy woman's breasts

- *Bottom Surgery*: The mutilation and surgical reconstruction of a man's or woman's genitals to mimic those of the opposite sex

The terms that have been chosen for these procedures have nothing to do with the truth or accuracy. Rather, they're meant to obscure the reality of what are clearly horrific crimes against patients. While the parent of a confused child is likely to blanch at the idea of chemical castration and physical mutilation, they are far more likely to agree to "gender affirmation care" and "bottom surgery." Ultimately, they're the same thing.

The new political correctness is also found in the slogans of the mainstream left. Again, these mantras sound harmless at first, but upon closer inspection they are revealed to be Trojan horses for radical policies.

Let's break down some of the slogans that are in widespread use:

## Diversity Is Our Strength

This slogan plays on America's long history of accepting immigrant groups into the fold and assumes that it's our differences that make us strong. The truth, however, is that there's nothing strong about diversity. A divided people are a weak people.

What makes people strong is unity. Men and women, for example, are strong when they're unified in raising a family. People of different races and ethnic backgrounds are strong when they're unified behind a common purpose. A nation is strong when it is unified behind common ideas.

The communist knows that unity is strength, but he wants the nation unified around *their* ideas—and against you, his enemy. What he really means when he says *diversity is our strength* is that America should be less white, less English-speaking, and less conservative, because he believes white, English-speaking conservatives are hostile to his ideas.

## It Takes a Village to Raise a Child

At first glance, this slogan seems both harmless and obvious, but if you want to understand how corrupt it really is, all you need to know is that Hillary Clinton decided to name her 1995 book *It Takes a Village.*

Community plays an important role in the life of a child, but raising a child is, first and foremost, the job of a family. Ideally, that family consists of a father and mother who instill in their children the morals of their faith, the traditions of their past, and the ideals on which their nation has been built.

The communist knows that family is the foundation on which children should be raised, which is exactly why he focuses instead on the "village." He can't control the family, but he owns the village.

What the communist really means when he says *it takes a*

*village to raise a child* is that *he* will raise your children. He will raise them in *his* schools, *his* institutions, and, most importantly, with *his* ideals.

## Equality for All

Again, this slogan plays into a value deeply ingrained in the American psyche. As Alexis de Tocqueville observed that Americans are "far more ardently and tenaciously attached to equality than to freedom." (Yes, I realize I used this quote earlier, but Simon & Schuster requires a certain word count and quotes like these chew up space.)

Go ask the next hundred people you see if they believe in equality. It doesn't matter their political persuasion. Whether they're the second coming of Joseph Stalin or the most hardcore right-winger you know, they will all profess to love and believe in equality.

But equality is a ridiculous concept—a myth that has no basis in reality.

There have never been two people on this earth who have been equal. You're not equal to me. I'm not equal to you. Neither of us is equal to some other fellow strolling down the sidewalk. Each and every human being was created differently—with unique talents and flaws. Sure, our souls are equal in the eyes of God (and we're *supposed to* be equal under the law), but that's where equality ends.

However, by accepting this myth as reality, many have come to believe that people are, and by right should be, equal in all things, paving the way for the evil that is "equity."

Wherever there is political correctness, there is an

enforcement mechanism. In the Soviet Union, a violation of political correctness might get you a visit from the Cheka or later
the KGB. In Mao's China, dissent could lead to a run-in with the
savage Red Guard. Unlike those nations, political correctness is
not imposed by the government in the U.S. (not yet, anyway).
Instead, the enforcement mechanism is crowdsourced to digital
mobs of anonymous malcontents and a handful of vocal activists.
We call this enforcement mechanism "cancel culture."

The communist cancel culture mob is America's version of
the Chinese Red Guard. They are constantly on the hunt for
offenses against political correctness and take pleasure in destroying the lives of those who cross them.

Cancellation usually begins with two simple words: "I'm
offended." However, the offense is rarely genuine. More often,
offending the mob means a person has simply expressed an opinion that contradicts their catechism. "I'm offended" is nothing
more than an excuse for the mob to begin its sadistic ritual.

Once it has acquired a target, the cancel culture mob will
pursue every avenue through which it can destroy their victim's
personal and professional lives. The consequences of being targeted by the cancel culture mob can be enormous. In addition
to the potential loss of your job and income, victims can feel
ostracized and socially isolated.

In some extreme cases, cancel culture has even led to suicide. For example, in an earlier chapter we learned about Mike
Adams, an associate professor of criminology at the University
of North Carolina at Wilmington. In 2007, Adams had sued officials at the university, claiming he was denied a promotion for
being outspoken about his conservative beliefs. While Adams
won his case in court, his ordeal was far from over. In the years

following the court case, he remained a punching bag for the cancel culture mob. He was harassed online, publicly denounced by students and school administrators, and forced into retirement as part of his settlement with the university. In 2020, at the age of fifty-five, Adams was found dead in his home, having taken his own life. While it's impossible to say that his suicide was entirely due to cancel culture, it would be naïve to think that the persistent harassment, vilification, and professional exile played no role.

Mike Adams's case should serve as a lesson about the goal of cancel culture: destruction—as complete and total as anything that could have been dished out by Soviet secret police or Chinese Red Guard zealots.

## Taking Back the Language

Political correctness has infected every corner of American society. It's in the media we consume. It's in the news we read. It's in the education our children receive—their history and even their math books.

The communist has shifted the language to make you accept his political program and invented new terms to conceal the horrors he wishes to unleash on you and your family. All the while, he is forcing you to adopt the new political correctness using social pressure, cancellation, and, in some cases, the law.

Defeating political correctness begins with changing our own habits. The first step in doing so is to reject his new language. Whether you're using politically correct language out of sheer habit, the desire for social approval, or the fear of cancellation, you need to stop. For the anti-communist, an undocumented worker is an illegal alien, your partner is your wife or husband, and a person of size is fat.

I understand that our society has become so infected by politically correct language that failing to use it may make the person you're speaking to uncomfortable. That's okay. As a matter of fact, that's the point. The communist's language is made up of euphemisms for horrors and platitudes that are designed to mask tyrannical goals. We *want* people to feel uncomfortable when confronted with, for example, the chemical castration of young people. It's horrible. We want them to face the horror, not hide it behind verbal camouflage.

Refusing to use politically correct language is not always going to be easy. Since cultural Marxism can be found in every aspect of society, you are now expected to use its language in places where resistance may be looked upon as a sign of insubordination or disrespect.

Let me give you an example: Imagine that you're asked to give your pronouns at the start of a meeting or conference call with your coworkers. It would be easy to just go with the flow and answer "he/him" or "she/her." What's the harm, right?

Wrong.

The anti-communist knows that this question has nothing to do with understanding who you are or how to properly address you. The communist simply wants you to participate in their ritual and, in doing so, publicly signal your acceptance of gender ideology.

Understand, there is no polite way out of this. You must refuse to participate in their game. If you're asked to give your pronouns, you should simply say, "I'm not comfortable with that," and move on.

In addition to showing that you won't play along, it will signal to other like-minded people that they don't have to play, either. The game only works when there are players.

Of course, refusing to play the game will inevitably make people uncomfortable, but you must learn to be comfortable being uncomfortable. And let me encourage you with this: as someone who angers communists daily, you may just learn to love it as I do.

Once you've stopped using their language, the communist will inevitably attack you. He'll call you a fascist. He'll accuse you of being racist or sexist. He'll label you a homophobe or transphobe. This brings me to the second step: you need to understand that their accusations are meaningless. Because you're a decent person, you don't want to be labeled any of the vile things he calls you. He knows this about you. So, he accuses you of these things to put you on the defensive. The second you begin defending yourself, you have allowed him to choose the battlefield and you have lost. *Never* allow him to use your values against you. Name-calling and accusations only work if you allow them to. For the most part, the people who matter don't believe it and the people who believe it don't matter.

I don't want to give the impression that refusing to use politically correct language is without risk. After all, Karen might have friends in the human resources department. There are too many examples of damaged reputations, ruined careers, and upturned lives to believe this is going to be a cakewalk. With this in mind, we must address cancel culture, the enforcement mechanism of political correctness.

The first rule is this: *do not apologize.*

When first confronted by cancel culture, many people will

immediately offer public penance in the belief that doing so will placate the mob.

Big mistake.

Remember, the communist loves to be offended. It gives him a sense of struggle and purpose. It should never bother you when he claims you've offended him because, deep down, he's thrilled.

Communism is a religion that does not offer forgiveness. No matter how sincere your apology may be, it's not going to convince the mob to back off. It's going to encourage them, like chumming the water for sharks.

The goal of cancel culture is not to extract an apology or get you to change. Like the struggle sessions of China, public expressions of remorse are nothing more than performances held for the entertainment of the mob. Ultimately, cancel culture is about destruction. The target of cancellation is a sacrifice to communism's sadistic god. He will not be satisfied until you are left mangled and broken like so much roadkill.

Let me take things a step further. Once you're in the crosshairs of the mob, refusing to apologize is not enough. The mob is predatory. It loves soft prey for the same reason a cat enjoys batting around a mouse before sinking its teeth in. You must go on the offensive.

Double down.

Triple down.

Let me give you an example from my personal experience.

In 2019, my oldest son participated in a Lego robotics program at his school. I don't want to bore you with all the details (I had to live through them, so I know how excruciating they can be), but in short, teams of students use Lego robotics to complete various tasks and the whole thing culminates in a big day-long tournament.

While I was at the tournament, I decided to have a little fun.

"I'm at a Lego robotics tournament for my oldest and you've never seen this many depressed fathers in one place," I tweeted. "We're all thinking, 'Other kids play football...'"

I also might have tweeted out a GIF of a man drinking poison when it was time for the closing ceremonies . . . and another of Alec Baldwin pouring himself a glass of whiskey when I found out my son had qualified for the next tournament . . . and a few other things.

Anyway, the commies went ballistic.

My comments resulted in a frenzy of losers, outrage-mongers, and CNN contributors (but I repeat myself) on Twitter calling me a garbage person, a horrible father, and worse. The story attracted media attention, landing in *Newsweek*, the *Houston Chronicle*, and the *Daily Mail*. I would even find out later that people had contacted the radio station at which I worked, demanding I be fired.

So, how did I respond? I leaned into it and fed them more of what made them angry.

"I hate the Patriots, but you have to give them credit," I later tweeted. "They're back in the Super Bowl. Winners play for championships. Losers do robotics."

When asked for comment by the *Houston Chronicle*, I told them that I wasn't sorry "even a little bit," and that "I'll probably do it again."

"I think it's hilarious," I added, "as does everyone with a sense of humor."

The backlash lasted around forty-eight hours. Once I made

it clear that I wasn't bending, they climbed back under the rocks from which they'd emerged. Nothing frustrates the mob more than the realization that you're not going to back down. Once they do, they'll move on to a new target.

No matter how much we fight back against cancel culture on a personal level by remaining persistent and frustrating the mob, there will inevitably be those who fall victim. There will always be weak-kneed employers who are ready to cut people loose when the heat is turned up. For those poor souls, we must build a safety net.

Let me explain what I mean.

If the far left is good at anything, it's taking care of their own. There's a system in place to support those who take risks to advance the cause. You might have noticed, for example, that every time you hear about some leftists who lost their government job for criticizing a conservative president or who was fired from the bureaucracy for "blowing the whistle" at a congressional hearing, the announcement of a deal to publish their memoirs inevitably follows. For example, Lieutenant Colonel Alexander Vindman gave testimony during President Trump's impeachment inquiry in November 2019. Within a year, he had a book deal. Similarly, former U.S. ambassador to Ukraine Marie Yovanovitch testified against Trump at House impeachment hearings that same month. Three months later, it was announced that she'd received seven figures to publish her memoirs.

To the untrained eye, these just look like standard book deals; publishing companies trying to make a few bucks off someone who's received some publicity. But do you really think the memoirs of an obscure Army bureaucrat like Vindman, or an ex-ambassador to Ukraine like Yovanovitch, are worth seven figures? Of course not. These book deals were essentially financial rewards for two people who were willing to go public: a safety net to cushion their fall and minimize their risk.

This financial safety net is not limited to publishers. Loyalists can also expect a cushy job as a "senior fellow" at some progressive think tank in D.C., or to become a paid contributor at CNN or MSNBC. There are entire networks of nonprofit organizations, media companies, and corporations that support those who are willing to take fire.

As anti-communists, we must build our own networks or parallel economies. We need our own publishers, think tanks, and corporations that are beyond the influence of the mob and are ready to catch those who fall victim to cancel culture.

Let me give you a perfect example from the nerdy world of comic books.

In 2018, artist Ethan Van Sciver—who worked on titles including *The Flash*, *Green Lantern*, and *Batman*—was exiled from the mainstream comic industry by woke colleagues and social justice warriors after he publicly supported Donald Trump for president. Instead of trying to find his way back into the good graces of the woke mob that shunned him, Van Sciver used his banishment as an opportunity. He rallied like-minded fans online and, less than a month after losing his job in the mainstream, began funding his own books independently. His first comic raised more than $500,000. His second effort raised more than $1.2 million.

His success inspired others to follow the same path. Over the course of several years, this collection of anti-communist artists and writers have established a parallel economy—free from the influence of social justice—that generates millions in revenue each year.

These parallel economies need to be established in every industry that the communist now dominates. And when they *do* emerge, you must support them with your dollars.

With a proper safety net in place, the risk of fighting back is reduced, and more people will be encouraged to do so.

Next, we must talk honestly about cancel culture itself. We hate when people we respect fall victims to the communist mob. We're horrified when it happens. It feels like watching a public execution. Watching it all unfold is so terrible that it's become popular on the right to label oneself an anti–cancel culture crusader who rejects the tactic as a matter of principle. We stomp our feet in indignation and scream, "I would never do that because I believe in free speech!" or we turn up our noses and say, "So much for the tolerant left."

Again, this is a huge mistake.

The communist does not care about free speech. He will not be dissuaded by your principles. He knows this is a war and he plans to win by any means necessary. Opposing cancel culture is shortsighted, and only allows the communist to feel comfortable while he destroys you. It's like unilaterally signing a treaty banning the use of a powerful weapon on the battlefield because your enemy is successfully deploying it against your troops.

Anti-communists do not oppose cancel culture. To the contrary, we embrace it. It's an important tool to achieve our goal: canceling communists.

We should use it against businesses that are driven by the cultural Marxist agenda.

We should use it against media outlets that publish communist propaganda.

And we should use it against teachers who push the communist religion on our children.

We have the numbers; we can't be afraid to use them. If you encounter a business pushing communism on its customers or a communist spreading his poison in the schools, employ the Jesse Kelly A.I.M. system:

**A**wareness: Rally the troops online and in your community. Spread awareness about the business or individual who needs canceling. Raise hell! If it's a business, publicly condemn them. If it's an individual, publicly expose them. Add your voice to the pile-on wherever you can.

**I**solate: Make them feel the walls closing around them. For businesses, go after their revenue streams. Threaten boycotts and follow through. Target advertisers. Make phone calls to corporate offices. Write letters and emails. For individuals, make them toxic. Pressure their colleagues to ostracize and condemn them.

**M**ake Demands: Demand apologies, policy changes, and public accountability for offending parties.

No matter what happens, keep pushing! Make them dance and squirm. Leave them broken and afraid. They should serve as an example to others who are considering their path.

I know this might make you feel uncomfortable, like you're *becoming* your enemy. "Don't become your enemy" is something that belongs in nursery rhymes. This is a cultural war. You must win it and win it by any means necessary. The victors will be the ones who decide what this nation looks like for the next five hundred years.

You know that old saying, "History is written by the victors"? The same is true of the future.

# ANTI-COMMUNIST ACTION ITEMS

- Eliminate politically correct language from your vocabulary, even if it makes the people you communicate with uncomfortable.

- Ignore name-calling and charges of "racism," "sexism," or "homophobia." They're meaningless.

- *Do not apologize!* It only encourages the mob.

- Establish and support safety nets for fellow travelers who have been "canceled" by the woke mob.

- Embrace "cancel culture." It's a powerful weapon and we should be using it against our enemy.

# CONCLUSION

D espite the clear danger that the communist poses, we've allowed him to infiltrate and capture every important institution in our nation. America's schools, media outlets, corporations, and laws are now, in part or in total, in service to his evil cause, which ultimately intends to destroy you, your family, and your nation.

For these reasons, the role of anti-communist is one of the most important you will fulfill in your lifetime. It must complement and inform every other role you play, whether as a parent, a faithful employee, or even as a servant of God. At all times, and in all decisions you make, the guiding principle of the anti-communist must remain at the forefront of your mind:

*Defeating the communist is all that matters.*

We have a long fight ahead of us, and my having it laid bare for you in such a frank way should have brought you to the end broken down and gasping for air.

Good.

While it's true that you will never see final victory, you can see to it that your children, or your children's children, will. If you demonstrate tenacity, refuse to compromise, and show the same level of dedication that the communist has for a century, future generations will be spared the horrors that befell so many millions before them. Victory is not within our sight, but it is within our power.

We are blessed in the fact that we have more tools with which to fight back than all of those poor souls who suffered communism's wrath in the past. Tools with which to organize, publish, and expose the enemy. With these tools, you will become a thorn in his side, your home will become a fortress, and your community will be saved.

Finally, understand that you don't have options. You don't have choices. You *must* do these things. You *must* become an anti-communist. I cannot save this country. Nor can your father, your son, or your neighbor. It must be you. Each and every one of us must become committed to eradicating this deadly religion from the nation we love. It will not be easy, and it will not be fast. But we *can* do this.

*Let us begin.*

# AUTHOR'S ACKNOWLEDGMENT

There are so many people I can thank for this book and how wonderful it is. But really, the person who deserves the most praise is me. None of this would have been possible without my incredible talent. So, thank you, from the bottom of my heart. Jesse, you're the best.

# AUTHOR'S WIFE'S ACKNOWLEDGMENTS

First off, let me apologize for my husband's behavior (not for anything he wrote in this book specifically, but it's generally how I begin all conversations about Jesse). I'd like to thank all the people who helped Jesse make this book a reality.

Nick Rizzuto, the book's coauthor, who I'm sure grew tired of having to say, "No, Jesse, that's not a real word." Also, his wife, Rosanna, and his children for loaning him out to Jesse on the weekends, and his mother, Roseann, whose kitchen table doubled as a writing desk for months.

Chris Balfe, Eric Pearce, and the team at Red Seat Ventures who encouraged Jesse to write this book and provided guidance throughout the process.

Natasha Simons, executive editor at Threshold Editions, who believed in Jesse even when she had no reason to. Hopefully, she has no regrets.

Keith Urbahn of Javelin for shepherding Jesse through the publishing process.

Julie Talbot, Dan Metter, Peter Tripi, and the Premiere Networks team, for providing Jesse a platform every weekday.

And, finally, I should probably thank myself, but I understand that putting up with this man on a day-to-day basis is my lot in life.

CHAPTER ONE

**The Communist and Anti-Communist**

7  *"the most advanced and resolute section"*: Karl Marx and Frederick Engels, *Manifesto of the Communist Party* (Chicago: Charles H. Kerr, 1906), p. 33.

7  *by all accounts his hygiene was better than Marx's*: Marx's hygiene was so vile that by the end of his days his skin was covered with reeking sores and boils. In an 1883 letter to Engels, Marx wrote, "I hope the bourgeoisie will remember my carbuncles to their dying day."

7  *A dandy who spent his evenings carousing*: In a letter to Marx from Paris in 1847, Engels wrote, "If I had an income of 5000 francs I would do nothing but work and amuse myself with women until I went to pieces. If there were no Frenchwomen, life wouldn't be worth living. But so long as there are *grisettes* [working-class women], well and good!" Gross.

8  *"The theory of the Communists may be summed up"*: Marx and Engels, *Manifesto of the Communist Party*, p. 34.

8 *"Just as Darwin discovered"*: Frederick Engels speech at the grave of Karl Marx, March 17, 1883.

9 *An estimated 1.7 million perished*: Steven Rosefielde, *Red Holocaust* (London: Routledge, 2010), p. 77.

10 *The resulting famine*: Mark O'Neil, "45 million Died in Mao's Great Leap Forward, Hong Kong Historian Says in New Book," *South China Morning Post*, September 5, 2010, https://www.scmp.com/article/723956/revisiting-calamitous-time.

10 *The United Nations estimates*: Letter dated November 7, 2003, from the permanent representative of Ukraine to the United Nations, addressed to the secretary-general.

11 *In one case*: Frank Dikötter, "Looking Back on the Great Leap Forward," *History Today* 66, no. 8 (August 2016), https://www.historytoday.com/archive/looking-back-great-leap-forward.

11 *In another instance of brutality*: Ibid.

11 *Still another man, Liu Desheng*: Isaac Stone Fish, "Mao's Great Famine," *Newsweek*, September 26, 2010, https://www.newsweek.com/maos-great-famine-72301.

12 *The regime abolished civil liberties and political rights*: USC Shoah Foundation, https://sfi.usc.edu/collections/cambodian-genocide.

12 *Between 1975 and 1979, the Khmer Rouge's rule*: National Research Council Roundtable on the Demography of Forced Migration; H. E. Reed and C. B. Keely, eds., *Forced Migration & Mortality* (Washington, DC: National Academies Press, 2001), p. 5; "The Demographic Analysis of Mortality Crises: The Case of Cambodia, 1970–1979," https://www.ncbi.nlm.nih.gov/books/NBK223346/.

13 *"the most terrible acts of barbarism"*: "10th Edition of International Symposium on the Piteşti Experiment, Re-education through Torture," Agerpres, October 1, 2010, https://web .archive.org/web/20170214002437/https://www.agerpres .ro/english/2010/10/01/10th-edition-of-international -symposium-on-the-pitesti-experiment-re-education -through-torture-18-14-45.

13 *All told, Marx's disciples racked*: Stéphane Courtois, Mark Kramer, et al., *The Black Book of Communism: Crimes, Terror, Repression* (Cambridge, MA: Harvard University Press, 1999), p. 4.

15 *"It is worth noting that not one communist"*: Whittaker Chambers, *Witness* (New York: Random House, 1952), p. 725.

17 *"A number of liberals"*: John Earl Haynes and Harvey Klehr, *Venona: Decoding Soviet Espionage in America* (New Haven, CT: Yale University Press, 1999), p. 17.

18 *"Socialism is precisely the religion"*: Roger Kiska, "Antonio Gramsci's Long March Through History," *Religion & Liberty* 29, no. 3 (December 12, 2019), https://www.acton.org /religion-liberty/volume-29-number-3/antonio-gramscis -long-march-through-history.

20 *"far more ardently and tenaciously"*: Alexis de Tocqueville, *Democracy in America*, vol. 2 (New York: Knopf, 1945), p. 94.

23 *"end point of mankind's ideological evolution"*: Francis Fukuyama, *The End of History and the Last Man* (New York: Free Press, 1992), p. xi.

CHAPTER TWO
## The University System: America's Communist Factory

29  *"for the purpose of promoting"*: Leonard D. Abbott, "The Intercollegiate Socialist Society," *Harvard Illustrated Magazine* 7,
no. 1 (October 1905): 90.

30  *"All over the place radicals sprang up"*: Eric Homberger, *John
Reed* (New York: Manchester University Press, 1990), p. 21.

30  *"a classless cooperative society"*: Philip G. Altbach and Seymour
Martin Lipset, *Students in Revolt* (Boston: Houghton Mifflin,
1969), p. 10.

31  *"a revolutionary communist party"*: Weather Underground
Organization, *Prairie Fire: The Politics of Revolutionary Anti-
Imperialism* (San Francisco: Communications Co., 1974),
https://onlinebooks.library.upenn.edu/webbin/book
/lookupid?key=olbp52159.

31  *"to lead white kids into armed revolution"*: Weather Underground, "A Declaration of a State of War," first broadcast in
1970 and read by Bernardine Dohrn.

31  *"were angry that a policeman didn't die"*: Bryan Burrough,
"Meet the Weather Underground's Bomb Guru," *Vanity Fair*,
March 29, 2015, https://www.vanityfair.com/culture/2015
/03/weather-underground-bomb-guru-burrough-excerpt.

33  *"believed that their immediate responsibility*: *No Place to Hide:
The Strategy and Tactics of Terrorism*, directed by Dick Quincer,
1982.

34  *"very respected and prominent in Chicago"*: Bob Drogin and
Dan Morain, "Obama and the Former Radicals," *Los Angeles
Times*, April 18, 2008, https://www.latimes.com/archives
/la-xpm-2008-apr-18-na-radicals18-story.html.

35  *"As Karl Marx's ideological heirs"*: Felicity Barringer, "The

Mainstreaming of Marxism in U.S. Colleges," *New York Times*, October 25, 1989, https://www.nytimes.com/1989/10/25 /us/education-the-mainstreaming-of-marxism-in-us-colleges .html.

38 *"Some of my young colleagues"*: Ibid.

38 *about 115 colleges have received*: Janet Lorin and Brandon Kochkodin, "Harvard Leads U.S. Colleges That Received $1 Billion from China," Bloomberg, February 6, 2020, https: //www.bloomberg.com/news/articles/2020-02-06/harvard -leads-u-s-colleges-that-received-1-billion-from-china.

39 *"avoid Chinese political history and human rights abuses"*: George Leef, "The Chinese Don't Like Academic Freedom, So American Schools Should Avoid Their Confucius Institutes," James G. Martin Center for Academic Renewal, September 20, 2017, https://www.jamesgmartin.center/2017 /09/chinese-dont-like-academic-freedom-american -schools-avoid-confucius-institutes/.

39 *"an important part of China's overseas propaganda set-up"*: "A Message from Confucius," *Economist*, Special Report on China and America, October 24, 2009, https://www .economist.com/special-report/2009/10/24/a-message -from-confucius.

40 Data on books assigned to students are from the Open Syllabus Project, https://opensyllabus.org/.

44 *dismantle societal norms* Jonathan Butcher and Mike Gonzalez, "Critical Race Theory, the New Intolerance, and Its Grip on America," Heritage Foundation, December 7, 2020, https: //www.heritage.org/civil-rights/report/critical-race-theory -the-new-intolerance-and-its-grip-america.

45 *"Distract them from learning something that is constructive"*:

Yuri Bezmenov's 1983 Lecture on Subversion, https://cosmo learning.org/documentaries/yuri-bezmenov-lecture-on -subversion-1983/.

48 *"I would be crucified"*: Jennifer Kabbany, "Poll: 73 percent of Republican Students Have Withheld Political Views in Class for Fear Their Grades Would Suffer," College Fix, September 4, 2019, https://www.thecollegefix.com/poll-73-percent -of-republican-students-have-withheld-political-views-in -class-for-fear-their-grades-would-suffer/.

55 *"'Seize the Endowments' will help open"*: Will Chamberlain, "Seize the Endowments," *Human Events*, March 30, 2020, https:// humanevents.com/2020/03/30/seize-the-endowments.

56 *Colleges and universities* United States Senate Permanent Subcommittee on Investigations, *China's Impact on the U.S. Education System*, 2019, p. 3.

## CHAPTER THREE
## Cultural Destruction

58 *"Put destruction first"*: "Circular of the Central Committee of the Communist Party of China on the Great Proletarian Cultural Revolution," May 16, 1966.

61 *"the past dominates the present"*: Marx and Engels, *Manifesto of the Communist Party*, p. 36.

61 *"the tradition of all dead generations"*: Karl Marx, "The Eighteenth Brumaire of Louis Bonaparte," 1852.

61 *"every picture has been repainted"*: George Orwell, *Nineteen Eighty-Four* (New York: Signet Classic, 1983), p. 128.

65 *an estimated 20 million by one count*: Courtois, Mark, et al., *The Black Book of Communism*, p. 4.

66 *"Beating drums"*: "Red Guards Destroy the Old and Establish

the New," *Peking Review* 9, no. 36 (September 2, 1966): 17–19, https://www.marxists.org/subject/china/peking-review/1966/PR1966-36m.htm.

67  *an estimated 65 million by one account*: Courtois, Kramer, et al., *The Black Book of Communism*, p. 4.

68  *"Zero for him and zero for you"*: Don Watkins and Yaron Brook, *Equal Is Unfair: America's Misguided Fight Against Income Inequality* (New York: St. Martin's Press, 2016), p. 208.

68  *an estimated 2 million by one account*: Courtois, Kramer, et al., *The Black Book of Communism*, p. 4.

68  *"Religion is the sigh of the oppressed creature"*: Karl Marx, *Critique of Hegel's Philosophy of Right* (New York: Cambridge University Press, 1970), https://www.marxists.org/archive/marx/works/1843/critique-hpr/.

68  *"the cornerstone of the entire ideology of Marxism"*: Vladimir Lenin, "About the Attitude of the Working Party toward the Religion," in *Lenin Collected Works*, vol. 15 (Moscow: Progress, 1973), pp. 402–13, https://www.marxists.org/archive/lenin/works/1909/may/13.htm.

69  *"the complete destruction of links"*: *Workers International News*, October 1945, http://www.marxist.com/religion-soviet-union170406.htm.

70  *"[W]e have torn down the plaque"*: Matthew Omolesky, "China's Three-Child Policy and the Philosophy of Reproduction," *American Spectator*, June 12, 2021, https://spectator.org/chinese-three-child-policy/.

73  *"The discovery of gold and silver in America"*: Karl Marx, *Capital: A Critique of Political Economy*, vol. 1, https://www.marxists.org/archive/marx/works/1867-c1/ch31.htm.

74  *"Objectivity is impossible and it is also undesirable"*: Larry De-

Witt, "Howard Zinn: The Historian as Don Quixote," History News Network, http://hnn.us/articles/58544.html.

75  *"Monuments to men"*: Nancy Pelosi, "Pelosi Sends Letter to Joint Committee on the Library Calling for Removal of Confederate Statues from the United States Capitol," June 10, 2020, https://www.speaker.gov/newsroom/61020-1.

75  *"If we're going to have bases"*: Felicia Sonmez and Paul Kane, "Trump Faces Clash with Congress over Confederate Names on Military Bases," *Washington Post,* June 11, 2020, https://www.washingtonpost.com/politics/trump-faces-showdown-with-congress-over-confederate-names-on-military-bases/2020/06/11/981d2178-abeb-11ea-94d2-d7bc43b26bf9_story.html.

75  *"[I'm] not opposed to it"*: Ibid.

75  *David Graham called Trump's slippery-slope argument*: David Graham, "Trump Knows Exactly What He's Doing," *Atlantic,* August 16, 2017, https://www.theatlantic.com/politics/archive/2017/08/trump-charlottesville-white-supremacy/537045/.

76  *NPR ran a "fact check"*: Steve Inskeep, "FACT CHECK: 'Whatabout' Those Other Historical Figures? Trump's Question Answered," NPR, August 17, 2017, https://www.npr.org/2017/08/16/543881696/fact-check-whatabout-those-other-historical-figures-trumps-question-answered.

77  *a committee reporting to Washington, D.C., mayor*: Andrew Kerr, "DC Mayor Embraces Report Calling for Removal or Contextualization of Washington Monument," *Daily Signal,* September 2, 2020. https://www.dailysignal.com/2020/09/02/dc-mayor-embraces-report-calling-for-removal-or-contextualization-of-washington-monument/.

CHAPTER FOUR
## Red in the Streets: The Foot Soldiers of Communism

87 *According to estimates*: Jennifer A. Kingson, "Exclusive: $1 Billion-plus Riot Damage Is Most Expensive in Insurance History," *Axios*, September 16, 2020, https://www.axios .com/2020/09/16/riots-cost-property-damage.

87 *In total, the street violence*: Lois Beckett, "At Least 25 Americans Were Killed During Protests and Political Unrest in 2020," *Guardian*, October 31, 2020, https://www.theguardian.com /world/2020/oct/31/americans-killed-protests-political -unrest-acled.

91 *"working people's comrades"*: Billy Moncure, "How Communists in Germany Allied with Nazis to Destroy Democracy," War History Online, September 28, 2018, https://www.warhistory online.com/instant-articles/communists-allied-with-nazis .html?D2c=1&A1c=1.

92 *According to the SA itself, a full 55 percent*: Timothy Scott Brown, *Weimar Radicals: Nazis and Communists Between Authenticity and Performance* (New York: Berghahn, 2009), p. 139.

94 *"Be careful not to leave fingerprints"*: "Fashion Tips for the Brave," CrimethInc., October 11, 2008, https://crimethinc .com/2008/10/11/fashion-tips-for-the-brave.

94 *"spraypaint, projectiles, slingshots"*: "Blocs, Black and Otherwise," CrimethInc., November 20, 2003, https://crimethinc .com/2003/11/20/blocs-black-and-otherwise.

95 *The group even has a hotline*: Whitney Mallett, "California Anti-Fascists Want Racists and the Trump Administration to Be Afraid," *Vice*, May 9, 2017, https://www.vice.com/en /article/3d9d4k/the-bay-areas-antifa-movements-are-alive -and-well-v24n4.

95  *On its website, the group compiles*: "Frequently Asked Questions: What Is Fascism?" Rose City Antifa, accessed January 2, 2023, https://rosecityantifa.org/about/.

96  *if their mug shots are any indication*: Seriously, look at these people: https://twitter.com/mrandygo/status/1347901451 188776962.

96  *According to a December 2012 Kenosha County*: Laura Collins, "Kyle Rittenhouse's second victim had a violent criminal past, assaulting family members by threatening to 'gut his brother like a pig' and burn down their home, defense for Kenosha shooter argues," *Daily Mail*, November 5, 2021, https://www.dailymail.co.uk/news/article-10169537/Witness-testifies-Kyle-Rittenhouses-victim-asked-bluntly-shot.html.

97  *Grosskreutz had a long history*: Laura Collins, "EXCLUSIVE: Prosecution's star witness in Kyle Rittenhouse case is a career criminal with a history of domestic abuse, prowling, trespass and burglary—but had charges DROPPED just six days before trial began and jury never learned of his past," *Daily Mail*, November 15, 2021, https://www.dailymail.co.uk/news/article-10203911/Sole-survivor-Kyle-Rittenhouse-career-criminal-charges-dropped-just-trial.html.

97  *In December 2002, a court in Pima County, Arizona*: Michael Ruiz and Paul Best, "Kyle Rittenhouse Trial: Who Are Joseph Rosenbaum, Anthony Huber, and Gaige Grosskreutz?" Fox News, November 17, 2021, https://www.foxnews.com/us/kyle-rittenhouse-trial-who-are-joseph-rosenbaum-anthony-huber-and-gaige-gross-kreutz.

98  *Kenosha County assistant district attorney Thomas Binger*: Eric Levenson, Carma Hassan, and Brad Parks, "Prosecution Says

Kyle Rittenhouse Provoked Fatal Shootings, While Defense Says He Feared for His Life," CNN, November 15, 202, https://www.cnn.com/2021/11/15/us/kyle-rittenhouse-verdict-wisconsin-national-guard/index.html.

98  *Willem Van Spronsen attempted*: Hannah Allam and Jim Urquhart, "'I Am Antifa': One Activist's Violent Death Became a Symbol for the Right and Left," NPR, July 23, 2020, https://www.npr.org/2020/07/23/893533916/i-am-antifa-one-activist-s-violent-death-became-a-symbol-for-the-right-and-left.

99  *In an Instagram post*: Lee Brown, "Man Suspected in Deadly Portland Shooting Calls Himself '100% ANTIFA,'" *New York Post*, August 31, 2020, https://nypost.com/2020/08/31/man-suspected-in-deadly-portland-shooting-is-100-antifa/.

99  *"We can take out the trash on our own"*: https://twitter.com/MrAndyNgo/status/1299956667287703553.

100  *a spray-painted message*: Andy Ngo, "How a Portland Radical Murdered a Trump Supporter—and Became a Hero for Antifa," *New York Post*, January 30, 2021, https://nypost.com/2021/01/30/how-a-portland-radical-murdered-a-trump-supporter/.

100  *"not a group or an organization"*: Eric Tucker and Ben Fox, "FBI Director Says Antifa Is an Ideology, Not an Organization," AP News, September 17, 2020, https://apnews.com/article/donald-trump-ap-top-news-elections-james-comey-politics-bdd3b6078e9efadcfcd0be4b65f2362e.

101  *According to the Armed Conflict Location & Event Data Project*: Lois Beckett, "At Least 25 Americans Were Killed during Protests and Political Unrest in 2020," *Guardian*,

October 31, 2020, https://www.theguardian.com/world /2020/oct/31/americans-killed-protests-political -unrest-acled.

101 *The summer of BLM is estimated*: Jennifer A. Kingson, "Exclusive: $1 Billion-plus Riot Damage Is Most Expensive in Insurance History," *Axios*, Sep 16, 2020, https://www.axios .com/2020/09/16/riots-cost-property-damage.

102 *Grant Napear*: Chuck Barney, "Sacramento Kings Announcer Grant Napear Fired after Black Lives Matter Backlash," *Mercury News*, June 2, 2020, https://www.mercurynews .com/2020/06/02/kings-announcer-grant-napear-fired-after -black-lives-matter-backlash/.

102 *Stan Wischnowski*: Marc Tracy, "Top Editor of Philadelphia Inquirer Resigns After 'Buildings Matter' Headline," *New York Times*, June 6, 2020, https://www.nytimes.com/2020/06/06 /business/media/editor-philadephia-inquirer-resigns .html.

102 *Several Cisco employees were fired*: Katie Canalesl, "A 'handful' of Cisco employees were fired after posting offensive comments objecting to the company's support of the Black Lives Matter movement," *Business Insider*, July 17, 2020, https:// www.businessinsider.com/cisco-employees-fired-racist -comments-black-lives-matter-2020-7.

102 *Tiffany Riley*: Amanda Woods, "Vermont Principal Placed on Leave over 'Insanely Tone-Deaf' Black Lives Matter Post," *New York Post*, June 15, 2020, https://nypost.com/2020/06/15 /vermont-principal-placed-on-leave-over-facebook-post-on -blm/.

102 *Heather McVey*: Nikita Biryukov, "Woman Fired for Posting anti–Black Lives Matter Comments Loses Appeal," *New*

*Jersey Monitor,* May 20, 2022, https://newjerseymonitor .com/2022/05/20/woman-fired-for-posting-anti-black-lives -matter-comments-loses-appeal/.

103   *"When I trained in sociology, we would read Marx"*: Julia Carrie Wong, "The Bay Area Roots of Black Lives Matter," *SF Weekly,* November 11, 2015, https://www.sfweekly.com/news/the -bay-area-roots-of-black-lives-matter/.

103   *"not possible for a world to emerge where black lives matter"*: Mike Gonzalez, *BLM: The Making of a New Marxist Revolution* (New York: Encounter Books, 2021).

103   *"We're talking about changing how we've organized this country"*: Dan Neumann, "Black Lives Matter Co-founder: Maine Can Be a Leader in Dismantling White Nationalism," *Maine Beacon,* June 28, 2019, https://mainebeacon.com/black-lives -matter-co-founder-maine-can-be-a-leader-in-dismantling -white-nationalism/.

103   *"I do believe in Marxism"*: Jeffrey Cawood, "'Trained Marxist' BLM Co-Founder Releases YouTube Video 'to Set the Record Straight,'" *Daily Wire,* December 22, 2020, https://www .dailywire.com/news/trained-marxist-blm-co-founder -releases-youtube-video-to-set-the-record-straight.

104   *Cullors spent her early years*: Juan Gonzalez and Amy Goodman, "'When They Call You a Terrorist': The Life of Black Lives Matter Co-Founder Patrisse Khan-Cullors," *Democracy Now!,* January 16, 2018, https://www.democracynow .org/2018/1/16/when_they_call_you_a_terrorist.

104   *In 2015, she penned a letter*: Opal Tometi, "Black Lives Matter Network Denounces U.S. 'Continuing Intervention' in Venezuela," VenezuelaAnalysis.com, December 16, 2015, https:// venezuelanalysis.com/analysis/11789.

104 *That same year, Tometi met with Nicolas Maduro*: "VIDEO: Venezuelan President Nicolás Maduro in Harlem: 'Put People Before Profits & Capital,'" *Democracy Now!*, October 3, 2015, https://www.democracynow.org/2015/10/3/video _venezuelan_president_nicolas_maduro_in.

105 *According to Human Rights Watch*: "Venezuela: Events of 2019," Human Rights Watch, https://www.hrw.org/world -report/2020/country-chapters/Venezuela.

105 *The regime also carried out raids*: Ibid.

105 *Following the death of Castro in 2016*: Black Lives Matter Global Network, "Lessons from Fidel: Black Lives Matter and the Transition of El Comandante," Medium.com, November 27, 2016, https://medium.com/@BlackLivesMatter Network/lessons-from-fidel-black-lives-matter-and-the -transition-of-el-comandante-c11ee5e51fb0.

106 *"Blacks in Cuba know"*: "A Barrier for Cuba's Blacks," *Miami Herald*, June 20, 2007, http://media.miamiherald.com/multi media/news/afrolatin/part4/index.html.

106 *In 2020 alone, the Black Lives Matter Global Network Foundation*: Nicholas Kulish, "After Raising $90 Million in 2020, Black Lives Matter Has $42 Million in Assets," *New York Times*, May 17, 2022, https://www.nytimes.com/2022/05/17/business /blm-black-lives-matter-finances.html.

107 *According to the group's financial disclosures*: Ibid.

107 *In October 2020, the group purchased a mansion*: Isabel Vincent, "BLM's LA Mansion Sold for 250 Percent More than the Price of Similar Homes in the Area," *New York Post*, April 6, 2022, https://nypost.com/2022/04/06/blms-la-mansion-sold -for-250-times-the-price-of-other-homes-in-the-neighbor hood/.

107 *In July 2021, the* New York Post *reported*: Isabel Vincent, "Black Lives Matter Sent Millions to Canada Charity to Buy Mansion," *New York Post*, January 29, 2022, https://nypost .com/2022/01/29/black-lives-matter-sent-millions-to -canada-charity-m4bj-for-mansion/.

107 *$1.4 million compound in Topanga, California*: Isabel Vincent, "Marxist BLM Leader Buys $1.4 Million Home in Ritzy LA Enclave," *New York Post*, April 10, 2021, https://nypost .com/2021/04/10/marxist-blm-leader-buys-1-4-million -home-in-ritzy-la-enclave/.

108 *In November 2020, ten chapters*: Zack Linly, "10 Black Lives Matter Chapters Pen Open Letter Criticizing BLM Global Network for Lack of Transparency in Decision Making," *The Root*, December 10, 2020, https://www.theroot.com /10-black-lives-matter-chapters-pen-open-letter-criticiz -1845850690.

108 *Fidel Castro, for example*: Keith Flamer, "10 Surprises About Fidel Castro's Extravagant Life," *Forbes*, November 26, 2016, https://www.forbes.com/sites/keithflamer/2016/11 /26/10-surprises-about-castros-extravagant-life/?sh=5f5d4 0366d76.

108 *Hugo Chavez is believed to have amassed*: Hugo Gye and Jill Reilly, "Was Chavez worth over $1bn when he died? Intelligence analyst claims he amassed huge fortune from country's oil wealth," *Daily Mail*, March 7, 2013, https://www.dailymail .co.uk/news/article-2289427/Was-Hugo-Chavez-worth-1bn -died-Claims-amassed-huge-fortune-countrys-oil-wealth .html.

110 *One vocal resident demanded that white people*: Isabel Vincent, "Protester in Seattle's CHAZ Demands White Demonstrators

Give Out Cash," *New York Post*, June 13, 2020, https://nypost
.com/2020/06/13/protester-in-seattles-chaz-demands
-white-people-give-out-cash/.

110  *One business owner, whose car repair shop*: Deedee Sun, "'Nobody showed up': 911 calls bring no response after break in
at auto shop near Capitol Hill protest zone," KIRO 7, June 15,
2020,   https://www.kiro7.com/news/local/nobody-showed
-up-911-calls-bring-no-response-after-break-auto-shop
-near-capitol-hill-protest-zone/O42CQ6VUXVDBHIB
3334DI7LPV4/.

111  *According to the Seattle Police Department*: KING 5 Staff, "25
Arrested during Overnight Protests after Seattle Police Dismantle 'CHOP,'" KING 5, July 1, 2020, https://www.king5
.com/article/news/local/protests/seattle-police-capitol-hill
-chop-chaz/281-6253a20a-127b-4cd7-93dd-43f3f008afd0.

111  *In a June 2020 article*: Andy Ngo, "My Terrifying Five-Day
Stay Inside Seattle's Cop-Free CHAZ," *New York Post*, June
20, 2020, https://nypost.com/2020/06/20/my-terrifying-5
-day-stay-inside-seattles-autonomous-zone/.

111  *"with an armed entourage"*: Ben Feuerherd and Laura Italiano,
"Rapper Raz Simone Accused of Being 'Warlord' in Seattle's
Police-Free CHAZ," *New York Post*, June 12, 2020, https://
nypost.com/2020/06/12/raz-simone-accused-of-acting-like
-warlord-in-seattles-chaz/.

112  *Seattle mayor Jenny Durkan described*: Ian Schwartz, "Seattle Mayor Durkan: CHAZ Has A 'Block Party Atmosphere,' Could Turn Into 'Summer Of Love,'" RealClear
Politics, June 12, 2020, https://www.realclearpolitics.com
/video/2020/06/12/seattle_mayor_durkan_chaz_has_a

_block_party_atmosphere_could_turn_into_summer_of
_love.html.

112  *Lori Patrick, a spokesperson*: Oliver Darcey, "Right-Wing
Media Says Antifa Militants Have Seized Part of Seattle. Local
Authorities Say Otherwise," CNN, June 11, 2020, https://
www.cnn.com/2020/06/11/media/seattle-antifa-protest
-trump/index.html.

112  *Washington governor Jay Inslee*: Heidi Groover, "Trump, Inslee
Trade Twitter Barbs over Capitol Hill Protest Zone Known
as CHAZ," *Seattle Times*, June 11, 2020, https://www.seattle
times.com/seattle-news/trump-inslee-trade-twitter-barbs
-over-capitol-hill-protest-zone-known-as-chaz/.

112  *"into a center of peaceful protest"*: Katelyn Burns, "Seattle's Newly
Police-Free Neighborhood, Explained," *Vox*, June 16, 2020,
https://www.vox.com/identities/2020/6/16/21292723
/chaz-seattle-police-free-neighborhood.

112  *"a peaceful realm"*: Rosette Royale, "Seattle's Autonomous
Zone Is Not What You've Been Told," *Rolling Stone*, June 19,
2020, https://www.rollingstone.com/culture/culture-features
/chop-chaz-seattle-autonomous-zone-inside-protests-1017
637/.

112  *"an anti-capitalist vision of community sovereignty"*: Hanna Wal-
lis, "The Rich Legacy of Autonomous Zones in the Americas,"
*Nation*, June 23, 2020. https://www.thenation.com/article
/society/seattle-chaz-chop/.

112  *"passionate about achieving racial equality and justice"*: Jack
Kelly, "Meet Raz Simone, the Alleged 'Warlord' of the Capitol Hill Autonomous Zone," *Forbes*, June 14, 2020, https://
www.forbes.com/sites/jackkelly/2020/06/14/meet-raz

-simone-the-alleged-warlord-of-the-capitol-hill-autonomous
-zone/?sh=5b6dfc45523f.

114    *the foundation contributed $1.5 million*: Robert Stilson, "The
Organizational Structure of Black Lives Matter," Capital Research Center, June 18, 2020, https://capitalresearch.org
/article/the-organizational-structure-of-black-lives-matter/.

114    *The W. K. Kellogg Foundation*: Ibid.

114    *In July 2020, Amazon announced*: Amazon, "Amazon Donates
$10 Million to Organizations Supporting Justice and Equity,"
Amazon press release, July 14, 2020, https://www.about
amazon.com/news/policy-news-views/amazon-donates
-10-million-to-organizations-supporting-justice-and-equity.

115    *"Violent, criminal acts committed"*: FBI, "What We Investigate: Terrorism Definitions," https://www.fbi.gov/investigate
/terrorism.

116    *In 2019, the pair introduced a resolution*: Ted Cruz, "Sens. Cruz,
Cassidy: Antifa Is a Domestic Terrorist Organization," July 18,
2019,   https://www.cruz.senate.gov/newsroom/press-releases
/sens-cruz-cassidy-antifa-is-a-domestic-terrorist-organization.

118    *"It's the least we can do"*: Larry Krasner, "District Attorney Krasner Statement on Trump Administration Actions Targeting
Cities," Philadelphia District Attorney's Office, July 20, 2020,
https://medium.com/philadelphia-justice/district-attorney
-krasner-statement-on-trump-administration-actions
-targeting-cities-f5a8add29d59.

118    *more than four hundred people were arrested*: Heather Che-
rone, "Foxx Pushes Back on Criticism from Lightfoot, Brown
after Looting," WTTW, August 10, 2020, https://news.wttw
.com/2020/08/10/foxx-pushes-back-criticism-lightfoot
-brown-after-looting.

CHAPTER FIVE
## American Red-ucation

121   *"Among the elementary measures"*: William Z. Foster, *Toward Soviet America* (New York: Coward-McCann, 1932), p. 316.

123   *"replace home education by social"*: Marx and Engels, *Manifesto of the Communist Party,* p. 40.

123   *"give me four years to teach the children"*: Harry J. Greenwall, *Mirrors of Moscow* (London: G. G. Harrap, 1929), p. 241.

124   *"the bourgeois clap-trap"*: Marx and Engels, *Manifesto of the Communist Party,* p. 40.

126   *In 1937, Richard Frank*: U.S. Congress, Senate, Committee on the Judiciary, Scope of Soviet Activity in the United States: Hearing Before the Subcommittee to Investigate the Administration of the Internal Security Act and Other Internal Security Laws of the Committee on the Judiciary, 84th Congress, 2nd session, May 31, 1956, p. 507.

126   *The most notable union*: U.S. Congress, Senate, Committee on the Judiciary, Subversive Influence in the Educational Process: Hearing Before the Subcommittee to Investigate the Administration of the Internal Security Act and Other Internal Security Laws of the Committee on the Judiciary, 82nd Congress, 2nd session, September 8, 9, 10, 23, 24, 25, and October 13, 1952.

127   *"skillfully inject it into their teachings"*: Scope of Soviet Activity in the United States, p. 2641.

127   *In it, Langford explains*: Howard Langford, *Education and the Social Conflict* (New York: Macmillan, 1936).

129   *"The rebelliousness of school children"*: Subversive Influence in the Educational Process, p. 382.

130   *"must interpret academic freedom"*: California Legislature,

Senate, Report of the Senate Fact-Finding Committee on Un-American Activities, p. 157.

135  *The School Superintendents Association promised*: AASA, "AASA Issues Statement on Recent Events and Racial Inequality in Our Nation," June 3, 2020, https://aasa.org/content.aspx?id=44754.

135  *the National Council for the Social Studies*: Max Eden, "The 'Anti-Racist' Drive to Turn Schools into Woke Propaganda Mills," *New York Post*, June 22, 2020, https://nypost.com /2020/06/22/the-anti-racist-drive-to-turn-schools-into -woke-propaganda-mills/.

135  *"apply the power of language and literacy"*: National Council of Teachers of English, "NCTE Takes a Stance Against Racism," June 1, 2020, https://ncte.org/blog/2020/06/ncte-takes-stance -racism/.

136  *Units of Study*: Daniel Buck and James Furey, "Units of Indoc-trination," *City Journal*, November 24, 2021, https://www .city-journal.org/critical-race-theory-in-the-classroom.

137  *Historian Leslie Harris*: Leslie Harris, "I Helped Fact-Check the 1619 Project. The Times Ignored Me," *Politico*, March 6, 2020, https://www.politico.com/news/magazine/2020/03 /06/1619-project-new-york-times-mistake-122248.

137  *Underrepresentation Curriculum Project*: "The Underrepresen-tation Curriculum Project," https://underrep.com/.

138  *"critical approaches to dismantling white supremacy"*: Sam Dor-man, "Oregon Promotes Teacher Program That Seeks to Undo 'Racism in Mathematics,'" Fox News, February 12, 2021, https://www.foxnews.com/us/oregon-education-math -white-supremacy.

138  *"Math Ethnic Studies Framework"*: Seattle Public Schools, "K–12 Math Ethnic Studies Framework (20.08.2019)," https://www

.k12.wa.us/sites/default/files/public/socialstudies/pub docs/Math%20SDS%20ES%20Framework.pdf.

138 *"Let's be clear: Critical race theory is not"*: Caitlin O'Kane, "Head of Teachers Union Says Critical Race Theory Isn't Taught in Schools, Vows to Defend 'Honest History,'" CBS News, July 8, 2021, https://www.cbsnews.com/news/critical-race-theory-teachers-union-honest-history/.

144 *homeschooled kids typically score 15 to 30 points above*: Brian D. Ray, "Homeschooling: The Research," National Home Education Research Institute, September 15, 2022, https://www.nheri.org/research-facts-on-homeschooling/.

145 *According to a 2015 study*: Michael G. Vaughn et al., "Are Homeschooled Adolescents Less Likely to Use Alcohol, Tobacco, and Other Drugs?," *Drug and Alcohol Dependence* 155 (2015): 97–104, https://www.ncbi.nlm.nih.gov/pmc/articles/PMC4652803/.

**CHAPTER SIX**

## Climate Communism: Green on the Outside, Red on the Inside

155 *In 2003, Jurassic Park author Michael Crichton*: Mark J. Perry, "Michael Crichton in 2003: Environmentalism Is a Religion," American Enterprise Institute, April 17, 2019, https://www.aei.org/carpe-diem/michael-chrichton-in-2003-environmentalism-is-a-religion/.

161 *If left unchecked, a full meltdown*: Lisa Horner, "Chernobyl: A Short History of the Human Impact on Ukraine and Its Neighbors," *Geohistory*, May 6, 2009, https://geohistory.today/chernobyl-short-history-human-impact/.

161 *Later effects included*: Erin Blakemore, "The Chernobyl Disas-

ter: What Happened, and the Long-Term Impact," *National Geographic*, May 20, 2019, https://www.nationalgeographic.co.uk/environment/2019/05/chernobyl-disaster-what-happened-and-long-term-impact.

161 *some experts claiming*: Story Hinckley, "Chernobyl Will Be Unhabitable for at Least 3,000 Years, Say Nuclear Experts," *Christian Science Monitor*, April 24, 2016, https://www.csmonitor.com/World/Global-News/2016/0424/Chernobyl-will-be-unhabitable-for-at-least-3-000-years-say-nuclear-experts.

162 *Radioactive material was absorbed*: European Parliament Briefing, "Chernobyl 30 Years On: Environmental and Health Effects," April 22, 2016, https://www.europarl.europa.eu/thinktank/en/document/EPRS_BRI(2016)581972.

163 *It wasn't until after the fall of the Soviet Union*: Francis X. Clines, "Soviets Now Admit '57 Nuclear Blast," *New York Times*, June 18, 1989, https://www.nytimes.com/1989/06/18/world/soviets-now-admit-57-nuclear-blast.html.

163 *The consequences of the incident remain*: Tony Wesolowsky, "The Russian Villagers Living in the Shadow of a Nuclear Tragedy," Radio Free Europe, December 16, 2017, https://www.rferl.org/a/russia-mayak-villagers-living-in-shadow-nuclear-tragedy/28921944.html.

164 *"40% of the Soviet people"*: James Ridgeway, "Environmental Devastation in the Soviet Union," *Multinational Monitor* 11, no. 9 (September 1990), https://www.multinationalmonitor.org/hyper/issues/1990/09/ridgeway.html.

164 *"arguably one of the greatest environmental crimes"*: Charles Homans, "The Most Senseless Environmental Crime of the 20th Century," *Pacific Standard*, November 12, 2013, https://

psmag.com/social-justice/the-senseless-environment-crime
-of-the-20th-century-russia-whaling-67774.

164 *Writer Charles Homans described*: Ibid.

165 *"Whalers knew that no matter what"*: Alfred Berzin, "The Truth
About Soviet Whaling: A Memoir," *Publications, Agencies and
Staff of the U.S. Department of Commerce*, 2008, https://digital
commons.unl.edu/usdeptcommercepub/12.

167 *U.S. National Academy of Sciences estimated*: Dr. J. Gordon
Edwards, "Malaria: The Killer That Could Have Been Conquered," *21st Century Science & Technology* 6, no. 2 (Summer
1993), https://calepa.ca.gov/wp-content/uploads/sites/6
/2016/10/CEPC-2013yr-Feb28-Comments-AppA_Ex17
.pdf.

167 *Carson also argued that DDT*: Robert Zubrin, "The Truth
About DDT and Silent Spring," *New Atlantis*, September
27, 2012, https://www.thenewatlantis.com/publications/the
-truth-about-ddt-and-silent-spring.

167 *Agriculture secretary Ezra Taft Benson*: Mark Stoll, "Rachel
Carson's *Silent Spring*, a Book That Changed the World," Environment & Society Portal, *Virtual Exhibitions* 2012, no. 1, Rachel Carson Center for Environment and Society, https://doi
.org/10.5282/rcc/3517.

167 *In the years that followed its publication*: Deepal Lal, "Bring Back
DDT," Cato Institute, April 26, 2016, https://www.cato.org
/commentary/bring-back-ddt.

168 *As a result, tens of millions of people died*: Paul A. Offit, "How
Rachel Carson Cost Millions of People Their Lives," *Daily
Beast*, April 11, 2017, https://www.thedailybeast.com/how
-rachel-carson-cost-millions-of-people-their-lives.

169 *Ira Einhorn*: *Commonwealth of Pennsylvania v. Ira Einhorn*, 2006, https://caselaw.findlaw.com/pa-superior-court/1030 703.html.

172 *"includes environmental equity and justice"*: U.S. Department of Defense, "DOD Announces Plan to Tackle Climate Crisis," Office of the Deputy Assistant Secretary of Defense for Environment and Energy Resilience, October 7, 2021, https://www .defense.gov/News/News-Stories/Article/Article/2787056 /dod-announces-plan-to-tackle-climate-crisis/.

172 *Texas Commission on Environmental Quality*: Brad Johnson, "Texas Governmental Agency Launches 'Environmental Justice' Initiative," *Texan*, April 30, 2021, https://thetexan .news/texas-governmental-agency-launches-environmental -justice-initiative/.

174 *"[W]e should facilitate"*: Thomas Robert Malthus, *An Essay on the Principle of Population: The 1803 Edition* (New Haven, CT: Yale University Press, 2018), p. 407.

175 *"The battle to feed all of humanity is over"*: Dr. Paul R. Ehrlich, *The Population Bomb*, rev. ed. (River City Press, 1975), pp. xi–xii.

176 *"Overt coercion became the rule"*: Robert Zubrin, "The Population Control Holocaust," *New Atlantis* 35 (Spring 2012): 33–54. (Adapted from Zubrin's book *Merchants of Despair: Radical Environmentalists, Criminal Pseudo-Scientists, and the Fatal Cult of Antihumanism.*)

177 *In 1976 alone, more than 6.2 million men*: Hannah Harris Green, "The Legacy of India's Quest to Sterilise Millions of Men," *Quartz*, October 6, 2018, https://qz.com/india/1414774 /the-legacy-of-indias-quest-to-sterilise-millions-of-men.

177 *"At long last"*: Dylan Matthews and Byrd Pinkerton, "'The

Time of Vasectomy': How American Foundations Fueled a Terrible Atrocity in India," *Vox*, June 5, 2019, https://www .vox.com/future-perfect/2019/6/5/18629801/emergency -in-india-1975-indira-gandhi-sterilization-ford-foundation.

181  *price tag of close to $100 trillion*: Douglas Holtz-Eakin, Dan Bosch, et al., "The Green New Deal: Scope, Scale, and Implications," American Action Forum, February 25, 2019, https:// www.americanactionforum.org/research/the-green-new -deal-scope-scale-and-implications/.

182  *The once-pristine area*: Valerie Richardson, "Dakota Access Protest Camp: Crews Haul Off 48 Million Pounds of Garbage, Debris," *Washington Times*, March 1, 2017, https://www .washingtontimes.com/news/2017/mar/1/dakota-access -protest-camp-crews-haul-48-million-p/.

182  *Army Corps of Engineers*: U.S. Army Corps of Engineers, "Corps Closes Federal Property Adjacent to Cannonball River for Safety, Environmental Concerns," press release, February 3, 2017, https://www.nwd.usace.army.mil/Media/News -Releases/Article/1071286/corps-closes-federal-property -adjacent-to-cannonball-river-for-safety-environme/.

184  *According to a 2021 study*: Caroline Hickman et al., "Climate anxiety in children and young people and their beliefs about government responses to climate change: a global survey," *Lancet* 5, no. 12 (December 1, 2021), https://doi.org/10.1016 /S2542-5196(21)00278-3.

185  *"each Federal agency"*: William J. Clinton, Executive Order 12898: Federal Actions to Address Environmental Justice in Minority Populations and Low-Income Populations, February 11, 1994.

186  *"EPA today may be said"*: Jack Lewis, "The Birth of EPA," *EPA*

*Journal,* November 1985, https://www.epa.gov/archive/epa
/aboutepa/birth-epa.html.

186 *Between 1979 and 2018:* "It's Time to End Subsidies for Renewable Energy," America's Power, April 17, 2020, https://
americaspower.org/its-time-to-end-subsidies-for-renewable
-energy/.

187 *announced in 2021 that it would invest:* Darren W. Woods,
"Why We're Investing $15 Billion in a Lower-Carbon Fu-
ture," Exxon Mobil press release, November 9, 2021, https://
corporate.exxonmobil.com/News/Newsroom/News
-releases/2021/1109_Why-we-are-investing-15-billion-in-a
-lower-carbon-future.

187 *federal direct subsidies:* Savannah Bertrand, "Fact Sheet: Proposals to Reduce Fossil Fuel Subsidies (2021)," Environmental and Energy Study Institute, July 23, 2021, https://www
.eesi.org/papers/view/fact-sheet-proposals-to-reduce-fossil
-fuel-subsidies-2021.

## CHAPTER SEVEN
## Communist Gun Control: Disarming the Victims

190 *"Political power grows out of the barrel of a gun":* Mao Zedong,
*Problems of War and Strategy, Selected Works of Mao Tse-
tung,* vol. 2, November 6, 1938, https://www.marxists.org
/reference/archive/mao/selected-works/volume-2
/mswv2_12.htm.

191 *"when the resolution to enslaving America":* George Mason, Debate in Virginia Ratifying Convention, June 1788, https://
press-pubs.uchicago.edu/founders/documents/a1_8_12s27
.html.

191  *"To preserve liberty, it is essential"*: Richard Henry Lee, "Federal Farmer XCIII," January 25, 1788, https://press-pubs.uchicago .edu/founders/documents/a1_8_15s11.html,https://teaching americanhistory.org/document/federal-farmer-xviii/.

192  *"Under no pretext should arms and ammunition"*: Karl Marx and Frederick Engels, "Address of the Central Committee to the Communist League," March 1850, https://www.marxists.org /archive/marx/works/1847/communist-league/1850-ad1 .htm.

195  *"What kind of militia do we need"*: V. I. Lenin, "Third Letter Concerning a Proletarian Militia," March 11, 1917, https:// www.marxists.org/archive/lenin/works/1917/lfafar/third .htm.

196  *"To ensure the sovereign power"*: V. I. Lenin, "Declaration of Rights of the Working and Exploited People," January 3, 1918, https://www.marxists.org/archive/lenin/works/1918 /jan/03.htm.

196  *members of the Communist Party were exempt*: José Niño, "A Brief History of Repressive Regimes and Their Gun Laws," Mises Institute, October 13, 2018, https://mises.org/wire /brief-history-repressive-regimes-and-their-gun-laws.

196  *"it is necessary to secure the Soviet Republic"*: Council of People's Commissars, "Resolution on Red Terror," September 5, 1918, https://soviethistory.msu.edu/1917-2/state-security /state-security-texts/resolution-on-red-terror/.

196  *"the anthem of the working class"*: Danny Bird, "How the 'Red Terror' Exposed the True Turmoil of Soviet Russia 100 Years Ago," *Time*, September 5, 2018, https://time.com/5386789 /red-terror-soviet-history/.

197 *"We are not carrying out war against individuals"*: Harrison E. Salisbury, *Black Night, White Snow: Russia's Revolutions, 1905–1917* (New York: Doubleday, 1978), p. 565.

199 *"This is how democracy works"*: "Cuba: Lay Those Rifles Down, Boys," *Time*, September 3, 1965, https://content.time.com /time/subscriber/article/0,33009,842045,00.html.

200 *"Fidel Castro defused the situation"*: Miguel A. Faria, Jr., "America, Guns, and Freedom. Part I: A Recapitulation of Liberty," *Surgical Neurology International*, October 29, 2012, https:// www.ncbi.nlm.nih.gov/pmc/articles/PMC3513846/.

200 *The island's state-run radio station Radio Havana*: "Cuba: Lay Those Rifles Down, Boys," *Time*, September 3, 1965, https://content.time.com/time/subscriber/article /0,33009,842045,00.html.

202 *It's estimated that between $11 and $300 billion*: "Black Gold in Swiss Vaults: Venezuelan Elites Hid Stolen Oil Money in Credit Suisse," Organized Crime and Corruption Reporting Project, February 20, 2022, https://www.occrp.org/en/suisse -secrets/black-gold-in-swiss-vaults-venezuelan-elites-hid -stolen-oil-money-in-credit-suisse.

202 *The number of murders, kidnappings, and armed robberies*: Girish Gupta and San Casimiro, "Will Venezuela's Pandemic of Crime Destabilize Hugo Chávez's Regime?" *Time*, September 25, 2012, https://world.time.com/2012/09/25/will -venezuelas-pandemic-of-crime-destabilize-hugo-chavezs -regime/.

202 *Venezuela's murder rate increased*: José Niño, "Gun Control Preceded the Tyranny in Venezuela," Foundation for Economic Education, January 22, 2019, https://fee.org/articles /gun-control-preceded-the-tyranny-in-venezuela/.

204  *the first being enacted by New Jersey in 1686*: Robert J. Spitzer, "Gun Law History in the United States and Second Amendment Rights," *Law and Contemporary Problems* 80 (2017): 55–83, http://scholarship.law.duke.edu/lcp/vol80/iss2/3.

204  *with Alabama even passing*: Ibid.

204  *In Arkansas*: Ibid.

205  *In subsequent years, states*: Ibid.

205  *"For some time this country"*: Congressional Record, Proceedings and Debates of the Second Session of the Seventy-Third Congress of the United States of America, Volume 78, Part 10, p. 11400.

206  *"A machine gun, of course"*: Ronald G. Shafer, "They Were Killers with Submachine Guns. Then the President Went after Their Weapons," *Washington Post*, August 9, 2019, https://www.washingtonpost.com/history/2019/08/09/they-were-killers-with-machine-guns-then-president-went-after-their-weapons/.

206  *Clyde Barrow, for example*: Jeff Guinn, *Go Down Together: The True, Untold Story of Bonnie and Clyde* (New York: Simon & Schuster, 2010), pp. 206–7.

206  *Bank robber John Dillinger*: Carson Gerber, "Peru Officials Seek Tommy Gun Stolen by John Dillinger," *Courier & Press*, March 25, 2016, https://www.courierpress.com/story/news/local/2016/03/25/peru-officials-seek-tommy-gun-stolen-by-john-dillinger/87127298/.

207  *Pretty Boy Floyd carried out*: FBI, "Kansas City Massacre and 'Pretty Boy' Floyd," Famous Cases & Criminals, https://www.fbi.gov/history/famous-cases/kansas-city-massacre-pretty-boy-floyd.

207  *purchased by his wife, Kathryn*: FBI, "George 'Machine Gun'

Kelly," Famous Cases & Criminals, https://www.fbi.gov
/history/famous-cases/machine-gun-kelly.

207  *"I do not believe"*: Michael S. Rosenwald, "The NRA Once
Believed in Gun Control and Had a Leader Who Pushed
for It," *Washington Post*, February 22, 2018, https://www
.washingtonpost.com/news/retropolis/wp/2017/10/05
/the-forgotten-nra-leader-who-despised-the-promiscuous
-toting-of-guns/.

208  *"the measure as a whole"*: Arica L. Coleman, "When the NRA
Supported Gun Control," *Time*, July 29, 2016, https://time
.com/4431356/nra-gun-control-history/.

208  *"I asked for the national registration"*: Lyndon B. Johnson,
Remarks Upon Signing the Gun Control Act of 1968, October 22, 1960, https://www.presidency.ucsb.edu/documents
/remarks-upon-signing-the-gun-control-act-1968.

209  *"The best kept secret"*: David Sherfinski, "Wayne LaPierre,
NRA CEO: Need for More Background Checks an 'Absolute
Fallacy,'" *Washington Times*, January 6, 2016, https://www
.washingtontimes.com/news/2016/jan/6/nras-lapierre
-need-more-background-checks-fallacy/.

209  *"[W]e all know there is more to be done"*: William J. Clinton,
Remarks on Signing Handgun Control Legislation, November 30, 1993, https://www.presidency.ucsb.edu/documents
/remarks-signing-handgun-control-legislation.

213  *a 2021 Pew Research survey*: Katherine Schaeffer, "Key Facts
about Americans and Guns," Pew Research Center, September 13, 2021, https://www.pewresearch.org/fact-tank
/2021/09/13/key-facts-about-americans-and-guns/.

214  *Even in New York City*: John R. Lott Jr., *The Bias Against Guns:*

*Why Almost Everything You've Heard about Gun Control Is Wrong* (New York: Regnery, 2003)

**CHAPTER EIGHT**
## Corporate Communism: The Devil's Alliance

219  *"We watch so that nothing"*: U.S..Congress, House of Representatives, Committee on Un-American Activities, Investigation of Un-American Propaganda Activities in the United Sates, 84th Congress, 1st session, February 6, 1947, p. 282.

220  *"despotic inroads"*: Marx and Engels, *Manifesto of the Communist Party*, p. 45.

221  *Marx laid out several key goals*: Ibid., pp. 45–46.

224  *"They were aggressive men"*: Matthew Josephson, *The Robber Barons: The Great American Capitalists, 1861–1901* (New York: Harcourt, 1934), p. vii.

225  *"We believe"*: League of Professional Groups for Foster and Ford, "An open letter to the writers, artists, teachers, physicians, engineers, scientists and other professional workers of America," October 1932, https://www.marxists.org/archive/foster/1932/foster01.htm.

225  *"seemed like the hope of the world"*: Matthew Josephson, *Infidel in the Temple: A Memoir of the Nineteen-Thirties* (New York: Knopf, 1967), p. 191.

225  *"Before people pass judgment on Comrade Stalin"*: Michael Kazin, *American Dreamers: How the Left Changed a Nation* (New York: Vintage Books, 2011), pp. 190–91.

226  *"a temporary condition of evil"*: Andrew B. Wilson, "A Blanket of Silence," *American Spectator*, September 14, 2018, https://spectator.org/a-blanket-of-silence/.

226  *"I have seen the future, and it works"*: Ibid.

226  *"Stalin didn't look upon himself as a dictator"*: Walter Duranty, *Duranty Reports Russia* (New York: Viking Press, 1934), p. 188.

227  *"appears to be quite free from symptoms of megalomania"*: Edgar Snow, *Red Star Over China* (New York: Grove Press, 1968), p. 94.

227  *"You are a very great producer Sam"*: Lou Lumenick, "How Hollywood Turned a Pro-Soviet Epic into Cold War Propaganda," *New York Post*, July 15, 2014, https://nypost .com/2014/07/15/how-hollywood-turned-a-pro-soviet-epic -into-cold-war-propaganda/.

228  *"I pledge myself to rally the masses to defend the Soviet Union"*: J. Peters, *The Communist Party: A Manual on Organization* (New York: Workers Library, 1935), https://www.marxists .org/history/usa/parties/cpusa/1935/07/organisers -manual/ch04.htm.

229  *"to pursue those policies"*: Howard R. Bowen, *Social Responsibility of the Businessman* (New York: Harper, 1953), p. 6.

229  *"[T]he doctrine of 'social responsibility'"*: Milton Friedman, "The Social Responsibility of Business Is to Increase its Profits," *New York Times Magazine*, September 13, 1970, http://websites .umich.edu/~thecore/doc/Friedman.pdf.

231  *If you're lucky enough to live near a Target*: Mey Rude, "Target Now Sells Chest Binders & Packing Underwear, Thanks to TomboyX," Out, May 11, 2022, https://www.out.com /pride/2022/5/11/target-2022-lgbtq-pride-collection-trans gender-nonconforming-tomboyx-binders-packing-briefs.

231  *Starbucks's $100 million pledge*: "Starbucks Expands Initiatives to Advance Opportunity, Equity and Inclusion in the Com-

munities It Serves," Starbucks press release, January 12, 2021, https://stories.starbucks.com/press/2021/starbucks -expands-initiatives-to-advance-opportunity-equity-and -inclusion-in-the-communities-it-serves/.

233 *"Movies can and do have tremendous influence"*: William B. Russell and Stewart Waters, *Reel Character Education: A Cinematic Approach to Character Development* (Charlotte, NC: Information Age, 2010), p. 37.

235 *Latoya Raveneau*: Alexandra Steigrad, "Disney Exec Cops to Advancing 'Gay Agenda' by 'Adding Queerness' to Shows," *New York Post*, March 30, 2022, https://nypost.com/2022/03/30 /disney-producer-cops-to-adding-queerness-to-animated -shows/.

235 The Proud Family: Louder and Prouder: Disney, "About Us: Disney Channels," DGEPress.com, accessed January 15, 2023, https://web.archive.org/web/20210121050804/https:// www.dgepress.com/waltdisneytelevision/about-us/disney -channels/.

235 *"Last summer we removed all gendered"*: Joshua Rhett Miller, "Disney Exec Vows More Gay Characters amid Huge Inclusivity Push," *New York Post*, March 30, 2022, https://nypost .com/2022/03/30/disney-executive-wants-more-lgbtqia -minority-character/.

236 *"bill should never have passed"*: "Statement from the Walt Disney Company on Signing of Florida Legislation," Walt Disney Company press release, March 28, 2022, https://the waltdisneycompany.com/statement-from-the-walt-disney -company-on-signing-of-florida-legislation/.

237 *As of November 2020*: Debbie Carlson, "ESG Investing Now Accounts for One-Third of Total U.S. Assets under Manage-

ment," MarketWatch, November 17, 2020, https://www
.marketwatch.com/story/esg-investing-now-accounts
-for-one-third-of-total-u-s-assets-under-management
-11605626611.

238 *Procter & Gamble and Hewlett-Packard*: "HP, Procter & Gamble Join Companies Pledge to Cut Emissions," Associated
Press, September 20, 2021, https://apnews.com/article
/business-climate-environment-and-nature-science--64ceb
7778952ca3a1d822c176a26addd.

238 *In 2022, researchers*: Sanjai Bhagat, "An Inconvenient Truth
About ESG Investing," *Harvard Business Review*, March 31,
2022, https://hbr.org/2022/03/an-inconvenient-truth-about
-esg-investing.

240 *The corporation essentially went quiet*: Robbie Whelan and
Arian Campo-Flores, "Disney Strategy Is to Stay Silent to
Soften Florida Gov. Ron DeSantis's Blow," *Wall Street Journal*,
April 27, 2022, https://www.wsj.com/articles/disney-strategy
-is-to-stay-silent-to-soften-florida-gov-ron-desantiss
-blow-11651089850

242 *According to Google, the decision*: Ashley Gold and Shawna
Chen, "Google Suspends Parler from App Store after Deadly
Capitol Violence," *Axios*, January 8, 2021, https://www.axios
.com/2021/01/09/capitol-mob-parler-google-ban.

242 *According to a report in Reuters*: Mark Hosenball and Sarah N.
Lynch, "Exclusive: FBI Finds Scant Evidence U.S. Capitol Attack Was Coordinated—Sources," Reuters, August 20, 2021,
https://www.reuters.com/world/us/exclusive-fbi-finds-scant
-evidence-us-capitol-attack-was-coordinated-sources-2021
-08-20/.

245 *Texas, for example, has blacklisted*: Richard Vanderford, "Texas

Blacklists BlackRock, UBS and Other Financial Firms Over Alleged Energy Boycotts," *Wall Street Journal*, August 24, 2022, https://www.wsj.com/articles/texas-blacklists-blackrock -ubs-and-other-financial-firms-over-alleged-energy-boy cotts-11661381425.

CHAPTER NINE

## Political Correctness: Euphemisms for Horrors

250  *In Canada*: Furvah Shah, "Trans, Non-binary Server Awarded $30,000 in Employment Dispute over Pronouns," *Independent*, October 4, 2021, https://www.independent.co.uk/news /world/americas/canadian-tribunal-transgender-nonbinary -restaurant-worker-pronouns-b1931972.html.

251  *In 1894, Lenin coined*: David Joravsky, Partiinost, 1998, doi:1 0.4324/9780415249126-E068-1, Routledge Encyclopedia of Philosophy (Taylor & Francis), https://www.rep.routledge .com/articles/thematic/partiinost/v-1.

252  *For Russian speakers*, pravda: And even those are just rough translations. True story: I asked five native Russian speakers what it meant, and they couldn't agree. Then they started argu- ing with one another about it. Thanks to Mike, Marina, Yuri, Dmitri, and Emilia. You were of no help.

252  *"The capitalists"*: Vladimir Lenin, "How to Assure the Success of the Constituent Assembly," October 15, 1917.

252  *Lenin's idea mutated over time*: Frank Ellis, *Political Correctness and the Theoretical Struggle* (Auckland: Maxim Institute, 2004)

253  *In the 1920s and '30s, Soviet babies*: "Russia's Revolutionary Names Live On 100 Years Later," *Hurriyet Daily News*, Octo- ber 29, 2017, https://www.hurriyetdailynews.com/russias -revolutionary-names-live-on-100-years-later-121547.

253 *"disclose and eliminate"*: Joseph V. Stalin, "Against Vulgarising the Slogan of Self-Criticism," June 26, 1928, https://www.marxists.org/reference/archive/stalin/works/1928/06/26.htm.

254 *"not to have a correct political point of view"*: Mao Zedong, *On the Correct Handling of Contradictions Among the People* (February 27, 1957), 1st pocket ed., pp. 43–44.

254 *In her 1987 book,* Enemies of the People: Anne F. Thurston, *Enemies of the People* (New York: Knopf, 1987), pp. xiii–xiv.

256 *"There were beheadings, beatings, live burials"*: "China Suppresses Horrific History of Cannibalism," *Hindustan Times*, May 11, 2016, https://www.hindustantimes.com/world/china-suppresses-horrific-history-of-cannibalism/story-6hbxXBtvWf9LSIS0yaYlIM.html.

256 *"This was not cannibalism because of economic difficulties"*: Jack Phillips, "Cultural Revolution Psychosis Prompted Murder, Cannibalism in a Small Chinese Town," *Epoch Times*, February 22, 2017, https://www.theepochtimes.com/mkt_app/cultural-revolution-psychosis-prompted-murder-cannibalism-in-a-small-chinese-town_2224397.html.

257 *"The fascist menace has grown"*: Earl Browder, *Fighting for Peace* (New York: International, 1939), p. 102.

257 *"The American government cannot"*: William Z. Foster, *History of the Communist Party of the United States* (New York: International, 1957), p. 387.

259 *"Our very existence is at stake"*: Earl Browder, *Policy for Victory* (New York: Workers Library, 1943), p. 5.

265 *In some extreme cases, cancel culture*: John Nolte, "Cancel Culture Victim Mike Adams' Death Ruled Suicide," Breitbart, July 28, 2020, https://www.breitbart.com/politics/2020/07/28

/nolte-cancel-culture-victim-mike-adams-death-ruled
-suicide/.

271  *Three months later*: Jon Levine, "Ex-Ukraine Diplomat Marie
Yovanovitch Lands Seven-Figure Book Deal," *New York
Post*, February 22, 2020, https://nypost.com/2020/02/22
/ex-ukraine-diplomat-marie-yovanovitch-lands-seven-figure
-book-deal/.

# THE WORLD-FAMOUS
## JESSE KELLY CHEESEBURGER

---

1 pound of the fattiest burger meat you can find (73/27 if it's available)

Any kind of general seasoning (I use Lawry's) and garlic powder

Chipotle TABASCO sauce

American cheese singles

FRESH hamburger buns

**Step 1.** In a large bowl, combine the meat with a dusting of seasoning. Not too much. The seasoning is not the star of the show.

**Step 2.** DROWN the meat in Chipotle TABASCO sauce. Pour in what looks like too much . . . then add some more. I personally use half a bottle for every pound of meat.

**Step 3.** Form four patties. Remember, a good burger is a THIN burger. You're not making meatballs.

**Step 4.** Cook the burger patties on a flat top. If you prefer a grill, you must use a flat top of some kind on the grill. I use a frying pan. A good burger cooks in its fat. Add two American cheese singles when you flip the patty, so it melts.

**Step 5.** Place cooked burger patties on your buns and enjoy.

**Note:** No condiments are needed for this burger because this is the greatest burger on earth. And don't you dare assault the World-Famous Jesse Kelly Cheeseburger with lettuce and tomato.